A Book in Every Hand

A Book
in Every Hand

Public Libraries in Saskatchewan

Don Kerr

COTEAU BOOKS
WWW.COTEAUBOOKS.COM

Edited by Dave Margoshes.
Cover and book design by Duncan Campbell.
Cover photo by Photonica.
Printed and bound in Canada by Marc Veilleux Imprimeur Inc.

Library and Archives Canada Cataloguing in Publication

Kerr, Don
A book in every hand : public libraries in Saskatchewan / Don Kerr.

Includes index.
ISBN 1-55050-313-8

1. Public libraries –Saskatchewan—History.
2. Regional libraries—Saskatchewan—History. I. Title.

Z735.S3K47 2005   027.47124'09   C2005-901726-0

1 2 3 4 5 6 7 8 9 10

COTEAU BOOKS

401-2206 Dewdney Ave.
Regina, Saskatchewan
Canada   S4R 1H3

Available in the US and Canada from:
Fitzhenry & Whiteside
195 Allstate Parkway
Markham, Ontario
Canada   L3R 4T8

The publisher gratefully acknowledges the financial assistance of the Saskatchewan Arts Board, the Canada Council for the Arts, the Government of Canada through the Book Publishing Industry Development Program (BPIDP), the Government of Saskatchewan, through the Cultural Industries Development Fund, the City of Regina Arts Commission, for its publishing program, and the Saskatchewan Library Trustees Association for support of this title.

The SLTA Library History Book Committee would like to express their gratitude to the following groups of people whose financial contributions made it possible to publish this book: The Saskatchewan Library Trustees Association; Provincial Library, Saskatchewan Learning; The Friends of the Saskatoon Public Library; Saskatchewan Centennial 2005; SaskCulture; Saskatchewan Library Association; Saskatchewan Lotteries; United Library Services; and SIRSI Canada.

To Frances Morrison and librarians everywhere.

To Judy Chuey and trustees everywhere.

CONTENTS

Preface

 A HISTORY BOOK OF THIS TYPE DOES NOT JUST happen. It started with a dream. The dreamer, Judy Chuey, spent six years on the Saskatoon Public Library Board and one year as a representative on the Saskatchewan Library Trustee Association (SLTA) Executive. I believe dreams are a result of passion and require vision and determination. At times it does not hurt to roll up your sleeves, even your pant legs and sometimes put on your hip waders and wade in deep to GET THE JOB DONE. This is exactly what Judy and her SLTA History Book Committee have done!

Don Kerr, former Board Chair of the Saskatoon Public Library, has woven together the tapestry of Saskatchewan Libraries in a marvellous way.

SLTA was established in 1967, made its first annual brief to the Minister in 1968, and was incorporated under provincial law in 1969. SLTA is a voluntary association currently representing 2,800 library trustees from across the province who are dedicated to providing library services, without a user fee, that will meet the needs of Saskatchewan people and thereby improve their quality of life. Resource sharing and co-operation are the fundamental strengths of what is called Saskatchewan's "one province" library system – a system that is the envy of the country.

On behalf of all SLTA current and former members, we invite you to come and celebrate Saskatchewan libraries with us.

The History Book Committee members are: Judy Chuey, Zenon Zuzak, Frances Morrison, Louise Cochran, Andre Gagnon.

Kathy Evans
President, SLTA

Introduction

THIS INTRODUCTION IS A MAP TO THE BOOK WHICH FOLLOWS. A central theme of the book is how one of the weakest library services in Canada became one of the best. The 1935 Dominion Bureau of Statistics Survey of Libraries included a comparison of American states and Canadian provinces according to circulation of materials per capita. Saskatchewan was 43rd of 59 jurisdictions, while with 82% of the province without library service, only West Virginia and Arkansas were worse off. The comparisons did not take into account Saskatchewan's major service, travelling libraries. They were however included in a bleak Saskatchewan Library Association (SLA) report presented to the provincial Reconstruction Council in 1944. "In the 49 libraries in the smaller centres of the province, the majority [of books] are old, worn, and out-of-date." The number of registered library borrowers in the province was 7.1% of the population, "while the book stock [totalled] 275,000 books or .3 books per capita." Adding the book purchases of public libraries and the provincial programs results in a figure of $25,151 for the year, "which represents 2.8 cents per capita as compared with 15 cents in Alberta, 31 cents in British Columbia, and 37 cents in Ontario." Saskatchewan's library system by 1944 was in an appalling state.

Yet by 1975 Saskatchewan had the best library system in Canada, and while it has been poorly funded by the province since 1986, it keeps reinventing itself as co-operative, sophisticated and committed to providing, according to its central legislative mandate, equitable library service to Saskatchewan people.

The story begins in 1890 with the Mechanics' and Literary Institute ordinance of the Territorial government, followed by the provincial Public Libraries Act of 1906. Except for Regina, Saskatoon and Moose Jaw, the libraries created by those two acts always had difficulty in renewing the book stock. The two early provincial services were the Travelling Library, begun in 1914, and the Open Shelf Library, begun in 1922. The Travelling Library was a box of 40 to 60 books mailed to rural Saskatchewan and was the province's pre-eminent service for 30 years, leading the country. The Open Shelf Library offered individual titles to anyone in the province.

The great change in library service was a result of a new government, the Co-operative Commonwealth Federation (CCF), and better economic times after the Depression and the war years. The new concept, borrowed from other jurisdictions in Canada, was the regional library. The first-ever government advisory committee on libraries, the Saskatchewan Library Advisory Committee (SLAC), hired Marion Gilroy in 1946 to survey the province and recommend the first region, which was North Central (later Wapiti), centred at Prince Albert, and formed in 1950. The expansion of that region and the creation of new regions was slow at first. Southeast (Weyburn) was created in 1966, Wheatland in 1967, Parkland (Yorkton) in 1968, Chinook (Swift Current) in 1971, Lakeland (North Battleford) in 1972, Palliser (Moose Jaw) in 1973.

In the middle of that process, the Library Inquiry Committee Report, 1967, was the blueprint for the one-library system, all of Saskatchewan connected to public library service. The report was the basis for the 1969 Library Act. That emerging one-library system was described in the report as one in which "Administration is centralized; public service decentralized." The system is hierarchical. At the centre is the Provincial Library, begun in 1953, as the central and coordinating library. There are two independent city libraries, Regina and Saskatoon, which act as resource centres for the regions. Each region has a central library that provides services to all the branches in its region, today for instance 45 branches in Wheatland, 55 in Wapiti. Each branch provides its own branch library, hires its own librarian, has its own library board, sends a representative to the regional board which elects an executive, chosen according to the kinds of municipalities in a region – cities, towns, villages, RMs, Indian bands. That executive and board determine local opening hours and provide changes of book stock at regular intervals. The regional libraries usually began with two professional staff, the regional librarian and the branch librarian. Later developments included resource centres, for instance five in Parkland: Melville, Kamsack, Wynyard, Canora, and Esterhazy, which had more books and longer hours.

There was one more region to organize, in Northern Saskatchewan, completed by 1986 with headquarters at La Ronge and with two new principles: that libraries were often in schools, and that the region, Pahkisimon Nuyʔáh, operated as a federation of independent libraries rather than as the unified regions in the south.

Libraries are funded primarily by a combination of provincial funding and local levies, usually based on a sliding scale, cities paying most, rural municipalities (RMs) least. The proportional payment scheme in Chinook, for instance, is RMs 1, villages 1.5, towns 1.85, city 3.25, so if there were a 10% levy increase, and for comparison we'll assume the proportions are dollar figures, RMs would pay 10 cents more, Swift Current 32.5 cents more, all based on levels of service. Provincial grants were a high proportion of funding at the beginnings of regions – which would have come into existence in no other way – while slowly over the years local levies have surpassed provincial grants in most regions. In Southeast over 30 years the changes are remarkable: In 1981 the region paid $177,000, the province $423,000; by 1992 the proportions were closer to equal, local levies providing $565,000, the province $602,000; by 2002 the positions were reversed, local levies providing $901,000, the province $724,000.

There is one attractive story of early support by the Allan Blakeney government. Don Meadows, provincial librarian in the 1970s, told me he went to Treasury Board to make his case for library needs, asked for, say, 17%, which under questioning he said was enough for the system to get by. Later, his minister, Ed Tchorzewski, said he had bad news and good news. The bad news was that the Treasury Board did not grant Meadows' request. The good news was they increased it to say 23%. When I asked Allan Blakeney about that story he said it must have occurred in 1973 or 1974, and they had the money to do it. Only a premier could have approved that increase. Ned Shillington, Meadows' favourite minister in charge of libraries, said Blakeney was the great supporter of libraries in those days.

Blakeney had a sense of rural isolation and said "filling in the spaces with services" was a part of his vision, a vision that goes back to first Liberal government of Walter Scott and the creation of the Travelling Library, though only the regional library could give adequate service. The concept of the regional library is also one part of Saskatchewan's long co-operative tradition, to overcome all that space with service. No library is an island. No one is left behind.

One of the perpetual difficulties for regions was those communities which wouldn't join or which gave notices of withdrawal (not allowed in the first five years of the region to give it stability, and with a two-year period before a notice of withdrawal came into effect, all according to legislation). In Lakeland, Joy Campbell, now provincial librarian, had to bring 20 libraries back into the fold. The process was costly in time and money. The 1967 Library Inquiry report had said if voluntary participation didn't work to make communities join the regions within a decade, then mandatory participation should be implemented. Needless to say that was a controversial issue. When 1977 arrived there was a plethora of letters sent to the government to support mandatory participation. The regions were then polled, internally to gauge the level of support, with these results: in Chinook, eight communities expressed support, including Swift Current; in Lakeland two said yes with the executive opposed; in Palliser the executive and four branches said yes, while four said no; in Parkland it was ten yes and four no, including Yorkton and Melville; in Southeast there were nine yes, including Weyburn, and three no, including Estevan. Neither Wapiti nor Wheatland replied. As well the Saskatchewan Urban

Municipalities Association (SUMA) and the Saskatchewan Association of Rural Municipalities (SARM) opposed the concept, which clearly wasn't going to be implemented by government. Yet mandatory or universal participation never died as an ideal and it was finally enshrined in legislation in 1996. Maureen Woods, provincial librarian, and two others attended a meeting with Ned Shillington who would guide the new library act through government. The committee had proposed a mild form of universal participation but Shillington, who had supported the concept as library minister in the 1970s, said let's do it, and it was done, introduced said Shillington at the end of a cabinet meeting, where he would summarize key issues, and it passed, as it did at Caucus, again after a long day and a brief summary, and that which was once a life-and-death issue now entered the library world with barely a murmur.

Automation is the chapter I didn't write and had planned to – two librarians said who'd want to read it? – and a great burden was lifted. Automation appears here and there in the text. Early automation included, from an account of Eston, the telephone, book shelves, the card catalogue, the pen, the typewriter. Later the electric typewriter appeared, and telex as a way to increase Interlibrary Loan (ILLO). The first important consequence of automation was the fiche replacing the card catalogue. The arrival of the computer and later the Internet had the most far-reaching consequences, the computer automating such services as cataloguing, circulation, ILLO, reference, finance. Then the Internet made the world accessible at rapid speed, for better or worse. The major original supplier of a machine-readable catalogue was the University of Toronto Library Automation System (UTLAS) while the provincial one-library automated network was the Province Wide Library Electronic Information System (PLEIS). The money for computers for all libraries came from three sources, the Canada-Saskatchewan Infrastructure Grant, grants from the Gates Foundation, and the Every Library Connected Project, so that all libraries in the province are now connected, though not all have high-speed Internet service. At a time when provincial support for libraries did not always keep up with inflation, there was money available to computerize, though that service added new costs as well as new opportunities. It's not uncommon now to find moderately sized libraries with ten or more computer stations.

Libraries now – a book for every hand, a machine for every finger.

Libraries now – sophisticated, connected, the world at your call. But everything began somewhere. Here are three stories of how young women discovered books. Isabelle Butters, who has been a trustee at regional, provincial, and national levels, attended a rural school south of Weyburn, Riverview School, where there was "one old-fashioned bookcase," full of "old stuff in fiction," but she read every one of the books, spent half her time in school reading. In the early '40s school dances were held to buy books for the school. She doesn't remember books in her own house, but a neighbour had all the Elsie and Anne books. She doesn't remember as a child being aware of a library in Weyburn. Later she became, as she said, "a volunteer for life."

Frances Morrison was raised in a book-reading family in Saskatoon – "we were never told we couldn't read anything," including a Dickens by the time she was ten. She read whatever was in the house, including books her mother was reading. She read the children's books at the early Broadway branch. There were only a few books at Victoria School, a small library at Nutana, and a subscription library at the Hudson's Bay Store downtown, from which she borrowed a book Saturday nights. Her best story is piano practice with a book to read rather than a music score. Reading helped make a librarian.

Judy Chuey wrote this account of her early reading habits:

I grew up on a farm in the small town of Pleasantdale near Naicam and Melfort. In the 1940s and 1950s there were no libraries near by. I really loved to read and was so thankful my aunt owned a nice selection of books. Sometimes the store in town had one of those boxes you could choose a book from but there weren't very many for ten-year-olds to read. In 1952 my parents and I were visiting in Regina with our friends. Their daughter said, "Why don't you come with me to the library and I'll take back my books and get some new ones." I thought that would be great because I had never been in a library. I couldn't believe my eyes. I had never seen so many books in one place before. The Regina Public Library was such a big building and had lots of books for people my age. I thought it must be the most wonderful experience ever to live so close to a library and have such a selection to choose from. For me that trip was a real experience. I sure thought those city kids were lucky.

The joy of the book. Here's one more.

An Interview with Me

Y FIRST LIBRARY IN SASKATOON WAS THE BRANCH on Broadway – I attended St. Joseph's School three blocks away. I remember a room lit only by electric light and filled with hardback books, all of them protected with red or green covers.

I was a specialist. I read dog stories, especially those of Albert Payson Terhune, *Lad a Dog, Bruce, Lochivar Luck,* and the like. I don't remember wanting a dog so much as wanting to read about them.

My second library was the school library at Nutana Collegiate. I didn't know I was lucky to be a city boy since so many composite high schools in the towns were just beginning to have libraries. I remember reading Rider Haggard's *King Solomon's Mines* and John Buchan's *The Thirty-nine Steps* and *Prester John,* and other boys' adventure stories. I bought my favourite reading all those years, Walt Kelly's comic book adventures of Pogo Possum, and I love them as much now as I did then: early reading that has not aged at all. In one of my favourite six-frame Pogos, Albert Alligator is pursuing a bug with a fly swatter, and it keeps escaping into margins and the next box until Albert swats it and that's how the semicolon was born.

When I went to university I never did use that library on the second floor of the Administration Building but spent lots of time in the new Murray Memorial Library, complete with those pre-machine pocket cards that were a local history of who had read the books.

Sometimes you were the first reader for thirty years. I always checked to see if my professors had previously borrowed the book. The shelves of literature are still where they were in 1956, and the carrels by the west windows are filled with the ghosts of all my friends who once haunted that floor.

I became more a book buyer than a book borrower, and returned in 1964 from two years in London with a trunkload of books (we came by ship), so cheap at the time, popular hardback series of dramas, essays, novels for six shillings or seven-and-six, about a dollar or less. Because they were my books, my tools, I could write all over them, as if I were going to teach each one of them.

I became a library trustee at the Saskatoon Public Library (SPL) in 1971, nominated by alderman George Taylor whom I'd supported in political campaigns. He asked me what civic body I'd like to be nominated for. I said the library. That board had on it two of the most significant men who had worked for libraries in the previous twenty years, and who you will meet in this history: Carlyle King, who chaired the Saskatchewan Library Advisory Council – advisory to the government – for the fifteen years of its existence, and Rusty Macdonald, who was a member of the Saskatchewan Library Inquiry which delivered the most important report on Saskatchewan libraries, and then was first chair of the Library Development Board. The chief librarian was Frances Morrison, whose name I later found over and over again in the early years of the Saskatchewan Library Association, the major volunteer organization for library work in the province. That was as true of her successor, Alice Turner. At that time in the 1970s I knew nothing of the library past and lived in the presence of meetings.

I became chair in 1977 for five years, and was for a number of years a management representative on annual negotiations with the staff association, which wasn't a union yet, though one year we negotiated a proper union contract, a rational but time-consuming process. At the time of high inflation we increased clerical salaries by 20% to bring them in line with equivalent city rates, and then said in future we'd follow the city in its annual agreements. It was hard to be a wage leader when the city provided the lion's share of the library budget through a portion of the mill rate. Negotiations sometimes served as an unofficial grievance process. We'd be asked to make an amendment to the agreement which we thought would work against staff, only to discover that the real issue was conflict between a supervisor and members of the staff.

I was on one provincial inquiry, The Automation Review Committee, 1980, representing the Saskatoon Public Library, and there met most of the regional librarians at the time, so when I write the history of the regions in the '70s I have faces for the names. The committee had little effect and there was never a single unified automation system for the one-library system.

There were, in those years, two excellent SPL forums, an annual board/staff meeting open to all employees at which department heads reported on their areas, and an annual meeting with city council at which we explained our realities and needs. Mayor Cliff Wright was clearly the friend of the library and once approached us, after the federal government three-year price and wage freeze was lifted, to suggest we raise the chief librarian's salary to levels consistent with the managers of the Mendel Gallery and the Centennial Auditorium; both men were paid substantially more than the librarian, who had a more complex organization to manage. Of course we followed such good advice.

Rusty Macdonald told me once "the smartest thing we did on the board was hire Frances Morrison." Later, the board Carol Copland and I chaired could make the same claim – the best thing we did was hire Alice Turner as head librarian.

And now they've all become edifices: the Frances Morrison Library (Frances was recently asked if she was named after the library), the Cliff Wright Branch, the Alice Turner Branch, the Rusty Macdonald Branch, the Carlyle King Branch. I officiated at that dedication to Professor King, and think now with shame of how little I knew of King's involvement in library development in the province, how caught I was by the present.

One advantage of a book like this is the abolition of the present and the joy of discovering the past where everything came from. In the beginning...

Chapter One

Early Days
1887 to 1906

IN THE BEGINNING, THERE WERE CANADIAN PACIFIC Railway (CPR) employee libraries; there was one important law, the 1890 Mechanics' and Literary Institute ordinance; there were the libraries and reading habits people brought with them to the west; there were important early libraries at Qu'Appelle and Grenfell; an early travelling library; and the one major library, the Legislative Library.

The CPR employee libraries along the main line were established at Moose Jaw by 1887 and at Broadview by 1890, both funded from the proceeds of annual employee picnics. Moose Jaw had a "commodious and comfortable reading room," subscribed to newspapers and magazines, and had 400 "of the standard English books." Non-members could join for $1.50 per year. Both libraries continued to buy new books.[1] Broadview's collection consisted of "a large number of books in a still larger book case."[2] By 1891 the CPR had installed "a fine large bath which all the members here have the right to use," making Broadview the only library in Saskatchewan with a bath attached (like the first University of Saskatchewan classes held in a downtown building so it could claim it was the only university in Canada with an elevator).

There had been an earlier CPR employees' library in Winnipeg by 1884, which published a catalogue of holdings the following year, half fiction, half non-fiction, with subscriptions to thirty periodicals and newspapers.[3] The CPR libraries were like true mechanics' and literary institutes since they were directly organized by and for working men.

The Moose Jaw establishment was an important early library – there was none in Regina in these years. Moose Jaw added 400 new books in 1892 while the company replastered and kalsomined the room, all to no avail, for a terrible fire in 1894 at the CP freight sheds "totally destroyed" the library and its books.[4] Fire is no friend to history or to virtue.

There's one book-reading anecdote set on a train, starring a drunken conductor and a man quietly reading until the conductor knocked the book to the floor: "We don't allow reading on this train." The story has a happy ending since the conductor was fired.[5]

The first library law, "An Ordinance respecting Mechanics' and Literary Institutes," was passed by the Legislative Assembly of the North-West Territories in 1890. To be formed, an institute needed at least thirty persons to subscribe one dollar each, to call a public meeting, and to follow the objectives of the ordinance:

> The objects of institutes organized under this Ordinance shall be to encourage mechanics, manufactures and arts generally:
>
> (a) By having evening classes organized for the imparting of practical instruction to its pupils:
> (b) By establishing a library of books on one or more of the following subjects, viz: mechanics, manufactures, agriculture, horticulture, philosophy, science, the fine and decorative arts, history, travels, poetry, biography, and fiction:
> (c) Establishing a reading room.

There are the usual directives for annual meetings, though an institute is required to report on every book, newspaper, and periodical purchased during the year, all to be noted in a journal, with an annual report forwarded to the Territorial Secretary. The ordinance makes no mention of funds but at some point fifty dollars became available to match reading materials purchased by an institute.

An Act on Mechanics' and Literary Institutes in 1940 is virtually unchanged from the 1890 ordinance, though now the funding is explicit: "a grant of one dollar for every dollar expended by any such institute on the purchase of books, magazines and newspapers" – still to a maximum of fifty dollars a year.

A word on where such institutes originated. The first was organized in London, England in 1823, "For the instruction of the members in the principles of the arts they practice or in the various branches of the science and useful knowledge connected therewith." There was to be a library, a reading room, and lectures. It began as a method of free education for working people, and it spread rapidly to a number of countries, entering Ontario within the decade, in Kingston by 1835, both to educate the mechanic and to keep him tractable, according to statements at the time. By 1847 they were eligible to receive a government grant of fifty pounds a year. The institutes were the major form of library service in Ontario until 1888, when a Free Public Libraries Act was passed, while in 1895 the name Mechanics' Institutes was dropped and all libraries became public libraries. The 1890 North-West Ordinance was a clear echo of Ontario's history of mechanics' institutes.[6] It was not therefore surprising that the first library ordinance in what would become Saskatchewan was this strange anomaly on the prairies, for in small communities there could hardly be many "mechanics," or working-class men. As in Ontario, such institutes would have to be more inclusive.

PEOPLE BROUGHT THEIR OWN LIBRARIES and reading habits to the prairies. In *Harbinger Farm*, 1975, John Wooff wrote that his father from Yorkshire was a well-read man, who'd learned from workers' institutes and libraries, and brought a small library with him across the ocean: Tennyson, Browning, Longfellow, Shakespeare, Felicia Hemans. At school, Wooff first read Canadian literature: Ralph O'Connor, Nellie McLung, Henry Drummond, Pauline Johnson, Lucy Maud Montgomery. Soon weekly publications entered the home: the *Farmer's Advocate*, the *Grain Grower's Guide*, the *Family Herald* and *Weekly Star.* As a boy Wooff also read Horatio Alger, G.A. Henty, Ballyntyne's *Coral Island,* Dafoe's *Robinson Crusoe,* and tales from the *Boy's Own Annual.*

There were elaborate home libraries. Nicholas Flood Davin, Regina newspaperman and politician, had such a library in his Regina home, with a set of law books on one wall, literature on the other. The Neatby family, which produced three writers, brought an elaborate 3,000 book library to their homestead in the Watrous area; the father spent his time reading rather than practising medicine. L.H. Neatby describes in detail his boyhood reading and the influence of his father.

> It would have done Dickens' heart good to have heard father re-enact a scene from *Martin Chuzzlewit,* the absurd burlesque of the drunken hypocrite Pecksniff making elephantine love to the coy mistress of Todger's rooming house and stuttering moral and philosophical platitudes to the gentlemen boarders as they hauled him off to bed.[7]

Neatby was so "captivated by Dickens that [he] began to study him on [his] own and read *Nicholas Nickleby* at the age of nine." He was a boy fortunate not to live in one Saskatchewan town, where a woman remembered that a yellow line was painted on the library floor and no child was to cross that line into the forbidden books of the adult world.

Neatby also read the adventure novels of the preceding century, as so many did, Ballyntyne as always, but also expensive illustrated books by W.H. Kingston, in one of which "the spectacle of an English family adrift on a huge tree trunk in the Orinoco with an anaconda writhing his way onto their log, his jaws distended...was breathtaking to view."[8] There was Fenimore Cooper, and Sunday piety books, magazines like the *Boy's Own Paper* and *Chums.*

Fredelle Bruser Maynard was also a reader of Dickens. Her father, a storekeeper, would borrow books for her. "I read whatever they had and [I] could read. I went through all of Dickens that way, breathlessly, because the set belonged to the preacher and there was a chance he might move to other points before I reached *Hard Times.*[9] I share the intoxication with Dickens. I read my first, *Bleak House,* when I was eighteen on summer evenings after a day working at a brewery. Later I did an M.A. on *Bleak House* and read, I figured, 18,000 pages in a year, going from joy to joy to joy, still the best reading experience of my life. But look how easy it was for me to get books, with good libraries in Saskatoon, including the University Library, good bookstores, books everywhere, and think back to a time when it was rare to get mail and often as rare to have books. "To most pioneers almost any kind of reading material was highly prized."[10]

Look how hard it was in pioneer days to get newspapers or letters. For people in the tiny village of Saskatoon, "In 1883 and 1884 we got mail when we could get it. Mail sometimes came to us from Batoche or Moose Jaw and whoever was in Batoche or Moose Jaw bound for this settlement would ask for the mail and bring it."[11] The newspapers and periodicals that did finally arrive included British papers, the *Times, Pall Mall Gazette,* the *Spectator,* and Canadian papers, the *Globe, Tribune, Family Herald, Winnipeg Free Press,* and various local papers from Ontario. A woman in Eastend in 1898 said, "We could only write when the opportunity rose to get them posted. The NWMP patrol from Maple Creek used to bring our letters out as far as the detachment. They would post our letter if we were lucky enough to catch them."[12]

Books were important to people. "To most pioneers, almost any kind of reading material was highly prized."[13] Everyone who brought books brought the Bible. Other favourites included *Pilgrim's Progress, Uncle Tom's Cabin,* Shakespeare, Dickens, Scott, Macauley's *History of England,* and the *Book of Common Prayer.* The newspapers and periodicals were those subscribed to in Saskatoon, the *Family Herald* and *Weekly Star* remaining especially popular.

There were two good books for people in the west, The Bible, of course, and Eaton's Catalogue. Tom Evans of Lashburn says an "insufficiency of reading material made the Eaton's Catalogue the most frequently read book of them all."[14] Maynard describes the Eaton's Catalogue lovingly for a chapter in *Raisins and Almonds.* As for her other reading there was, in English – she also read Yiddish – the stories of O. Henry, and a favourite, *Skinner's Dress Suit*. "Few classics have left in me a more lasting impression than that tale of a poor young man who rises rapidly through the ranks after he purchases a suit from "Tip Top Tailors.""[15] She learned from that book that "virtue is all very well but it's tailoring that counts."[16]

THERE WERE TWO EARLY TOWN LIBRARIES in the south of the province, at Qu'Appelle and Grenfell.

Qu'Appelle "had its first library in 1888 when a Mr. Bulyea, who operated a furniture store, opened a reading room with daily papers, magazines and a library of fifty books."[17] Yet in 1891, "Under the auspices of the Sons of England a reading room and club has been opened in the town, which is open to all on payment of a small fee: $1.00." There was "a good range of daily and weekly newspapers and all the leading magazines" available, as well as "refreshments of a light kind,"[18] at what was called the Royal Standard Reading Room. It was located in a house that had been used as a drugstore. The newspapers and magazines included ten Canadian, five American, and five British, a kind of balance of forces creating the West.[19]

The Grenfell Mechanics' and Literary Institute was formed in the fall of 1892, its objectives a copy of those outlined in the 1890 ordinance. It had a library and one form of evening classes: debates. In 1892 topics included: Have the North West Indians received just treatment?; Is the North West a success?; Is Capital Punishment justifiable?; That Novel Reading has done more good than harm. At the 1893 annual meeting there were 67 paid-up members, while the Grenfell Library Association presented 250 books, so they now held 336 volumes. They decided to rent a reading room and to admit boys under sixteen at half price. As the Reading Room was cold and dark, it was most unsatisfactory. A Miss Thompson was offered the job of librarian for "25 dollars a year." A set of bylaws were passed, including opening hours – 9 a.m. to 10 p.m. – a fiat against card playing or gambling, regulations on borrowing and fines (five cents a day). In 1894 they had lectures, Nicholas Flood Davin on the advantage of reading, Hon. W. D. Purley on creameries in connection with agriculture, and more debates. By 1896 the society sold its reading-room furniture and discontinued subscriptions to magazines and newspapers. The experiment had lasted but four years.[20]

The Grenfell institute surfaced again in 1904 and was incorporated by 1907. The books were housed in Ellis Hall, in a Mr. Coy's residence, in a jewellery shop, then in the town office. In 1920 it became a public library under the new 1906 Public Libraries Act.

THERE WAS ONE TRAVELLING LIBRARY before the provincial service began in 1914, with books provided by the Aberdeen Association, later by the Lady Minto Libraries, initiatives launched by wives of Governors General to make books more widely available. Literature was distributed to Doukhobor colonies by 1901, mostly books collected in Great Britain. There was a Lady Minto Library in Hillview, West Assiniboine, near the present-day Harris. Circulating Library XVIII at Hillview is a black book that lists the holdings and readers: the winning (most popular) book, *The Second Son* had five readers, while those we might recognize, *Plutarch's Lives, Hard Times, Letters of General Gordon,* had two each. Many were unread.[21] The library was extant as late as October 1979 according to a letter to Wilbur Lepp, local history librarian at the Saskatoon Public Library, from Janet Etter. Miss Etter is concerned about where she'll keep the books now she is eighty-four years old and in a small house: "We didn't ask for the books in the first place...[they were] left in our care, because from 1905 to 1928 the post office for the district was in the hands of my family." She preferred the later travelling libraries which were changed every six months. "The Lady Minto Libraries were never collected so that is why they are still at our place."[22] Another resident recalls receiving by 1905 a box from the Lady Minto Library, which was never recalled. The libraries were usually located in post offices, one at Paynton having five or six hundred books.[23]

There was one great library in Territorial days, the Legislative Library in Regina. John Hawkes, a legislative librarian, tells the physical story of the library, as "the eventful history of this most unfortunate library, which has existed in rat holes and basements, has been bombarded with cyclones, and has been moved three times in seven years under my jurisdiction."[24] Home one: in what had been the original Indian Office Building on Dewdney. The room "was about the size of a fairly spacious dining room, ill-lighted and insalubrious," with the reading room off the lobby containing a table the size of a kitchen table. The provincial bacteriologist worked upstairs, his experimental animals in the basement, and they could create an aroma "not precisely that of Araby the Blest." Home two: a room in the basement of the Land Titles Building on Victoria Avenue. Hawkes recalls, "I had to utilize parts of the engine and ventilating rooms to eke out the rooms." Of course books had to be unpacked, shelves moved each time. Home three: the unfinished Legislative Building. "Then came the [1912] cyclone and smashed the whole business into a confused mass of plaster, broken glass, wood, books and papers, on the floors," with two holes 20 or 30 feet long in the library rooms. They had a makeshift library ready in time for the legislative session.

The Legislative, or Territorial, Library was books too, originally a collection of law books based on Governor Laird's law collection.[25] By 1891, Mrs. Kate Hayes had a catalogue printed. That year 1,379 law books were transferred to the Regina Court House, other books purchased and the contents classified in August 1891, including:

Religion . . . . 134 volumes
Canadian Section . . . . 168 volumes
History . . . . 254 volumes
Historical Biographies . . . . 137 volumes
Political Economy and Sociology . . . . 134 volumes
Belles Lettres (fiction, etc.) . . . . 518 volumes
Science . . . . 236 volumes
French Section . . . . 150 volumes

and so on, including magazines, 33 from the Territories.[26] The library was moved from the control of the Lieutenant-Governor to the Executive Committee of the Legislative Assembly in 1893. Rules were established, including this one on borrowing privileges: "Not more than one book may be lent to any person, other than a Member of the Assembly, at the same time, except by special permission of the Executive Committee."[27] Clearly the Legislative Library was not a public library, yet twice in its existence the library, or the legislative librarian, were at the centre of public library service. Under the jurisdiction of Hawkes both the Travelling Library and the Open Shelf Library were instituted. In 1944, after the Co-operative Commonwealth Federation victory, Legislative Librarian Jesse Bothwell also became in effect provincial librarian at the heart of all library services in the province until her retirement in 1952. Until the advent of a provincial librarian in 1953, the legislative librarian was the central figure in provincial library service.

Chapter Two

Town and Village Libraries 1906 to 1968

HIS CHAPTER HAS BEEN THE MOST DIFFICULT TO WRITE and organize, partly because of different amounts of information on different libraries, with anything like completeness rare; partly because there isn't a clear cause-and-effects story as there is with travelling libraries or regional libraries; and partly because towns literally are all over the map.

My major sources of information are individual library histories that Judy Chuey, a Saskatoon trustee, organized with the assistance of trustees who chaired their regions, so I was also the recipient of a wealth of stories, some slim, a few that were wonderful, and many with lovely bits, of which my favourite is the Melville library's statement on overdues – "You have our book. We have your kids." The passages without references come from this source. There was also material in a twenty-fifth anniversary publication from the Southeast region; in tenth anniversary newsletters from Palliser and Lakeland; in other newsletters; in the *Saskatchewan Library Association Bulletin;* and various government records.

After defining the 1906 Public Libraries Act, I'll start with a statistical overview of town and village libraries, continue with stories of the origin of libraries, stories of three libraries – Wolesley, Unity, and

Shellbrook – and then one thing after another, including homes for libraries and concluding with services to children.

In 1906, the province a year old, the Liberal government of Walter Scott passed an act to provide for the establishment of Public Libraries (Chapter 37) with this subheading, "Establishment of Free Libraries." No library of course is free. Literary institutes were paid for by subscribers, free libraries by taxation. They were then free for patrons. Such public libraries could be set up by petition, by 10% of resident electors, followed by a binding bylaw if supported by 60% of the qualified voters. There were the usual administration regulations, that the management committee – or library board – was to be appointed by the municipality each January, comprising the mayor or head official ex officio, plus four others. There were duties for the board, on purchasing materials, looking after the physical home of the library, submitting an annual budget in May, and raising debentures if necessary. The library was to be paid for by an annual levy not to exceed one mill on all ratable property, the government matching expenditures on the purchase of books, magazines, newspapers, to a maximum of two hundred dollars a year. There was a penalty for "rude or indecent" behaviour, maximum fine twenty dollars, while the janitor could be appointed as a special constable to preserve "the peace in the rooms of the library." The janitor might be the only male employee in some libraries.

There was no newspaper report of that first "Act to provide for the establishing of Public Libraries." It was introduced on the second day of the first sitting of the Saskatchewan Legislature, March 29, 1906, received second reading April 23, and was assented to on the last day of that sitting, May 26, along with 62 other bills, and so was lost in the crowd.

STATISTICS

In the Dominion Bureau of Statistics Survey of Canadian Libraries, 1929-30, the first clear cross-section of library service, there's a list of those Saskatchewan public libraries and Mechanics' and Literary

Institutes (MLI) which completed a questionnaire, including date of
origin: Carnduff, 1907; Regina, 1908; Frances MLI, 1910; Estevan and
Sintaluta, 1911; Moose Jaw, Prince Albert, and Wolseley, 1912;
Saskatoon and Weyburn, 1913; Lanigan, 1914. These are the libraries
listed before the Great War. Then came North Battleford, 1916; Swift
Current, 1918; Lemberg, 1919; and these in the 1920s: Assiniboia,
Kindersley, Macklin, Neudorf MLI, Ogema. The list was incomplete.
When Violet McNaughton, women's editor for the *Western Producer,*
asked for a list of libraries in Saskatchewan a year later, she received
such a list, name only, of 21 public libraries and 31 MLIs.

By 1949 there were 35 public libraries, both town and city. Town
libraries receiving the full government grant of $200 included Canora,
Hafford, Rosetown and Rosthern, while public libraries established in
the previous two years were at Arcola, Canora, Hafford, Kerrobert,
Radville, Watrous, and Watson. There were 29 MLIs: those receiving
the maximum $50 grant included Cabri, Eatonia, Freemont,
Glentworth, Hughton, Lashburn, Leader, Mervin, Ogema, Preeceville,
and Woodrow; while those created in the previous two years were at
Bapaume, Bounty, Glentworth, Sceptre, and Trossachs. One library,
Lloydminster, changed from a MLI to a public library.[1]

By 1953 the town public libraries receiving the full $200 grant
were Rosthern, Watrous, Watson, and Wynyard.[2] Between 1953 and
1958 there were ten new public libraries established – these were
growth years for libraries across the country – and four new MLIs,
called Community Libraries after the 1961 Library Act. Who gave
how much to libraries? In Saskatchewan Library Statistics for 1958,[3]
with 47 public libraries and 32 community libraries in existence, the
per capita spending by municipalities was $2.13 for the three largest
cities, including Moose Jaw (with Regina's $2.52 the highest); an
average per capita of 67 cents in the next six cities (with North
Battleford's $1.50 the highest and Prince Albert omitted as already in
a region); an average per capita in the towns of 21 cents. The government grants were miniscule, 5 cents per capita for public libraries, 11
cents per capita for community libraries – and $55,260 to the first
region, the North Central Region, including the initial book grant.
It paid to organize a region.

The Annual Provincial Library Reports from 1953 on include statistics for each year, until 1986, when the report, in the Department of Education, virtually disappeared. We were protected from information. There was a modest rise in the number of public libraries in the late '50s and early '60s, from 37 in 1958 to 42 in 1961, the year the government cancelled grants to community libraries (as well as to travelling libraries). When community library grants were cut, Alameda replied: "Starting from scratch we have been struggling to make a success of our new community library since 1953 and have just now reached the point where we have a Building of our own and have built up membership 'til we are now entitled to the full grant, which now no longer exists."[4] Allan Blakeney, then minister of education, replied that community libraries were cut "partly to save some funds, but also because it was our belief as a principle that libraries are best financed as public bodies rather than by membership fees."[5] The government saving – the grants in 1961 totalled $1,433 – was hardly an amount worth antagonizing 25 local communities over. After 1961, the balance slowly shifted, four community libraries disappearing that year, one, Davidson, becoming a public library, as Unity had in 1958, and Leader in 1960.

1965 was the year with the highest number of town libraries, 52, before the next regions, in Southeast and West Central (Wheatland) went into operation. The town libraries with the largest circulation were Biggar, Canora, and Leader, with over 25,000, while Eston, Kerrobert, Meadow Lake, Rosetown, and Rosthern had circulations over 10,000. Among the villages Spy Hill did best at over 4,100 circulation, while Beechy and Lampman were over 3,000. Book stock was modest, rarely over 6,000, while opening hours varied from two – Herbert and Macklin – to 13 in Biggar. Those who report being open 40 hours per week or "anytime" must have had their libraries in their town offices. In community libraries, the statistics are bleaker, opening hours averaging two to four, book stock rarely over 2,000 (3,448 in Preeceville) and circulation over 3,000 only in Alameda, Lashburn, Luseland, Ogema, and Preeceville. By 1972 there were only 21 town and village libraries and two community libraries. Libraries were joining the new regions: in 1971 Chinook, in 1972

Lakeland, in 1973 Palliser. Once regions formed, all kinds of new towns and villages, with Rural Municipality support, opened their own branch libraries, so today there are 290 libraries in Saskatchewan, though it's a shifting number.

ORIGINS

Origins are fascinating. Every library in Saskatchewan had its own particular beginning, like its own signature.

Women were more involved than men in starting libraries, and various chapters of the Imperial Order of the Daughters of the Empire were more instrumental in beginnings than any other organization. The IODE started a library in Kerrobert in 1926, which it turned over to the town 25 years and 2,000 books later. In Shaunavon "The first mention of a library is in the January 8, 1914 issue [of the *Shaunavon Standard*] that states: "A complete lending library has been opened to book lovers of Shaunavon, and vicinity, by F.O. Bransted of the Empire Billiard Hall. The best books of such modern writers as Rex Beach, R. Charles, G. Parker, R.W. Service, Ralph Conner, and many others, could be read for the small sum of 10 cents each." But still it was the IODE that formed the first public library in 1927 and continued to operate it for 23 years, until 1950, when the Shaunavon Public Library was born. In Humboldt the IODE sponsored a library in 1932, operating it for many years with volunteer help. In Melville the Robert Combe Chapter of the IODE began library service in 1936, though the transfer to the town took place only a year later. In Balcarres in the mid '50s, the local IODE began the first permanent library, donating and collecting books, and volunteering as librarians, typical of their role in many early town libraries.

The Homemakers' Clubs were instrumental in starting library service in Nokomis. "On June 2, 1917, a board of six ladies, two representatives from each of: Mount Hope Homemakers' Club, Wereford Homemakers' Club, and Bonnockbury IODE met in the Rest Room...and after some discussion, drew up a draft of an agreement for managing such room," which they did, for over 30 years, until 1955, when the Nokomis Public Library was formed. In Govan "The White Heathers Homemakers' Club was the group responsible for the first make shift library... It was kept in the home of one of the club's members and the club gathered books from each other and other people in the community... In 1915 it was in the house of Mrs. Puffer, who would also eventually become librarian." In Davidson "Our library was started by the Homemakers' Club... in 1914 and was housed in a small room called the 'Rest Room in the Davidson Town Hall.'" The first librarian was Beatrice Lick, and this story was told by one of her nieces: When Miss Lick was ill late in life in a Saskatoon hospital, a nurse said, "Lay down, Miss Lick," who replied, librarian to the end, "it's lie down."[6]

In Meadow Lake the library was "started originally as a Children's Library by the Stagettes, a business girls group, 1948. It was open one day a week for two hours. In 1953 the building burned but the books were saved." It was then moved to cupboards on the walls of the Council Chambers, the cupboards "locked when not in use."

In the Kelliher area the Garnock Homemakers' organized a library in the Garnock School, and when it was closed, in 1960, the books were moved to Kelliher. Home and School Clubs in Arcola and Lampman invited Marion Gilroy, the first organizer of regional libraries, to speak to them, in 1948, and both towns formed libraries. In Kamsack it was the Business and Professional Women's Club that instigated for a library, and they were joined by the Chamber of Commerce and the Kamsack Film Council, and a library board was formed by 1955.

Men's groups were fundamental in forming libraries too, one in Rosthern. "The history of library service in Rosetown dates back more than 55 years to October 2, 1943. It was on this date that the Men's Service Club of Rosthern held a Harvest Festival, from which $400 of the proceeds were marked for a library fund." The library started January 16, 1945, housed in a room at the school. The Rotarians first sponsored the Yorkton Public Library in 1947, and supported the Lloydminster Public Library, founded in 1929, for many years.

There was no predicting how libraries might begin. The Prince Albert Library was created from the Mechanics' Institute Library in the Empress Hotel, in 1913. North Battleford began in splendour in 1917 in their Carnegie Library (one of only two in the province – the other at Regina). It now houses the Allen Sapp art collection. The Warman Literary Institute began in 1933 when the municipality won a $500 community award in the CNR Community Progress competition and put $250 into library books.[7]

In Yorkton a man wrote a letter to the editor in 1904, "stating that young men might not frequent billiard rooms and hotels so often if library services were available," which they were, three years later, housed in the lower entrance of the new Town Hall. Watson Library "began at a meeting in December, 1946, a committee seeking books and cash; $150 from Watson Board of Trade, Order of Foresters, Catholic, United and Anglican ladies groups, and the Daphne Willing Workers." The library began in the Reliance Lumber Office. In Rockglen "in the late 1960s a group of avid readers in our town wanted a place to exchange pocket books they had been reading. They got together and established a small set of shelves in the lobby of the Dew Drop Inn, Rockglen's only hotel. Interested people dropped off their old books and traded them in for new ones. The 'collection' consisted mainly of old Harlequin Romances, the latest Louis L'Amour, and every Agatha Christie thriller ever written."[8] That kind of swap library still exists in the 8th Street Co-op in Saskatoon and in the Sasman RM office in Kuroki.

Broadview started three times, first as the CPR library in 1890, then as a public library in the 1930s, taken over by the Broadview Legion. In 1961 it started for the third time with Donalda Putnam of the Provincial Library providing the spark for Broadview and the Qu'Appelle Regional Library (which was to form half of Southeast); Kathleen Fafard served as the Broadview representative, and for years as the town's librarian. Foam Lake opened modestly, "a project of the IOOF [Independent Order of Odd Fellows] and Rebekah Lodges of this town. On January 10, 1952 the 'doors' of the Foam Lake Community Library opened to the public – but the library only had one 'door' – to a cupboard in the office of the Rural Municipality of Beaver on the main street of Foam Lake."⁹

Individuals were often responsible for starting libraries. "It was the hard work of Eva Davis, Iris Nicholson, Cynthia Donald, Ethel Harmel and John Branton [that was] responsible for getting Maidstone's Public Library off the ground," in 1973. In Hewlett, "An early pioneer from north of Manor, Mr. Arthur Hewlett, passed away and left a bequest of one thousand dollars with which to start a library," and through the work of others a library opened in 1967. The Ogema Library "actually started in 1917 with Ed Kilpatrick as librarian. Ed kept the books in a corner of his bakery shop. He made great efforts to keep his lending library going for 28 years. At that time the library housed 118 books." Estevan's public library began in "Lockhart's Law Office on February 18, 1908. Mayor Hastings acted as chairman for this first meeting." By April 4, books had been ordered and a room was being sought. June 6 witnessed the creation of bylaws which included this statement: "No person shall be permitted to handle the books except for the Librarian and members of the Board." In Watrous, "One evening in May 1948 Faye Labelle and Esther Gibney decided to do something about having a library in Watrous. The next morning with a pen and pad they set out on foot in different directions to collect names for a petition. There they met in the evening after many interesting receptions; they had a list of approximately 400 signatures."

So many people worked to make books available in town after town. Perhaps we take libraries a bit for granted, because they've always been there. Yet they exist in towns and cities now because people worked for, fought for, the right of books to take their place in our lives.

WOLESLEY

The town that claims the status of supporting the longest continuous library service in the province is Wolesley. The first library, 1883, was a Farmers' Institute, whose first financial statement showed 59 members paying a dollar each, with a $50 grant from the territorial government,[10] while their books and magazines were on agricultural matters. The library changed its name the next year to the Wolesley Mechanics' and Literary Institute, and then began the journey to find a home, from hardware store to drugstore to news office, to a reading room in a front parlour of a home. By 1900 the town made its first grant, $20; by 1903 the institute published its first catalogue, of 358 titles. In 1912 Wolseley, following the Public Library Act of 1906, became a public library, situated now in the new town hall. By 1927 it had 2,200 books and a circulation of 2,600 volumes, and would survive the Depression.

Wolesley's sense of independence can be felt in its presentation to the Library Inquiry Committee at Regina, November 24, 1966, written by Library Board member Mrs. L.J. Conn. That year the board had six members "who act as volunteer librarians two afternoons a week." For years, beginning in 1894, the library had exchanges with Grenfell and Indian Head. In 1964 the town renovated and enlarged the library as a Saskatchewan Jubilee project. What was needed, said the delegates Mrs. Conn and Mrs. Bell, was help from professional librarians, with book selection, incentives to buy expensive non-fiction, plus recommendations on school libraries. In the discussion, the delegates said regions might be good for others, but their library was established and they had the Public Information Library as excellent backup. Before the region there were only five libraries in the Southeast. Mrs. Conn finally said, "We are too much attached to our library; they are going to send our books away."

In the 1950s, according to statistics in the annual reports of the Provincial Library, it was a normal library for its size, the town growing from 885 to about 1,000 people with a gradually increasing book stock, around 5,000, with a growing circulation, up to 7,000 and then 9,000. It never was able to utilize the full government grant of $400 in any year, a grant that was cancelled after the Report of the Library Inquiry Committee as a way of encouraging participation in regional libraries. There was an end, in 1971, to interlibrary loans from the Provincial Library as well, again as an act to support the region.

A response by Virna Thompson, a member of the Wolseley Board and a writer for the *Wolseley News,* on March 11, 1969, contrasted costs in Wolseley, 30 cents per capita in town, 13 cents per capita in the RM, with that of Southeast region, 73.7 cents per capita, and North Central, 90 cents per capita. She said the local library gave good service. There was a response by Southeast Chair J.S. Porter, then a reply by Mrs. Thompson, who said the regional library "is a wonderful thing for towns and villages that never had a library," but Wolseley had had a library, and "a darned good one," continuously since 1884. In one way, she said, Wolseley was superior to the region because it had no non-participation fees and therefore discriminated against no one. All children were treated as equals. But now interlibrary loans had been discontinued: "because we are a local library and not a member of a regional library system, we can no longer receive this service. They are beginning to tighten the noose around our neck, and force us into the regional system." The regional library concept was defended in notes by Harry Newsom, provincial librarian." There was a sudden jump in circulation for Wolseley, from 9,196 in 1966 to 14,000 in 1967, and circulation remained at that level or higher through 1973 when it disappeared from the statistics, listed neither as a member of Southeast nor under town libraries.

WILKIE

Library history in Wilkie is like a bookmobile, so often did the library move during the years, from place to place to place. The story was splendidly told by Frances Love in 1988.

Before 1910 there was a circulating library in a fancy goods and stationery store, by 1912 a lending library at St. John's Anglican Church, subscriptions a dollar a year. An attempt to form a public library that year failed, but in 1920 the Mechanics' and Literary Institute was formed and housed in the back of Whelpton's Electric Store, with 250 books and Mr. Whelpton as librarian, though part of the collection was housed in the Wilkie Rest Room.

> The Wilkie Room maintained by the [Homemakers'] Club is in constant use by country shoppers. It is steam-heated, has an oil stove on which shoppers frequently make a cup of tea before starting on their drive home, has magazines for those who wish to read and rest, and the Public Library from which one book may be borrowed for five cents, or a year's membership for one dollar.

At the end of the '20s the library moved across the street to a Mr. Whitworth's store, and he became the librarian. In the harsh years of the Depression the library moved to the school but as it was less accessible there, it moved again, with the help of the Wilkie Ministerial Association, to the former R.G. Moore oil office. That was in 1938 and was move number seven. In 1940 the library moved upstairs in the former council chambers, until 1945, when it perambulated one more time, to the back of what became Boucher's Agency, though the Rest Room remained a constant. In 1959 the province contributed $253 to the library, the town of Wilkie $200, the RM of Buffalo $25. In 1962 there was an amazing occurrence – the library had enough money to pay a librarian for the first time.

Frances Love, the author of the library history, came to Wilkie in 1966 and saw a library that "was in a dark room, not very large, with shelves all around the walls. The books were all hard covered and a lot of them quite old. There were four removable doors, with padlocks, that Frances Weber had to take off every time the library was opened." In 1968 the library joined Wheatland region, which meant new quarters had to be found, first in the basement of the Community Medical Clinic, then in 1982 in rented quarters with a grand opening, then in 1986 in a building that originally housed a credit union, and a second grand opening in 1988.

Many communities moved libraries from pillar to post in early years. Wilkie's is the most moving experience of them all.

SHELLBROOK, 1979-81

Shellbrook was the location of a "Community Awareness Project" from May 1979 to May 1981. The project was created by Patricia Cavill, public relations consultant at the Provincial Library, and Karen Labuik, who did public relations for Wapiti. They published their findings in *Impact,* a Community Awareness Project, 1984, CLA. They'd received a small fellowship from the Library Development Board which covered costs. They surveyed the community with a questionnaire in May, 1979 (with a sample of 88 out of 1,231), ran a series of promotional ads in the local newspaper from January, 1980 to April, 1980, were then brought up short by a council resolution to hold a plebiscite on participation in the region at the fall elections. Library supporters undertook a massive campaign that was successful. That was followed by a second survey in May, 1981.

I'm choosing for comparison some items from Section II of the survey, the Attitude Interview:

			Agree
(f)	The value of the library is high compared to its cost.	1979	(42%)
		1981	(74.5%)
(r)	The library is a good place to find information on current events.	1979	(40.9%)
		1981	(41.8%)
(t)	The library is very useful to adults who are trying to educate themselves.	1979	(65.9%)
		1981	(83.6%)
(z)	The Town of Shellbrook has an excellent regional library branch.	1979	(62.5%)
		1981	(80%)

One ad in the Shellbrook campaign

In between the surveys there was the advertising campaign, the ads all different, sophisticated and sometimes witty. "IT'S *YOUR* LIBRARY...ALL SASKATCHEWAN LIBRARIES ARE THE SAME SIZE!" one proclaimed, because they were all part "Of An International Loan Network." In their evaluation the authors say repeating the same message over and over would have had a greater impact. The most effective ads, they say, were those that featured local librarians and board members.

The most exciting part of the story was the unplanned event. On August 6, 1980, Town Council passed a motion, "whether or not to maintain our branch of the Regional Library due to the cost involved." Then the campaign for the library was on. Battle plans were drawn up. The library board resigned in September and became "the Friends of the Library." Letters were sent out, 800 of them to ten target groups, the two authors fully involved. Handbills were distributed, with grocery stores putting them in grocery bags. Senior citizens phoned every resident twice. There was a forum, open-line radio, stories by CKBI, Prince Albert, and excellent ads: "One month's library service, a cup of coffee," illustrated with a coffee mug sporting slogans, and others of the like. The question on the ballot was simple: "I am [or am not] in favour of retaining our branch of the Wapiti Regional Library." The results of the vote and the excitement on voting day are captured in an October 23, 1980 letter from Labuik to Cavill, who had subsequently taken a regional librarian's job with the Primrose region in Alberta.

It was an incredible day. I had volunteered to answer phones and for rides to the poll.... A family from town joined the library yesterday, saying they had been planning it for a long time, and they hoped it wasn't too late. We waited – oh, how we waited – for the results. Finally, after three hours they came...43 against, 374 for. Never had there been so many ballots to count. We cheered, and then called you.

One of the great days in the history of Saskatchewan libraries.

LAKELAND AND BRANCH LIBRARIES

Lakeland region publishes three times a year a magazine, *Reflections,* circulated among its branches. I read a sampling and learned many things about village and town libraries. Libraries sometimes began small. "In Denzil, the first library was housed in a room comparable in size to a walk-in closet. There was not even space...for a librarian and a desk. This first library has since been converted into a washroom" (July 1987). "Considering that the population of Makwa is 107 and the story hour attendance was nearly fifteen every week, I think this was great" (July 1987).

There was black news too in rural Saskatchewan.

"Like most little towns, Paynton's population seems to be decreasing. It's heartbreaking to lose a family with five or six readers" (December 1998). You could give a program and no one would come. "I cannot say our senior story time was a success, in fact due to no attendance we gave up" (April 1990). Or a bookmobile didn't stop there anymore. "Fielding, once a busy stop, has been deleted from the schedule of visits. The children in the area have grown up, graduated, and moved to other centres" (August 1991). Schools closed and that affected bookmobile stops. "As of the end of June two schools on my run were closed. I sure miss not only the circulation...but all the children that I got to know" (December 1993).

There were joys, too. At Turtleford, "Our star reader was a six-year-old with a reading difficulty. He read 104 books aloud to his mother...and greatly improved his reading ability. He now loves to read!" (December 1993).

There were changes over the years. Borden changed venues. "So we now have a pleasant, carpeted, well-lit space instead of the cement floor; a furnace, complete with caretaker, rather than the balky oil burner which went out whenever the wind blew from the N.W. at over 40 mph.; a bathroom down the hall rather than one block away at the Co-op store. Inevitably pre-schoolers had the urge when no other parent was present so the entire story hour group had bathroom parade" (Fall 1992). Bob Wandler reflected on years of driving bookmobile in all kinds of weather and sundry other conditions: "dragging of a block exchange from the vehicle to the library on a toboggan (Goodsoil) because the snow was piled so high. Then there was the incident of interrupting a funeral service in Maidstone for the branch was located in the local Anglican church...there was one branch in particular (without mentioning Lashburn) which was long and narrow as a cigar...good thing I am a long drink of water or the books would have been falling like dominoes as one squeezed by" (Fall 1992).

Village and town libraries were community centres. At Maidstone over the years, "We have hosted a plant swap, babysitter's course, hobby and craft shows and sales, street painting, parade floats, puppet shows, pumpkin events, used book sales, exhibits at trade fairs, Discover Choices, children's skill games, and entertainment for Canada Day including Canada quiz, giving face painting, garden slides, PLEA programs, a recycling and environmental awareness; also a display on tools and aids for the disabled" (Fall 1992). This is a longer list than usual but not atypical. Libraries were books and story hours. They were also social and cultural centres. They raised money for their support too, beyond town, RM, and regional support. In Cutknife, over the years, "Other income has been raised by the following: Mother's Day Bake Sale, Garage sale along with pie and coffee, Silver Collections at demonstrations and Canada Day tea, Sale of numerical order telephone books, Monster Cookie Sidewalk Sale, Monster B.B.Q. dinner, Pie Sale at Atton's Lake, working at Chamber of Commerce Bingo, Renting a backroom for two months, Renting the library for classes, and Selling tickets on an inflatable monster" (December 1993.) Whew. Librarians at work.

HOMES FOR LIBRARIES

A number of libraries, like those in Wilkie, Nokomis, and Rosthern, were located in Rest Rooms, which in Rosthern was a considerable expense, $8,000 in 1947, and it had its downside. "Summer 1951 had the library closed until such a time as the cesspool from the restrooms was cleaned and the odour in the library was not so bad as to make people sick any longer."[12] There was water damage on books in 1977 and the library moved back to the town hall. At Nokomis in 1945, two Homemakers' clubs, still looking after the Rest Room and library, began a building bee. "Mrs. E.J. Edwards (Aunt Alice) was a great organizer and before we knew it the lot where the hospital is built was owned by the Homemakers' – often referred to by their husbands as the 'Homebreakers.' The husbands came with cement mixers, sand, shovels, etc....The Lee house arrived and the Homemakers' fixed up the library quarters, rest room and library."

Libraries often had strange bedfellows. In Kindersley the library spent a year at the curling rink, while Manor was pleased to get a room at the new rink, which also served as a doctor's waiting room once a month. In Wapella, "A new building was erected to house the Laundromat and the new library."[13] In Midale, "Winter is busy here as the Library is in the Civic Centre along with the curling and skating rinks." Val Marie, also by the rink, was quiet in the summer. Saskatoon branch libraries went into civic centres too, the Carlyle King branch in a building with a rink and gymnasium. In Glenavon "we are downtown between a grocery store and the Café, in the newly refurbished 'old pool hall.'"[14]

Cabri was for a time in the annex of the old theatre, Lashburn for a time in Gully School mentioned in Mary Heimstra's novel *Gully Farm,* Meadow Lake in a former RCMP building. In Ogema in 1984 the library was moved "to the old pool room and barber shop owned by John McKerricker." A year later the new town building housed the "fire hall, town shop as well as library." The current Shellbrook library is in a strip mall next door to a liquor store. It's either books and booze or booze and books, depending on your sense of values.

There were even libraries close to jail. In Gull Lake, "the town supplied the room which was away at the back of the town hall. To get to it you could go through the fire engine room, or through the town council chambers or through a door in the north of the building. If you went through the council chambers or through the north door you had to pass the jail. There were two cells and each had a bunk with a dirty mattress and an equally dirty blanket. When the cells were empty the children used to go in to see what it would be like to be in jail. When there were prisoners they were afraid and hurried by. Sometimes the prisoners would be happy and glad to have someone to chat with and sometimes you were very glad the vicious looking ones were locked up. It was an eerie experience to sit there alone even with the door closed."

At Meadow Lake, in the 1950s, the first librarian recalls "the room in which the books were kept was used as a Town Hall. There was a connecting door to the part where the cells for prisoners were situated. Many evenings, there was quite a noise from that part. Also the men employed as guards often came in for a book. Some days a trial was still on and we couldn't open the library till later."

In Ponteix "From 1971 until March of 1996 the Ponteix library has been in jail – the town jail to be exact...One cell was the children's section, another was the non-fiction and the hallway held fiction."

BOOK SELECTION

Book selection in early pre-region days was often done by trustees. In Cabri, "Adult books are selected by two or more members of the Board, and the Librarian selects the books for children. Selection is based upon publishers lists, reviews in newspapers, and requests of borrowers." At Estevan in 1966, "Two members of the library board work together with the librarians to select books." In Kamsack, "Four or our Board members belong to the Book Buying Committee," and they cater to younger readers. In Weyburn, "In the past two members of the Library Board submitted book selections which were added to the librarians' selections."[15] In 1921 Weyburn asked "Professor Marshall, Principal of Weyburn Collegiate, to compile a book list choosing fifty of each of Everyman's Library and Home University Lists." Even in Saskatoon at a board meeting of October 9, 1932, two motions were passed, one that no book by an unknown author "be circulated, that these be first read by a member of the board, or their nominees," and that all books ordered be approved by the board. Board members were sometimes better read than librarians, who were not trained in the field. In Saskatoon the arrival of one of the great Canadian librarians, Angus Mowat, was the first time the city had a professional librarian; he revolutionized the system and ordered the books.

CHILDREN IN THE LIBRARIES

In Yorkton, an early strict librarian said: "Children had to show clean hands before handling a book." Bill Morrison was chairman of the Yorkton Library. His daughter Nancy tells an anecdote: "A library worker had made a rule that children not be allowed in the library because it would be too disruptive. On the other hand, [my] father felt strongly that children should have access to this community resource. He managed to have the librarian agree to a six-month pilot project allowing children to use the library. At the end of the test period the librarian told [him] that she preferred having children around than adults."

In Estevan, "The board had already dealt with the challenge of children in the Library. In 1913 the board passed a motion 'that the Privilege of the Library not be extended to children under the age of fourteen unattended.'" By 1917 it passed this motion: "all boys under fourteen years of age are required to make application, by letter from their parents, to the librarian, promising good behaviour, and careful handling of magazines and papers while in the Library."

Rosthern had a more positive story. "At the suggestion of Peter Worobetz, 1948 saw the beginning of library service to the country schools for rural children. Five boxes of children's books were prepared and sent to the schools. *The Saskatchewan Valley News* reported that students read 1,757 books in a one-year period due to these book boxes." Melville had the great statement on overdue books: "You have our book. We have your kids."

Children have memories of library services, like Janice from Frontier: "I was about four years old when I first climbed the three tall stairs into the library. I remember Sharon's ready smile....The shelves were right to the ceiling and were close together, looking like sky scrapers to me. I was very proud to use my library card at noon hours once I was in school. I often filled my book bag with as many as I was allowed, dragging it back to school. On the bus I read all the way home."

In North Central Aina has a detailed story: "About four years ago when I was really beginning to read I kept wishing I was a millionaire so as to buy as many books as I wanted to. A year later when mummy told me there was to be a library in Prince Albert and I could go take books out whenever I wished, I thought a miracle had befallen me. Every day I asked her and she just kept on with that aggravating 'soon,' until I could bear it no longer. So one evening after school I went to the library, a big brick building mummy had pointed out to me some time ago. I didn't have a card or anything. I just went upstairs where the library lady had said the childrens books were. When I got there I began looking for the book I wanted, *Anne of Avonlea.* A kind little lady at the desk asked me what I was looking for. I promptly answered *Anne of Avonlea.* Then she said they didn't have it and asked me if I had a card. I didn't know what she meant but still I said no. She said I couldn't take out books without a card, so she gave me a white card to take home and said they would order *Anne of Avonlea.* I was so surprised that I kept telling mummy how nice she was and how she was going to order a book just for me."

There were summer reading programs for children, and the best account is that of Peter Eyvindson, a favourite storyteller for years, talking of his 1984 tour when the theme was A Monstrous Adventure, with library after library featuring dinosaurs. Prince Albert had 450 dinosaurs, one for each child in the summer reading program. In Rouleau children made boxes decorated with dinosaur stickers. In Caronport children completed dinosaur jigsaw puzzles.

Melfort had dinosaur footprints on the wall, with special treats under them. Wadena had a dinosaur tree full of dino eggs, one for each reader. Children in Duck Lake were playing Dinosaur Bingo. Canwood had a jar of dino eggs (jelly beans). Kids at Davidson made a dinosaur out of papier mâché. The biggest dinos were at North Battleford and Weyburn. At Cut Knife the dinosaur was fed bones with the titles and authors of books the children had read. There were other monsters but dinos won hands down.

Eyvindson also told stories of the pleasures of children learning to read. An elderly woman, Ruby, told of how she learned to read as a child who'd come from library-rich Ontario to library-poor Saskatchewan. "Every night Ruby and her mother would read the same stories over and over until Ruby, following her mother's voice could read the stories just as well as her mother. The pride in her face still shone as she finished her story by relating that when [she] went to school, [she] could already read."[16]

Eyvindson heard a boy in Moose Jaw tell a story with stuffed animals, a story about how all the animals had a voice but one, the owl. "Each animal talked to the owl – only to discover the owl was no fun as he didn't talk. Finally a fierce and madly talking bird came out of the sky to scare the owl. But the owl said Whoo! and the fierce bird was frightened off! The owl discovered that talking did have benefits and continued to talk!" Two years earlier, Eyvindson said, the boy who told the story was an autistic child who had attended an autistic story hour in Moose Jaw. It's the tale of a mute child learning a voice. Books, too, free the imagination and give voice to so many things we cannot imagine them all.

One such imagination is the topic of Eyvindson's next story, of a boy in Hafford responding to a story of Robert Munsch, *The Dark,* "The concluding line sent him into a convulsive fit of laughter and as he rolled on the floor enjoying his hilarity he shouted – 'That doesn't make any sense – because as soon as the sun comes out there will be shadows.' At this point he became very somber and his eyes as big as plates 'unless,' he said very slowly, 'the dark ate the sun.'"

Swift Current began a reading program for children in grades two to four who were poor readers, as identified by their parents.

They were helped by volunteers one on one, and at the library, borrowing books, they were joined by preschool siblings who were read to in groups of three or four. "Picture a Wednesday morning with forty to fifty children sitting on chairs, cushions, or scattered about on the floor, in groups of two to four. Needless to say circulation jumped for that particular day of the week."[17] The librarians had special pleasures: "seeing the bottle top collection (five in all) of a four-year-old boy. It takes some doing for a four-year-old to stand up in front of a group of fifty children and adults and talk about his collection." They also learned from the kids, and their tonnette-and-Mickey-Mouse-banjo band, a new song, "Rockin' Robin."

Summer reading programs didn't work everywhere. "We didn't participate in the summer reading program this year as most of the children, or perhaps I should say *all*, were out of town for the two months. They went to summer camps, summer homes, hockey schools or went on vacation to various parts of the country." That was Abbey in 1979. At Ponteix they built a bookworm. "For every book read by a child, fourteen years and under, a part was added to the body. On August 30th we put the tail on and we were pleased to say it consisted of 321 parts."[18] How many acts of imagination, from librarians, books, readers, make up the outer and inner world of the library?

Chapter Three

Travelling Libraries
and Open Shelf Libraries
1914-1987

F ROM 1914, WHEN THE TRAVELLING LIBRARIES WERE first implemented, until 1961 when television and the spread of the regional libraries made them obsolete, the Travelling Libraries were the way most people in rural Saskatchewan had access to books. Author Maria Campbell remembers a box of books arriving at Park Valley, a road-allowance Metis village at the west side of Prince Albert National Park, when she was a little girl. When the books arrived at the post office a horseback rider would bring the good news. "I was so excited. I didn't know what a library was." Campbell's mother, convent-educated, was the only one in the community who could read, so after supper she would read for anyone who wanted to visit, and then later to her children in bed. That's how Campbell and her sister learned to read, and to love books. Campbell says all her siblings have big libraries now, "all from those travelling libraries." When she went to school she couldn't speak English but she could read it.

On July 13, 1913, Legislative Librarian John Hawkes presented the first detailed recommendations on libraries to Premier Walter Scott in his second role of minister of education. Hawkes visited

Toronto, Chicago, and Madison, Wisconsin. While much of his report was given over to detailed recommendations for a proper legislative library and other library services, he also recommended that the province institute a scheme of travelling libraries.

> Roughly the position is this – that at a comparatively small expense a current of literature can be kept going through all the rural arteries, to the instruction, entertainment and great moral and educational uplift of the country people of this province.[1]

Ontario Travelling Libraries had begun in 1909 and by 1912 about 200 libraries (40 to 60 volumes in pinewood boxes) and 10,000 books were circulated, primarily to Women's Institutes and Farmers' Institutes, while specialized technical libraries were also in circulation. In Wisconsin a great deal of money was spent, Hawkes said, "to keep abreast of that making of books which is without end."[2] The state exhibited its travelling libraries at country fairs, and promoted them with talks at various institutes. Wisconsin even employed another approach to the travelling library, prefiguring the bookmobile, with wagon delivery of books "taken to the farmer's door,"[3] while the traditional travelling libraries served 609 communities in 1911-12, and included service in other languages – German, Norwegian, and Polish.

When the Saskatchewan government introduced the scheme in December of 1913, Premier Scott gave a genealogy of travelling libraries, beginning in Scotland in 1810, then in order travelling to Sweden, the United States, Australia, England, and Germany. There were now 25 states south of the border with travelling libraries, while even in Saskatchewan they had been at work in a small way because a professor at Regina College had sent out eighteen boxes of books from McGill University Extension to an area within a hundred miles radius of Regina.[4] One year later, an information letter explained how the system would work. A library would consist of 45 to 60 books, with 40% fiction, including books for children. "It is useless to send people books which people ought to read but won't read.... Heavy or high brow literature will be discounted."⁵ That's an early selection policy. Libraries should go out for three to six months, and would all be returned to Regina to be checked before remailing. Library boxes could be used as bookcases. Libraries would be sent to a local board created for the purpose, with one person appointed as local librarian.

By March 1915 Hawkes listed 42 locations which had received travelling libraries, and they'd been everywhere: to Theodore, Beadle, Beverley, Maryfield, to Lemberg, Stoneyview, Govan, Unity, to Lang, Kelliher, Meyronne, Marshall, to Horizon, Chaplin, Caron, Fillmore and lots more, with 32 other communities registered and waiting for service and 30 letters of enquiry. The program was a success at once. Only rarely in these early years were letters from recipients published in reports, but Margaret McDonald, manager of the system, would occasionally do so.

> A woman from Junor, sixty miles from a station, said:
> I often wonder if you people in charge can possibly know how we appreciate being able to read good books, and if you can imagine them taking the place of church, lodge, theatre and social and nearly all business transactions. It is a noble mission these good books travel on.
> A letter from Central Butte gives this information:
> We have one girl in the district, who finished her third grade certificate last Spring, and on account of an invalid mother will have to stay on the farm to keep house. The books will help her to stay contented and the mother is quite a reader. Then another woman who is alone every day from 8 a.m. to 6 p.m. (her husband drives the van) says she will not dread this winter, having good reading material.⁶
> She says with amazement that even her husband has read four books.

By 1917, 125 libraries were in circulation and 164 libraries sent out, to a much-extended list of communities, some of which had already received five libraries. There was substantial work to be done at headquarters in the Legislative Building.

Each library...is unpacked and checked, records examined to ascertain the circulation of each book, worn-out books are replaced with new ones, and in many cases changes are made in the selection of books, in order to suit the readers of the district to which the library is to be sent next.[7]

The same year, replying to criticism of the program as inadequate by Regina librarian J.R.C. Honeyman, Hawkes said economies were necessary, for "The Late Minister of Education gave me strict instruction only to expend what was absolutely necessary." The effect of the Great War on the provincial budget was severe. Staffing problems were acute, since the Legislative Library, with a staff of five, also administered the travelling library program. "It is not a reproduction of any other system; it is especially adapted to Saskatchewan,"[8] Hawkes observed. He gave a quick sketch of other library service in Saskatchewan that year: four city libraries; six towns organized under the Public Libraries Act, in other words free libraries (in Wolesley, Carnduff, Estevan, Oxbow, Sintaluta, Lanigan); and 20 libraries organized under the Mechanics' and Literary Institutes Act, or subscription libraries.

The story from 1918 to 1921 showed a sharp increase in demand and the constant need for more money. Hawkes said, "ever since the first library was sent out I have had to discourage propaganda, and avoid publicity as much as possible to prevent being overwhelmed with applications we had not the money to fill."[9] That year the whole budget would be spent four months before the end of the year and without a supplement the service would have to close down. As well, many of the early books "are being read practically to pieces"[10] and needed to be replaced. In 1919 it was the same story, not enough money to finish the year, costs rising, 65 libraries behind, the winter rush about to happen, and a recent communication from the Saskatchewan Grain Growers' Association asking for information to send all their locals. "The probable result if we were to comply with their request would be appalling"[11] said McDonald. By 1920 Hawkes said an additional $17,760 would clear off all the arrears; the 1920-21 budget was $8,500 so the need was enormous, partly because of demand (600 libraries in circulation by 1921) and partly because of increased costs (50% over 1914). They received $15,060, almost four times the 1918-19 figure, but not nearly enough, said McDonald in a report for Hawkes. She projected they would be out of money by October. The 200 new libraries they created that year were costly, at $100 each, but necessary. "Practically every application received after November last year was filled with this year's appropriation."[12] McDonald reckoned an annual circulation of 60,000 books.

Premier W.M. Martin, also minister of education, spoke on the virtues of the system in an article printed in the *Saskatoon Phoenix,* December 6, 1919. Travelling Libraries, he said, were ordinarily sent to isolated Saskatchewan districts, "where books are a blessing many times over in homes remote from the centres of population." In particular, "Many of our soldiers are settling on the land. They want books, and 'field workers' in connection with the Soldiers' Settlement board are sending in appeals for help from book-hungry districts." It's attractive to have a premier defending library service.

Later in 1919 the government decided to create a Bureau of Publications to administer Travelling Libraries, the new Open Shelf Library, and other government activities including moving pictures. Under Hawkes, the program had already begun the process of becoming its own government unit, with one staff position transferred from the Legislative Library budget in 1919-20 and a second the following year. W.A. MacLeod, the new commissioner of publications, immediately recognizing the significant financial needs of the travelling libraries, suggested to government that it publicize community libraries as a way to substantially reduce costs; but that initiative would have to wait until the 1950s when a provincial librarian was finally appointed. The costs for the Travelling Libraries for 1921-22 was $27,060; by 1922-23, $60,292.

A second service, the Open Shelf Library, was begun in 1922. A 1945 report said the library was organized "at the request of the Women Grain Growers."[13] In this case a L. Craig visited the Extension Department at the University of Alberta, which had been created in 1913 to assist people who wanted to read systematically in an area, or acquire knowledge for debates and public discussion.

Circulation there had increased from 1,081 in 1917 to 3,249 in 1920. Only two of all those books were not returned in that period. Craig recommended that government rather than the university handle the work, that the basic book stock for the program come from the Legislative Library or Travelling Library (22,000 and 26,500 books respectively), and proposed a rough breakdown of the kinds of books needed – literature, history, and biography leading all the rest.[14] There are two fascinating pages of statistics on Open Shelf books and readers in 1922-23. Over 6,000 books were mailed, 946 in fiction, 709 in history, 702 in sociology, 675 in literature and so on, while users were overwhelmingly farmers (640), then teachers (215), married women (190), and clergymen (122).[15] The early controversy over the Open Shelf Library was its overwhelming use of the Legislative Library. With little money of its own to build a basic library (a little over a hundred books), it listed in its catalogue about 3,000 volumes from the Legislative Library. MacLeod said the government must make up its mind to transfer those books from the Legislative Library that were little or never used to the Open Shelf, as many as eight or ten thousand books.[16] The matter was debated for a year and an agreement reached September 5, 1923 in a meeting between all the major players at the time: Premier Charles Dunning, also minister in charge of the Legislative Library; S.J. Latta, minister in charge of the Open Shelf; Hawkes and MacLeod. As a result, the Open Shelf would have its own space; Hawkes would examine his books to see which could be given to the Open Shelf; all magazines after three months were to be transferred to the Open Shelf; and debate material would be handled by university extension.

There were catalogues of books published in 1923, 1925, 1931, 1941, and 1943. The latter was 170 pages long with 43 headings: major ones like History and Travel, minor ones like Journalism and Philately, sometimes with no information (like *Elements and Perspective,* John Ruskin, n.d.), sometimes with adequate information (like *Study in Canadian Immigration,* 1920: "Immigration laws and their operational problems of rejection and deportation; education; crime; citizenship."). A Catalogue Supplement, for rural service, had 65 pages listing books purchased between April 1945 and

March 1946, followed by a section for boys and girls, then a section for hobby-followers and fact-seekers.

In the transfer of work away from the legislative librarian, the last word should go to John Hawkes. In 1921, cabinet responsibilities for libraries changed because Premier Martin was no longer both president of council and minister of education, and Latta was minister of education, so the Travelling Libraries moved to his portfolio. Hawkes recollected those humble beginnings in 1914, in the depression following the boom and during the years of the Great War. There were 600 libraries now in rural districts and that meant 600 unpaid librarians. "These librarians, who perform their duties as a labour of love, deserve I think the best thanks we can give them." After he praised the services of Margaret McDonald, he said, "The Travelling Library is a light-bringer in thousands of homes in Saskatchewan." He was proud of the privilege of organizing and supervising it. "I feel that if I have done nothing else I have not lived altogether in vain."[17]

Until 1923, government records on libraries, including travelling and open shelf libraries, were substantial and detailed. Suddenly government sources dried up for 20 years, until the 1944 election of the Co-operative Commonwealth Federation, which like the first three Liberal governments donated full records to the archives, and so to the public. What happened in between can in part be explained by a letter written by Jessie Bothwell, long-time Legislative Librarian. It was the day after the CCF victory in 1944. Because of where Bothwell lived she always entered the Legislative Building by the back door.

> The very next morning after the election I arrived to find the door blockaded by two trucks being loaded with files. In charge of it was Stevenson (afterwards made a Senator) and he suggested that I should go in the front door as they had two other trucks coming to be loaded. He also asked me if there was anything in the Library that should be removed.
>
> I do not know on whose authority but the next day a member of the RNMP. came to the Library and said he had orders to look over the books. He came down from the gallery in a few minutes (I noticed he had looked at a piece

of paper on which he had some notes) and had in his hands G.D.H. Cole's book and another which I cannot recall. I asked him for a receipt for the books but he refused and said he was acting under Government orders.[18]

In such an autocratic state as that, as exhibited by the Patterson Liberal government's exit, libraries as a defence for democracy gain new meaning in the province.

1930s-40s

Information for these years comes primarily from two sources, the provincial government's Public Accounts, which includes the Saskatchewan Bureau of Publication expenditures, and the Dominion Bureau of Statistics which published semi-annual accounts of Canadian libraries, and which sometimes provided comparative provincial statistics on travelling and open shelf libraries, from which two basic conclusions can be drawn, that Saskatchewan led all provinces in travelling libraries, often by a wide margin, while Alberta led open shelf service. The provincial statistics tell us what we probably know already, that service was good in the 1920s, dwindled during the Great Depression and World War Two, and was revitalized after 1944-45. The statistics are not always uniform, but book purchases, one criteria of service, are clear from 1921-22 to 1931-32 and again from 1938-39 to 1947-48, which is the year the provincial and legislative librarian inherited the service, and statistics from this provincial source come to an end. The fourteen thousand dollars worth of books purchased in 1921-22 was the highest expenditure, though book purchases remained healthy through the 1920s, were down to $7,877.53 in 1931-32, and sank, by my estimate, to $21.23 in 1932-33. The book purchases remained largely on hold for fifteen years ($1,176.74 the largest expenditure) until after the war, when over $13,000 was spent on book purchases in each of 1945-46 and 1946-47. The Open Shelf purchases followed the same pattern, usually at about 10% of the expenditures on travelling libraries, occasionally up to

20%. Circulation patterns followed their own curve. In 1929-31 about 3,000 books a year were circulated. In 1932 about 1,000; then from '33 to '35 about 650; while annual statistics went up to 10,000 in '37; to 16,000 in '38; to 37,000 in '40; to 58,000 in '41; and to 84,000 in '42.[19]

From the Dominion Bureau for Statistics for 1935, using figures for the prairies only, Manitoba had 10,700 volumes in travelling libraries, Alberta 12,075, and Saskatchewan 100,000 volumes; Manitoba sent out 182 boxes, Alberta 345, and Saskatchewan 2,200 boxes. Travelling libraries were Saskatchewan's central service, well beyond that of any other province. British Columbia came second with 50,000 volumes and 570 boxes sent out. The best chart comparing all sources for travelling libraries from 1937 and 1943 appears in the 1942-44 Dominion Bureau of Statistics.

TRAVELLING LIBRARY SOURCE	BOOKS AVAILABLE	LIBRARIES SENT OUT	AVERAGE BOOKS PER LIBRARY	CIRCULATION	EXPENDITURE ON BOOKS & REPAIR
Acadia University					
1943	1,000	1	25	75	—
1937	970	11	25	—	—
Dalhousie University					
1943	2,096	46	30	510	$150
1937	1,317	24	30	—	—
St. Francis Xavier University					
1943	7,300	—	—	—	—
1937	7,800	—	25	—	—
Macdonald College					
1943	17,345	162	40	6,440	$1,138
1937	16,500	207	40	—	—
Ontario Dept. of Education					
1943	60,000	1,508	40	65,320	$8,000
1937	30,526	622	45	64,440	—
Sask. Bureau of Publications					
1943	125,000	1,784	45	510,000	$435
1937	98,369	1,917	50	—	—
University of Alberta					
1943	9,000	246	35	10,420	$2,600
1937	5,025	387	35	14,345	—
B.C. Library Commission					
1943	40,785	571	71	—	$5,500
1937	74,526	—	—	—	—

The 1935 Dominion Bureau of Statistics Survey of Libraries in Canada, one of the most interesting, includes the first survey of regional library service in Canada and the first comparative statistics between state systems in the United States and provinces in Canada, listed in order according to circulation per capita. They exhibit the superiority of American funding, with Ontario the first Canadian representative, in 21st place, and Saskatchewan 43rd of 59 jurisdictions, with a circulation of 1.4 books per capita (Ontario 4.1, Alberta 2.1). With 82% of the province lacking library service – though that would not include travelling libraries, obviously – Saskatchewan was third worse; only Arkansas and West Virginia were lower.

THE SASKATOON STORY – 1935-39

In that same 1935 survey there's a great story on how Angus Mowat, appointed chief librarian at the Saskatoon Public Library in September, 1932, had instituted a travelling library scheme. He "solicited and received used books from the public libraries in eastern Canada, and the IODE," had them boxed in Saskatoon and mailed to rural communities, "mainly in the drought areas of the south-west part of Saskatchewan and newly settled districts in the extreme north." In fact, a later map shows a wide distribution of books across the province. Over two years, 716 boxes and almost 40,000 books had been distributed, and sometimes exchanged with other communities. This is a remarkable story and makes Saskatoon the third largest service of its kind in Canada. There were 278 boxes sent out in 1933-34, 438 in 1934-35, 303 in 1935-36, 241 in 1936-37, 540 in 1937-38, and 150 by December 1937.[20] The program ceased with the beginning of the war.

The plan started this way. Mowat visited a settler in northern Saskatchewan who had been forced north by the drought from his home place in the south. "Mr. Mowat discovered an intelligent and well-read family that had been reduced to a few tattered newspapers as their only winter's supply of reading material."[20] He laid the gen-

Angus Mowatt standing next to a CPR freight wagon loaded with about 55 cardboard boxes filled with books, each bearing the label "Ten Thousand Books/ Given by the Public Library Board of the City of Toronto/ to the people in rural districts of Saskatchewan/ to be distributed at the direction of / Angus Mowat, Esq./ Librarian of the Public Library/ Saskatoon, Saskatchewan." *(Photo courtesy Queen's Quarterly.)*

eral dilemma before George Locke, chief librarian of the Toronto Public Library, and Locke contributed 5,000 discards and began to talk to his colleagues. Through Locke's discussion with the minister of transportation, both railways delivered the books free, as Red Cross shipments. Mowat too wrote letters to other libraries and books came pouring in from everywhere: from Amherst, Dundas, Galt, Guelph, Orillia, Stratford, Walkerton, Queens, Brockville, Mimico, Woodstock, and McGill.

George Stephen, vice-president of the CPR, arranged for 2,000 books. The greatest source of books, however, was the IODE, which arranged through its branches for 40,000 books to be sent. The Saskatoon service depended entirely on these donations. The increase in service in 1937-38 over the previous year coincided with Mowat taking a new job as Inspector of Ontario Libraries and so increasing the Ontario contribution one more time.

Saskatoon's contribution to what was called the Rural Book

Distribution Scheme was to build the boxes, to contain about 60 books each, and then to ship them, though borrowers had to pay shipping costs (usually less than a dollar). Very few were returned to Saskatoon. To receive a box a simple letter of request was all that was required. Teachers could apply for their schools. Local libraries with a small stock could apply. Four hundred books were sent to the Saskatoon Relief Camp. The books were sent out once a year, in the fall. The cost to the Saskatoon Public Library, other than for staff time, was small. At its December 1933 meeting the library board passed a motion "That Mr. Mowat be authorized to spend $25 on boxes in which to ship books for distribution in the country." The service cost $797.19 in 1934-35 out of a $34,000 budget. The amount went down year by year to $122.67 by 1938-39.

Letters of appreciation were published in the October 7, 1937, *StarPhoenix*. "I am humbly appealing to you for books.... I hope my application will not be in vain, for this would mean another pent-in Winter in an isolated district with no other recreation than an hour of leisure reading, but nothing to read whatever." The writer says the neighbours are in the same condition, "They all love books but cannot afford them." Another writer expresses enthusiasm: "I was never so glad in my life when I lifted the box from the station and knew they were books, books to read." Neighbours came over that night for the pleasure of the books. When they were done they passed them on to another district, partly because they couldn't pay the freight rate back to Saskatoon.

Because so few books were added to the provincial Travelling Libraries in the '30s and because that program could not fulfill all the demands, the Saskatoon initiative was especially important.

1944 AND THE CCF

When the CCF came to power in Saskatchewan in June of 1944, it inherited the two provincial library systems, the travelling and open shelf libraries, which after hard times and few book purchases had ceased to be effective. The government suspended service in

September 1944. A survey of the libraries was undertaken by T.H. McLeod (who would later co-author a biography of Tommy Douglas) "who generously offered his services."[22] Potential users were informed the service was suspended, and it was resumed in February 1945. The new librarian in charge of the Travelling Libraries, Mrs. R.J. Brandon, wrote a detailed letter on the world she had inherited (to apply for a job reclassification). The Travelling Library had already been moved from the basement of the Legislative Building to the Education Annex at the rear of the building, but had never been organized. Returned boxes "were stacked almost to the ceiling in aisles and every bit of space in the main office" was taken as well as the shipping rooms.[23] There was tension in the staff, a number of people retiring, and a request from Jessie Bothwell to get the libraries out again. The libraries were rundown; there were no accurate statistics kept by the previous librarian and former cabinet minister, S.J. Latta; many books were not fit for circulation, as "worn out, outdated, the print too fine," and so on; the library boxes were in disrepair, and had to be mended, scrubbed, and – when in the shortages after the war, paint was even available – painted. There had been no system of cataloguing and with the assistance of the new provincial cataloguer the task was completed, though, reported Brandon, to cross-file by both title and author was time consuming. By 1946 statistics on service were compiled monthly.

A request from Bertha Oxner of the University of Saskatchewan that the Lady Tweedsmuir Travelling Libraries be identified book by book was "*a long and tedious task.*" Eventually the collection as a unit was transferred to the Legislative Library "where they [were] to be assembled as an historic unit – of the 'dirty thirties.'" That was one way to dispose of books. There were also many discards made throughout the system, about 3,000, but some discards were sent one last time to "folks who were bed-ridden or crippled who ask for certain works to pass the time." To those who had the least were given the least. At the same time the CCF government had increased the book budget substantially and pocket additions were added.

The Open Shelf Library, fallen into disrepute, was renamed The Public Information Library. It too was culled of about 3,000 books, the Juvenile section "limp and worn."[24] Twelve hundred adult books and 200 children's books were added, as well as pamphlets. Books in demand included travel, 13%; literature, 12%; fine arts, 11%; history, 10%; and so on, while the 835 new users of the program included students 40%; farmers 24%; housewives 14%; teachers 9%; and so on. It was assumed the student increase "is traceable to the cancellation of the fifty cent fee."

There were many letters of appreciation for the Travelling Libraries. "We are all pleased with the improvement in Travelling Libraries in the last two years," wrote Frank Meakes of Lestock. "Our school enjoyed the last library very much. We all thought the selection of books was particularly good. (32 readers)," wrote Elma Wudrick of Aberdeen. "I am very anxious to procure a Library for my school. I believe there will be over thirty readers, and there is no good library nearby" wrote Miss L.M. Mossip from Macklin. That's a selection from sixty or so letters.[25] There was one remarkable letter in 1947, from Fond du Lac, where the freight arrived twice a year, June 7 and September 7. "We all (Mr. Black, Mr. Kostner, Father Danto, Father Gamache, my little daughter included and I) have had many hours of real enjoyment from a very fine selection of reading material...We will look forward to another library next year."[26] By 1946 the service went to 135 schools in the province, to some of them more than once. They've been everywhere, to Alvena, Beaubier, Candiac, Carnduff, Clair, Cochin, Cupar, Drake, Gray, Gronlid, Hazel Dell, Hubbard, Jedburgh, Kelvington, Keppel, Kuroki, Marengo, Merle, Mikado, Mossbank, Nokomis, Osler, Riceton, Robsart, Stonehenge, Tessier, Veregin, Watson, Wolfe, Wymark, Zealandia, and Zelma.

The Travelling Library remained active through the 1940s, though service appeared much constrained compared to those 1930 and 1940 statistics; 130,000 books circulated in 1943. The library sent out 490 boxes and 25,000 books in that year of suspended service, 1944-45; sent out 583 boxes the following year; and over 600 boxes and 40,000 books from 1947 to 1950.[27] Brandon had been asked to provide statistics for 1943-44. She said Latta had published a pamphlet, *Saskatchewan, A Few Facts* which claimed, "Nearly 2000 libraries circulate approximately 100,000 books to Saskatchewan people." When Brandon examined the shipping records for 1943/44, she said 589 libraries had been sent, not 2,000. She said Latta must have included boxes in the country that hadn't been returned and dormant boxes in the store room. It is possible that Saskatchewan's great lead in the circulation of fiction, a mainstay of the travelling library, may have been part fiction itself.[28]

1953 TO 1986

The story is picked up again after 1953 in the annual reports of the new Provincial Library. The 1953 report defines the kinds of books sent in those boxes:

> Because the [travelling] libraries are for recreational reading the book collection is predominantly fiction: novels, westerns and mysteries, with some non-fiction, particularly biographies and books about personal experiences and travel. Children's books are included in a library when requested.

One of the people who enjoyed the travelling libraries was Ned Shillington, who would one day be minister in charge of libraries. As a boy, Shillington attended Grayburn rural school, northwest of Moose Jaw. The school received travelling libraries, in military boxes, the length of a rifle. "We read whatever came." The school owned but one book, a 1923 Encyclopedia, so travelling libraries were important for reading kids.[29] By 1954 there was one innovation. "A small public or community library, however, may borrow a box containing children's books only." According to the 1957 Provincial Library Report, numbers were down, under 500 boxes sent out. "According to letters received this is due to TV, moving away, and lack of time." It's also the year Brandon retired. The following year questionnaires were sent to users and 271 responses were received. "Over 75% were genuinely pleased with the service. Three custodians in entirely different sections of the province stated they had appreciated the service for 38, 30 and 25 years respectively." In 1959 the loaning of boxes to small libraries "includes small collections of children's books, the display collection for Young Canada Book Week and the non-English collection," though that year of 328 libraries sent out, 68 went to schools and only 17 to libraries.

In 1960 Frontier College instructors "asked if boxes of books could be sent to the summer work gangs in Saskatchewan," and six boxes were sent. But that was the last new service for travelling libraries. Use had been declining during the decade, from the over 500 boxes until 1955, to 477 in 1956, 468 in 1957, 297 in 1958, 328 in 1959, and 311 in 1960, the last full year of service.

The reasons for the service's demise in 1961: "improved roads, electricity, curling, radio and television, telephones and paperback books in many stores have all contributed." The books were being redistributed, some to the Public Information Library, others to pioneer lodges, to jails, hospitals, and to libraries if they came and chose. But the service begun in 1915, a central service for over half a century, had come to an end. "The sturdy grey travelling library boxes which, since 1915, were such a welcome sight on most railway station platforms will soon be only a memory."

As the travelling libraries came to an end the Public Information Library went from strength to strength, in circulation, in answering reference questions, and later in providing interlibrary loan requests. In 1953 reference services were provided to "students, members of book clubs, Home and School Associations, Homemakers' and individuals" – responding to 678 questions in all, in such subjects as Calypso music, the story of Christmas cards, racial prejudice, censorship, how to mount a deer's head, the United Nations, how to make a parrot talk, and stage makeup. Circulation increased from 44,873 in 1953 to 115, 371 by 1961, and 152,491 in 1967. By 1959, "biography is the most popular subject, followed closely by travel and books in useful arts, including how-to-do-it." That doesn't take into account children's story and picture books. There were no novels in the service. "More children, students, farmers and housewives are registered as borrowers than other groups, but the files indicate...service is also given to a cat operator, a beekeeper, welder, entertainer and sheep herder." When the travelling libraries were abolished in 1961, "the demand for books for adults and children continue[d] to increase."

By 1963 people were asking for help on current topics: Russia, independence of African states, an ecumenical conference in Rome, analogue computers, space travel, atomic energy, automation. "The tremendous increase in student requests for help in term papers caused such a drain on resources that the staff was hard-pressed to cope with the situation." The annual reports often included a few letters of appreciation for the service, like this one from 1963:

> My family and I have eagerly anticipated the parcel of books as we live out in the country on a farm and can devote much time to reading. I have received books from your library that have fostered life-long interests such as amateur astronomy and experimental chemistry....I believe that it is largely due to your service that I am now able to leave home for the University of Saskatchewan at Saskatoon where I will study sciences.

There were changes in how and what was done, including a photocopying machine to copy encyclopedia passages and the like. According to the 1965 report, the media became important. "Television and radio programs definitely have a strong influence on library use and it was necessary to buy multiple copies of books by two Canadian authors, *The Comfortable Pew* by Berton, and *Terror in the Name of God* by Holt, to meet the demand controversial publicity had created." By 1966 reinforced paperback books replaced books out of print. Interlibrary loan had begun, with 2445 interlibrary loans (ILLO) received in 1966, 4,624 a year later, 10,614 by 1969, and 50,151 in 1973. That was one sign of the growing regionalization of the province: Southeast library region was formed in 1965, Wheatland in 1966, Parkland in 1967, Chinook in 1971, Lakeland in 1972, and Palliser in 1973.

Toward the end of 1968 "it was decided that those residing in established regions should be encouraged to borrow from the Regional Library through their local branch," both to increase numbers in local branches and to make people aware that the Provincial Library "will eventually end this service," which it did on April 1,

1969, withdrawing all service to rural people if they lived within a regional library area. "Hundreds of replies poured into the library. They varied in tone from acrimonious political denunciation to resigned acceptance of the deprivation, but many wrote letters of appreciation for the service they had received for years." There were those unfortunate people who resided within a regional library's jurisdiction, but whose community had not joined. For them library service as they had known it came to an end, so the better world for most imposed hardships on the few.

Harry Newsom notified all residents within established regions (four of them on February 10, 1969) that as of March 31, 1969, the mailing of books to anyone living in a region would cease, so as to promote local library service through the regional system, not of course a universally popular decision. There were two letters of protest from Redvers. "Our taxes are high enough we should get library service even by mail,"[30] wrote one woman. A second woman from Redvers protested "vehemently." The nearest libraries were in Manor and Mayfield, 22 and 25 miles away, while her family did its business in Redvers, where there was no likelihood, she said, of a branch library being created. They'd been using the Information Library for five years:

> My husband has used electric reference books to supplement technical magazines in the radio and television field. Our children have exceptional reading ability and a wide variety of hobbies and interests....Family hobbies include oil painting, stamp collecting, music, antiques and current events, on all of which subjects we received reference books during the last year.

Now there would be "a real vacuum in our family."[31] Another woman, who belonged to a branch library at Manor, found "we do not have the reference books at our disposal, nor the variety of reading material."[32]

Another who felt library rights were taken away was a seventeen-year-old boy from Theodore, who found, once Parkland had been established, "that I would have to pay ten dollars a year and travel nearly twenty miles on a poor road to Jedburg if I wanted library books." He was told in reply – I assume by form letter – to work to make his own municipality join the region. "I need the services of a library now. And then why should I stay here," for, he argued, "city people get far more services though rural taxes are higher."[33]

For the next year, 1970, circulation went down from 127,853 to 110,865, while ILLO requests sharply increased, from 10,614 to 17,967 in one year, suggesting many people had responded to the change.

The Provincial Library collection became by 1970 "an ever increasing back-up to the libraries of the province," and 1971 circulation statistics were on the rise, while the library created "kits on those subjects for which there ha[d] been a great demand," often from students choosing identical topics like problems of Pakistan, Northern Ireland, Quebec, Vietnam, or drugs. There must have been good teachers in Saskatchewan to assign such topics. Readers in Chinook lost their direct service in 1973. "The two newest regional libraries, Lakeland and Palliser, decided that unlike the other regions they do not want their members cut off from direct service." Yet Lakeland residents were sent letters of discontinuance in June 1975, Palliser a year later. The Provincial Library was now sending kits of books to other libraries on topics of the day: the metric system, Watergate, the energy crisis, Remembrance Day, and so on, as well as, in 1975, "advance reference materials and blocks of books to the regional, public and government libraries," and to the community colleges. "Instructors request 15 to 30 books at a time for students." There was still direct service to the far north, to handicapped residents, and to individuals when requests were received from other libraries, and thus the dramatic increase in ILLO, up to 79,118 requests in 1977 and 93,643 in 1982.

Technology began to transform services. The telex sped up the reference service – to a turnaround of 48 hours. Computer searches had begun in a small way in 1978, with 807 searches. The Provincial Library report includes a 1980 Canadian comparison on ILLO, as one sign of how much more integrated the Saskatchewan system was by

COMPARISON OF INTERLIBRARY LOAN – 1980

LIBRARY	TITLE* REQUESTS RECEIVED	PROFES- SIONAL STAFF	TECHNICAL STAFF	CLERICAL STAFF	TOTAL	RATIO STAFF: REQUESTS
Alberta Library Services Branch	12,098	1	2	—	3	1:4,032
British Columbia Library Services Branch	12,783	3	—	3	6	1:210
Manitoba Public Library Services	4,492	—	1.5	0.5	2	1:2,246
New Brunswick Library Services	2,232	—	0.5	0.5	1	1:2,232
Newfoundland Public Library Services	4,943	—	2	2	3	1:1,647
Nova Scotia Provincial Library	9,548	1	—	—	4	1:2,387
Saskatchewan Provincial Library	72,543	2	4	4.5	10.5	1:6,908
Yukon Library Services Branch	1,280	—	—	1	1	1:1,280
Northwest Territories Public Library Services	1,82	0.5	1	1.5	3	1:60
National Library of Canada	145,000	8	4	21	33	1:4,393
Canadian Institute for Scientific & Technical Information	184,000				44	1:4,181
Pacific Northwest Bibliographic Centre	63,853	10.5	2	2	14.5	1:4,403
Ontario	no central ILLO service					
Prince Edward Island	no central ILLO service					
Quebec	no central ILLO service					

* Reference requests are not included.

that year than other provinces.

One principle of the Provincial Library was to "facilitate equal access to library resources for all the residents of Saskatchewan," and in 1985 it targeted "children, persons who are handicapped, seniors and ethnic groups." The library sponsored tours by children's authors, purchased talking and large-print books, purchased and circulated materials in eight languages. 1986 was the last year in which an independent and detailed Provincial Library Report appeared. Circulation was 182,583; ILLO 81,136.

Then in 1986-87 the Provincial Library Annual Report was folded into an Annual Report of Saskatchewan Education under Conservative Minister Lorne Hepworth. 1986 was also a black year for regional libraries, when the Progressive Conservatives cut the budget by 11.7%. The new report contained no statistics and almost no narrative. In 1991, under the returned New Democratic Party, the Library was transferred out of the Department of Education, where it had resided from its beginning in 1953 and where all library services had their home since 1914, to Community Services. There was marginally more information, even statistics for 1992: circulation at 98,067 in 1991 and 89,452 in 1992; reference questions around 5,000; ILLO requests at 63,845 in 1991 and 62,678 for 1992; and that's that, government decisions limiting public knowledge of a major public institution, one of whose central aims is to convey information.

Chapter Four

The Depression and the CCF
1930-1945

THE FIRST VIEW OF SASKATCHEWAN LIBRARIES IN THE 1930s was part of the first survey of libraries in the country, *Libraries in Canada, a Study of Library Conditions and Needs*, published in 1933 by Ryerson Press,[1] though the survey itself was completed in 1930, by a Commission of Enquiry made up of John Ridlington, librarian at the University of British Columbia; Mary J.L. Black, librarian at Fort William Public Library; and George Locke, chief librarian at Toronto Public Library. Their ideal, to simplify a rich passage, was the "desirability of providing access to knowledge" (p. 7) in the Canadian democracy, with books the great source of education, yet, as they discovered in their survey, "four-fifths of the Canadian population...[were] utterly without library service of any kind" (p. 139). Their recommendations were three: larger library units (the Fraser Valley experiment with a regional library system as one of their touchstones), extension of library service through branches and library trucks, and more trained professional librarians.

When they visited each province they began with basic statistics. For Saskatchewan – 925,000 people, two-thirds on farms, many races represented, no large cities. They mentioned five urban libraries.

"The Regina Library is without question, the best public library in Saskatchewan." Saskatoon was statistics only without comment. Moose Jaw had a good library building and good service. The Prince Albert Library worked under the most difficult position with only a $3,000 annual grant, but did as best it could. North Battleford, the commissioners said, could be criticized for staff, administration, and book stock. They spoke briefly of the Open Shelf and the Travelling Library, commenting on the latter: "Supposing that fifty people made use of each case of books (a far too liberal estimate) this would mean that only 75,000 people had been reached out of a rural population of 550,000" (p. 78).

Yet the commissioners expressed hope for Saskatchewan. While the province had many social problems, they noted that "it has the power and will to meet these bravely and successfully...and the whole province is permeated and animated by a spirit of confidence, initiative and progressiveness" (pp. 75-76). They were especially impressed with Attorney General Murdoch MacPherson and Premier Anderson, who both knew of the Fraser Valley experiment and were "keen on enquiring if there was a possibility of putting into operation a similar demonstration in Saskatchewan, if the government were willing to go halfway" (p. 79). "To sum up, Saskatchewan is a most hopeful and promising province for a comprehensive and creative library experiment." There was even more praise, not least of all for the government. What was needed, they said, was an organizing librarian, a commission of interested laymen, and a demonstration library. They concluded, "no part of this great dominion combines at once such need and such hopeful promise" (p. 80).

No one in 1930 could predict the devastation that would visit Saskatchewan for the rest of the 1930s. After 1944, a new government, in better economic conditions, could finally begin the experiment that would lead in time to a superb library service, fulfilling the hopes expressed fifteen years earlier.

The single best local source on Saskatchewan libraries in the 1930s was a questionnaire sent out to Homemakers' Clubs by Bertha Oxner, director of womens' work at the University of Saskatchewan, and information gleaned from her tour of rural libraries, both in

1935. She said the survey was inadequate because not everyone replied to her questionnaire. Still, sixty-nine Homemakers' Clubs said they ran libraries, either free or fee paying, with ten libraries started in the last year (October 1934 to March 1935). Book stock was acquired through Travelling Libraries and the Saskatoon Public Library travelling service, as well as through donations and purchases. Oxner's negative conclusion was on "the fragmentary way in which the work is being carried on," on duplication, and on the failure of coordination between libraries, though some, she felt, would like to co-operate "but [were] puzzled how to proceed."[2]

In her tour, she said, there were libraries all along the line from Chamberlain to Davidson, plus Dundurn, but all had acted individually to select books. When she spoke at the Homemakers' convention of the Davidson district, she suggested a district library committee. She then presented a number of small success stories in coordination. There were 115 non-resident borrowers living outside Saskatoon who received library service for a fee of a dollar a year plus postage. The Halcyonia (rural) Homemakers' Club had made arrangements with the IODE library at Kerrobert. At Warman, the school districts operated under the Mechanics' and Literary Institute Act, received the government's $50 annual grant, and exchanged books between schools. The Garnock Homemakers' Club, under the same act, distributed 600 books in two rural locations and in the town of Kelliher. Oxner suggested Nokomis as a potential centre for a small regional library experiment, with smaller libraries at Tate, Venn, Simpson, and Semans as part of the experiment.

Oxner learned there were difficulties with the two provincial programs. Many, she said, would like to use the Open Shelf library but didn't, "as they [found] it difficult to make a selection from a catalogue list." Six of eight Homemakers' Clubs were unable to secure travelling libraries because they weren't available.

Oxner realized that co-operation between libraries was limited because of weather and roads, so only communities near each other could join together. Still, hers is an early account suggesting regional libraries as the Saskatchewan solution. By 1935, Prince Edward Island, Ontario, and British Columbia were engaged in regional experiments. The Saskatchewan reality was fragmentation.

The third basic document of the period is a brief, "Post-War Library Service for Saskatchewan," presented by the Saskatchewan Library Association (SLA) to the Saskatchewan Reconstruction Council. That body had been set up under a Liberal government but reported to the new CCF government. The SLA brief, written by chair Cecil Lingard, secretary Emma Bell, and Arthur R. Stevens, was dated March 1944 and presented in a Regina meeting. Their ideal, "education for democratic living," could partly be realized by an extension of library service. They presented a picture of library service in the province which was both detailed and bleak. "There's a fair degree of adequate service in Regina, Saskatoon, and Moose Jaw." Other large collections served their own audience: the Legislative Library, the university and college libraries. In rural Saskatchewan there were 23 free libraries and 26 Mechanics' and Literary Institutes, but for both services they reported, "the great majority of books [were] old, worn, and out-of-date." There were other smaller services, such as the Wheat Pool Library which circulated its 1,100 books to its members. There was the limited service of the Saskatoon Public Library, the Lady Tweedsmuir Library, "the small circulation homemakers' libraries," and finally the Open Shelf and the Travelling Library. Their statistics were drawn from the Bureau of Publications. School libraries were inadequate, the ten-dollar requirement in the act used by schools and school boards more as a maximum than a minimum. There were correspondence classes and extension courses from the university, both with inadequate books, and an inadequate library service from the Legion War Services Education Board which offered classes. How bad was library service in Saskatchewan? "Existing library services in this province are in no way adequate to the task that lies ahead." The number of registered public library borrowers in Saskatchewan was 69,500 or only 7.1 percent of the population, while the library book stock totalled 275,000 or .3 books per capita. The total book stock purchases of the public libraries and the two provincial programs added up to $25,151.74 for the year, "which represents 2.8 cents per capita in Saskatchewan as compared with 15 cents in Alberta, 31 cents in

British Columbia, and 37 cents in Ontario." If you took away the Regina expenditure of 92 cents and Saskatoon's 70 cents per capita, "the figure of 2.8 cents per capita for all Saskatchewan reveals an appalling fact."

Their recommendations revolved around a single concept, the creation of a library commission for Saskatchewan which would: "supervise all Saskatchewan library affairs including Open Shelf and Travelling Libraries; extend library service; be adequately funded; be the granting agency; set standards; and provide training opportunities for librarians. The commission should apply to the Carnegie Foundation for a survey and to "institute an initial Regional library experiment," and should look to the British Columbia model of service.

Chapter Five

Regional Libraries and North Central
1944-1962

THE FIRST EXPERIMENT, TROSSACHS AND WEYBURN,

1944-45, AGNES WEWELER

N THE SUMMER OF 1944 AGNES WEWELER OF TROSSACHS
(17 kilometres west of Weyburn) began a campaign to introduce regional library service in her area. By that fall a South
Saskatchewan Regional Library Committee had been formed,
with Weweler as secretary-treasurer, four members from Weyburn,
one from the RM of Brokenshell, in which Trossachs was a village,
one from a Homemakers' Club, and a superintendent of schools.
Weweler was clearly the moving force. She'd earlier written the
American Library Association and the Canadian Library Council
(CLC), asking the latter for 200 copies of the excellent pamphlet by
Nora Bateson, *Rural Canada Needs Libraries.* Her plan was to create
a region of 20 rural municipalities, one city, four towns, and 26 vil-
lages.[1] Mrs. Weweler was an unknown but John Lothian, English
professor and Saskatchewan representative on the CLC, asked
Bertha Oxner, head of women's work at the University of
Saskatchewan, about her and she replied, "Mrs. Weweler is a trained

and experienced librarian who is doing excellent work at Trossachs."[2]

By September, Weweler said little had been done but to contact groups, and it was slow work. "Since making my first contact with various organizations regarding the possibility of this type of service, not one person has said, 'Oh, yes, I have heard about regional libraries.'"[3] No one on the Weyburn Library Board, she said, had heard of the experiments in British Columbia or Prince Edward Island, and no one from the Weyburn Library Board was on her committee. The Saskatoon branch of the SLA passed a motion of support including this phrase: "in particular...supporting and publicizing the effort to secure a regional library experiment in the Weyburn-Trossachs area."[4] A second motion offered a representative of the SLA to accompany the Weyburn-Trossachs delegation to meet with Premier T.C. Douglas who had only come to power a few weeks earlier. Weweler had already written to Douglas September 26, hoping that Carnegie funding could assist a regional experiment in her area, and said she had conducted a miniature regional library in Brokenshell, "since the fall of 1940, serving two village and five rural schools."[5] When she learned that four boxes of books were waiting she said they would "inter-loan" 100 books to Ogema.[6]

The Saskatchewan Library Association met on October 17 with Premier Douglas and two cabinet ministers, Woodrow Lloyd, minister of education and therefore in charge of libraries, and John Sturdy, minister of reconstruction. (They took a full package of information with them, including the 1933 Ridlington Report, regional legislation in BC and PEI, the 1933 and 1935 Dominion Bureau of Statistics reports, plus information on the SLA.) An undated SLA report, but which must have been part of their presentation, included this central statement: "We support [Weweler] in her zeal for realizing the great need for Rural Library Service in Saskatchewan, and particularly in her own district. We feel any such experiment in regional library service should be made as part of a larger province-wide project."[7] They proposed a survey which would determine the best site for a regional experiment. The memo also promised Carnegie support without any evidence that this would be forthcoming, and indeed it wouldn't be. Saskatchewan would have to go it on its own.

Weweler and a delegation of two met with Douglas in November, a good meeting, she said: "when legislation for regional libraries is provided, it will be in line with that of Nova Scotia.... The dollar for dollar plan is the best incentive for local support."[8] Part of her advocacy was a resolution for a regional library in southern Saskatchewan, and 102 communities (including Weyburn) and school districts submitted such a petition.

The most extensive information on the South Saskatchewan Regional Library, and on Agnes Weweler herself, is in correspondence with Violet McNaughton, women's editor of the *Western Producer.* The communities which signed a resolution for a demonstration area for a regional library included Griffin, Fillmore, Morton, Tecumseh, Radville, Halbrite, Carievale, Tribune; a number of groups, like home and school associations, also signed. Weweler speaks of her own joys in libraries:

> All my life I had the idea that it would be wonderful to be able to go to a town and in addition to a little shopping and getting the mail, go to a library and get something to read. But I never was all my life where it was possible to use a library.... I should add that I lived over eight miles from a post office and that there is not a single person living beside the road in all these eight miles. In the winter there is a period of three to four months when I never leave the farm and never see a single person from the outside.[9]

She decided to organize a library and spent time in the Regina Public Library in the winter of 1937. "When I was in Regina this fall the girls who were there at that time reminded me of how I wept that first day." She had never experienced the joy of being a borrower before. Then she enrolled in 1938 in the library course at the University of Toronto. Here is part of a report on her work there, as supervised practice in a Toronto branch: "She is aggressive in a quiet way, makes herself always the centre of the stage, and would advertise anything with which she was concerned. She seemed to realize that the work of a Branch was to maintain a distance between books and people."[10] The war slowed down her plans, but she organized the Trossachs Community Library, under the Mechanics' and Literary Institute Act, though with some difficulties, including the local Homemakers' Club: "Whenever I talked library service the members just clutched their purses and glared...I believe some of them took to sitting on them!"[11]

Her view of regional libraries is close to what came to pass: "Libraries organized on the co-operative plan, under provincial direction, of course, but regional in scope, with local control and as much local support as possible."[12] That same month Weweler knew there would be no Carnegie money, said her library activities "are done on the fly between the kitchen and the cradle," and asked for articles on the Fraser Valley System.[13]

An article celebrating the Trossachs-Weyburn experiment appeared in the February 15, 1945, *Western Producer*. It included the motion the group made to the province – a general motion on the need for a demonstration regional library. Weweler had learned to do book repairs in her time in Toronto, and was doing them now at Trossachs, at five cents a book, using gunny sacking for worn covers, unbleached cotton or flour sacking for hinges, brown paper for end papers, flour paste and harness thread for sewing. She would saturate the gunny sacking with paste and then press for a good finish. Saskatchewan as a make-do province. There were 2,000 books in the Trossachs Library, and books were sent to the schools, changed two or three times a year.

One response to the article was negative, from Suzie Gaught, on behalf of a Homemakers' Club which felt betrayed by the omission of its contribution. A sidelight of considerable interest in Gaught's letter is her commentary on crop conditions in the area year by year: 1935 – "Rust caused the grain to grade very low"; 1936 – "the crop nearly made expenses"; 1937 – "the crop didn't even provide fodder for the stock"; 1938 – "most farmers had enough Thatcher wheat to provide seed for the next year"; 1939 – "Every year since this the crops have been bumpers." All of which meant it was easier to support libraries than it had been.[14] Mrs. Weweler replied to charges and returned the compliment. She also suggested "that a book pool be set up in

Saskatchewan from which small communities could receive a few hundred books as a new nucleus." She added, "It is a heart-breaking experience trying to organize a library from scratch."[15]

LIBRARY ON WHEELS, NATIONAL FILM BOARD, 1944-45

The National Film Board of Canada made its first film on libraries in 1944 and the Canadian Library Council (which became the Canadian Library Association in 1946) was consulted. "The National Film Board has been interested in producing a regional library film in their Community Projects Series." The main shooting, Elizabeth Morton, secretary of the CLC, said, would be of the Fraser Valley experiment. However, "If any interesting organization moves [were] being made in Weyburn-Trossachs, Mr. Macdonald might consider stopping off to take some 'shots' there of a regional scheme in the organization stage."[16]

The Saskatchewan response was to see if money might be forthcoming to support filming in Saskatchewan. On August 11, J.S. Thomson, president of the University of Saskatchewan, suggested Morton contact J.S. Latta. On August 14, John Lothian suggested the chair of the SLA, Emma Bell, should contact the premier, the minister of highways (Open Shelf), the minister of education, and Morley Toombs, head of audio-visuals in the department of education. Toombs did approach Lloyd and Douglas and they wanted information on the purpose of the film and financing. The NFB sent a representative to Weyburn, who was there on August 24, and who "made a report back to the Board and the Board now has a unit in BC."[17] Lothian was friends with fellow Scot and NFB Commissioner John Grierson, and had talked to him as early as 1943 on linking library service with radio and film.

The film focused entirely on the Fraser Valley experiment, the first regional service in Canada, begun in 1930.[18] Its purpose: "By describing the Fraser Valley project, *Library On Wheels* may provide workable ideas to people in other areas where good books are now a luxury for the few, rather than the common possession of all."[19]

That's an excellent formulation of one central principle of libraries in general and regional libraries in particular.

Eighty prints of the film were released to rural Canada in September and October of 1945, and reports collected, two of them from Saskatchewan, one negative, one positive. D. Sharples was negative; saying, "I found a passionate lack of interest in libraries in the people of my district." But then, "they have no library facilities to turn to." Teachers and others knew their worth. B.L. Korchinski was positive and even thought regional libraries were on the way in his area. "At Parkside and Debden, committees were set up to explore the situation and report to the audience at the next program," he said. There was an active response at Hoey; people would ask their MLA to take up the matter at the next session, "and to introduce necessary legislation providing service to rural areas." Domremy "has a banker as its chairman, and a lawyer, a merchant, a farmer's wife and seven rural school teachers as its members." Wakaw and Rosthern were active and it all pointed to a Saskatchewan River Valley Regional Library Service.[20] Two of the communities, Hoey and Domremy, were in at the beginning of the North Central Library Region.

SASKATCHEWAN LIBRARY ADVISORY COUNCIL
AND HIRING MARION GILROY, 1945-46

The new CCF government renewed the Open Shelf (now Public Information) and Travelling Library. It also created a Saskatchewan Library Advisory Council (SLAC) whose terms of reference from an Order in Council were:

> To study the library system of the Province with the view of making recommendations to the Government as to necessary library extensionand to advise upon all matters concerning the Library Department that may be referred to them by the President of the Council and by the Lieutenant Governor in Council.[21]

The SLAC was a more moderate government response than the library commission proposed by the 1944 SLA brief to the Reconstruction Council. Carlyle King, chair both of the CCF party and the SLAC, and education minister Woodrow Lloyd, had talked the matter over. "I am inclined to agree that we are not ready for a regional library commission on a statutory basis as yet,"[22] Lloyd wrote. King had raised the matter earlier because Jesse Bothwell didn't feel she should or could supervise the regional librarian. SLAC would eventually be responsible. Indeed at that first December 5, 1945 SLAC meeting this crucial motion was passed:

> Resolved that we write to the proper official of the Canadian Library Council and make enquiry as to chances of obtaining a trained librarian through the Canadian Library Council to make a survey of library needs in Saskatchewan.

Those words are the beginning of regional library service in the province. The continuation of that first meeting on January 4 and 5, 1946, resulted in eight recommendations: first that government pass enabling legislation to allow for regional libraries; that its contribution be $10,000 to assist in establishing the first regional library; that it pay dollar for dollar with the region to maintain the library; and that an organizer for regional libraries be hired. A second series of motions spoke to the need for trained librarians in the province, asking the Department of Education to hire such librarians in its jurisdiction, including normal schools – a rate scale was included – and that scholarships for library study be implemented. There was also one recommendation on the need for more space for public information and travelling libraries. One member of the committee, Mrs. Harrington, was important to King, because she was a Saskatoon library trustee, and a practising librarian interested in library extension.[23]

In early 1946 King wrote letters to school superintendents and others, asking their advice on extending library service in Saskatchewan. One superintendent talked of "lack of reading experience among students," partly because of the depression years, where "books were luxuries which often went by the board in the struggle for existence." There was no library in many of the towns he visited, only a few books in schools, and he recommended "reading material geared to the age and interest of the individual."[24] The Saskatoon Library Association had the most sophisticated recommendations, copying in part the SLA 1944 submission to the Reconstruction Council, suggesting the appointment of a library board or commission which would be in charge of library development. They suggested a minimum of 40,000 books for a region and a grant of 50¢ per capita.[25] A letter from Betty Davis, a Prince Albert trustee, also said the first action should be to hire a library supervisor. Then she gave black news about the Prince Albert Library at the time of the 1933 Ridlington Report, which had praised Prince Albert without, she said, the commissioners ever visiting it. In fact, the library advertised for discarded books, while, "No attempt was made to catalogue the books or to place them in the shelves. Pages were missing." All the librarians did was mark the books in and out. "They were unable to tell if the library contained books asked for or to find any book they were known to have in the library,"[26] an example of how bad the library had been. Yet it was in Prince Albert where regional library service would begin, Davis one of its great early supporters.

By April 1946 King had asked Elizabeth Morton, secretary of the CLC, for advice on appointing an organizer of regional libraries. The minister of education had authorized the SLAC to find an organizer. Four names had been forwarded including that of Marion Gilroy. King asked about wages for such a position and planned to be in Hamilton in June at the CLC Conference, and the American Library Association Conference in Buffalo, hoping to meet as many people as possible who might consider the job. King interviewed candidates at Hamilton, thought Gilroy best, talked to her again in Buffalo, then recommended her to Woodrow Lloyd.[27] In the years that followed she became the most important person in Saskatchewan libraries. It was also at that meeting in Hamilton in 1946 that the Canadian Library Council became the Canadian Library Association (CLA).

When Gilroy arrived in Saskatchewan on November 2, 1946, she had already been head of the Nova Scotia Regional Library Commission. Born in 1912 in Springhill, Nova Scotia to book-reading parents, she had received a BA in history from the University of Wolfville (one of her fellow students was Grace Campbell, who would work with her at North Central), taken a job in the Public Archives in Halifax, met Nora Bateson who had worked in the Fraser Valley, and began to take library studies, at McGill and Toronto. She did a regional library survey in Cape Breton, attended a summer library school at Columbia University in New York, then came the Nova Scotia library position – and attendance at the CLC meeting in Hamilton, the meeting with King and her arrival in Saskatchewan, in April 1946, as described by Max Braithwaite, in *Like Being a Millionaire.*

On a cold, miserable blustery night of November 2, 1946 a short, slender woman of thirty-five with remarkable dark eyes that took everything in at a glance stepped off the CPR transcontinental train onto the platform in Regina, Saskatchewan.[28]

She was met by Provincial Librarian Jesse Bothwell who invited her to stay at her home. There was a general housing shortage in Canada after the Depression and war years. Marion Gilroy had arrived at the beginning of a winter that became, as Braithwaite said, "the most cussed winter that Saskatchewan people had endured for forty years, and broke all records for blizzards, cold, icy road conditions and stalled railroad trains."

MARION GILROY ON THE ROAD, 1947

Gilroy made two detailed reports to SLAC , one on her travels to April 1, 1947, and one from April 1 to November 16, 1947. She had been sent out on the road to survey libraries in Saskatchewan, to discover which area might be best for a regional library experiment – which communities were indeed interested enough to tax themselves. She was given those instructions at a SLAC meeting November 25, 1946. She first met with government officials from various departments, partly to see what other models of service, like health districts, already existed. In Saskatoon she met with university people, in Extension for instance in early January, and attended Farm Week where she showed *Library on Wheels.*

She visited the southeast part of the province first, that is, when she could, since 1946-47 was a famous cold and snowy winter. One trip had to be postponed because the train to Weyburn was not running. In that area she found progressive library boards in Weyburn and Estevan, and smaller less adequate libraries in Oxbow and Carnduff, which had no active board. She couldn't meet with the Homemakers. "Their Sunday meeting was postponed because of the severe cold and closed roads." Her conclusion: "The Weyburn Area has elements of hope as a regional library unit," but the lack of space for a headquarters "would make it impossible to start a library at present." Agnes Weweler's work was dismissed: "It was difficult to assess the effect of Mrs. Weweler's efforts with the proposed 'South Saskatchewan Regional Library,' which it was hoped would be financed by Carnegie funds."

After Gilroy found it impossible to travel in early February "because of severe storms," she finally visited Prince Albert. "The library board, part of the members of which had been somewhat unconvinced of the value of regional service, gave the idea complete support after our discussion." There was a lively public meeting with Mayor John Cuelenaere in the chair and highly supportive. She then visited Rosthern, Star City ("This is only the third winter the library has been operating, so fortunately it has fewer moribund books than some of the other libraries visited."), Tisdale (where a high school girl kept the library open a few hours a week), Melfort (weak but the librarian wanted to know how to improve the system and catalogue the books), Kinistino (where people were very enthusiastic though they had no library).

Gilroy then visited a series of towns in other areas: Watson ("The Council is largely made up of foreign-born non-readers but they showed interest"), Wadena, Melville (where the city had just voted $1,000 to replace Rotary support, and the mayor planned to talk to provincial people about a library-museum building). The Battleford area hosted her in March. North Battleford's Carnegie Library "is a real community centre, and the librarian and board chair are both enterprising people." The Battleford Library, however "is stagnant." The Rotary Club supported the Lloydminster Library and the board supported regional libraries, but a visit to the secretary-treasurer of the Rural Municipality was not encouraging.

Gilroy outlined her future plans and expressed disappointment with provincial aid; the budget submitted by the Regional Libraries Division (just her) cut down the line, allowing for no assistant, and barely enough money for travel and promotion. Most important, "whereas the Superintendent [Gilroy] had been informed before coming to Saskatchewan that the Cabinet had agreed to pay half the annual maintenance cost of regional library service, the appropriation cuts this from one-half to one-quarter." She was not optimistic this amount would be adequate to start a regional system.[29] She also spoke of the need for a short course in library techniques for all the untrained librarians in the province. Her most important conclusion saw the Prince Albert area "as the most hopeful," especially the work already done "by interested individuals and local organizations."

In February a delegation from Prince Albert, including Mayor Cuelenaere, L.F. McIntosh, the CCF member from the city, and Betty Davis, had already visited Legislative and Provincial Librarian Jesse Bothwell, to support the regional library coming to Prince Albert. Davis, Bothwell said, "was formerly Miss Elizabeth Andrews and was for some years Librarian of the Government's Open Shelf Library and has always been greatly interested in Library Work."[30] Her husband was editor of the *Prince Albert Daily Herald*.

By the time Marion Gilroy was on the road again it was in a car bought as a way to reduce travel expenditures. It also speeded the work and allowed her to take displays with her, which she set up, for instance, in a store window in Lloydminster, at fairs at Melfort and Nipawin, at Homemakers' conventions in Wadena and Kamsack, and so on. She also displayed books which people were allowed to borrow. Clergymen read Reinhold Niebuhr's *Discerning the Signs of the Times* and C.S. Lewis's *Screwtape Letters*. An agricultural representative read Stuart Chase's *Rich Land, Poor Land;* a Wheat Pool field representative read Tawnwy's *The Acquisitive Society;* a mother read *Your Child's Development and Guidance.* People borrowed books on house plans, quilting, photography, carpentry, bee culture, radio, and so on. "Two small girls who came in with their mothers...were overjoyed to have *Mary Poppins* and *Smokey, the Cowhorse* for a week."[31]

Gilroy was a steady worker snow or shine. Here's a two-week itinerary:

> July 9: Meeting Saskatoon, Co-op School at University
> July 10: Meeting Prince Albert, Co-op School at Army Camp
> July 11: Melfort to make final arrangements for display at Fair, etc.
> July 12: Ridgedale to help with establishment of library
> July 14: Nipawin and Codette to make arrangements for display
> at Fair and if possible meetings with Homemakers, etc.
> July 15: Ethleton, Kinistino, Birch Hills, etc.
> July 16: Watrous
> July 17, 18, 19: Melfort Fair
> July 23: back to Regina[32]

This itinerary shows the steady work, the usefulness of a car, and most importantly, her focus on the Prince Albert and northern district, which indeed had been her mandate on a recommendation from the minister of education. She did meet with three difficulties in organization. "This year the crop in the part of the province which the library would serve is the smallest ever known," so there was no extra money for libraries. As well, some municipalities' residents were largely foreign-born, which meant that their first language wasn't English; they "read and [wrote] English with difficulty," and so were less likely to support a library. There was also the low level of the grant, said Gilroy. While the grant made by the community of Star City would actually go down if a regional library were introduced, in Melfort the $300 spent by the community would rise to $805. Tisdale would go from an inadequate $125 to $475, Nipawin from $290 to $602. The service would improve dramatically but there was a cost for it.

What was needed next, said Gilroy, was a meeting of representatives from municipalities that might form a region, and a higher grant structure as recommended by SLAC ($35,000 for the initial book stock and half the annual operating costs). By November 21, 1947, Lloyd outlined the government's position at a SLAC meeting:

- To proceed in the Prince Albert-Melfort area
- To advance $1.00 per capita as an initial grant
      and 25% of maintenance
- To pay the salary of the Regional Library Supervisor
      and make her available for two years, or longer if necessary
- To include the $10,000 budgeted this year
      as part of the initial grant

A final word on Marion Gilroy as an advocate, from stories recounted by Max Braithwaite:

Marion went to see Clifford Groat, Mayor of Melfort, who had been lukewarm on the project, and talked and talked until she had a signed statement which read... "After due consideration, I feel the advantage of the Regional Library will be well worth the cost." After signing it, he mopped his brow and stated, "Lady, I wish I could talk like you. I'd be prime minister."[33]

There's the story of meeting the *StarPhoenix* editor in January 1947:

According to Marion, B.J. Richardson asked her bluntly, "Are these libraries going to be propaganda agencies for the socialists?" Whereupon Miss Gilroy's dark eyes flashed and her Scottish temper flared and she told the editor, "Sir, I'll have you know I am a professional librarian. I consider your remark an outrage." Whereupon the editor apologized and became a supporter of the library.[34]

Day after day, week after week, year after year, Marion Gilroy made the pitch for regional libraries.

NORTH CENTRAL REGION BEGINS, 1948

The meeting Gilroy spoke of as the next step occurred January 31, 1948, at the Prince Albert Council Chambers, with Mayor Cuelenaere as chair and representatives from the villages of Kinistino, Porcupine Plain, White Fox, and St. Brieux, and the rural municipalities of Porcupine, Flett's Springs, Star City and Prince Albert, as well as representatives from organizations like the Homemakers' and the Wheat Pool, about fifty people in all. "Delegates from the west...and the town of Melfort were unable to get through because the roads had been blocked by the storm the previous night." David Smith of the Department of Education represented Mr. Lloyd, who was ill, and presented the government's offer. Gilroy explained the advantages of a regional library, showed the possible boundaries and the likely level of taxation. In the discussion, Louis Demay of St. Brieux suggested a large board and a small executive would work best to involve people, and this was in fact the way regions would be governed, with a representative from every participating community and a small executive representing each type of member, city, town, village and so on. A committee of five was elected "to promote and study ways" to establish a regional library. The elected members were Gilroy; Dr. Tannahill, Prince Albert librarian; S.J. Branion, secretary of the Prince Albert Library Board; W. Scott, Kinistino; and H.W. Reid, secretary of the RM of Prince Albert. They would operate out of a motion passed by the delegates:

> Resolved that this meeting go on record as favoring the formation of a Regional Library forecast in mimeographed material presented and in explanation given, and that we recommend to the municipalities special consideration of the scheme of combination of property tax and per capita levy.[35]

The game was afoot.

Gilroy's mimeographed statement was a detailed 2,000-word document. The size of the region was 200 miles west to east and 70 north to south and it should have a minimum of 40,000 people to begin. A regional library would have additional books, "particularly children's books and practical and technical books." Books would be changed in branches at least once a year. She explained the 1946 Regional Libraries Act, including the large board and the small executive. "For the cost of a magazine in taxation we can have access to thousands of good books each year through the regional library system. As one rural woman said, 'We can't afford not to have it.'"[36] A second document listed the total population of the area and proposed methods of taxation, either one half mill on all municipalities (a Melfort householder at $1.20 annually, farmer at $8.00 a year), or one quarter mill and 20 cents per capita, which Gilroy recommended.

Gilroy wrote Bothwell on the success of the meeting. "The Prince Albert people went all out for the plan." They agreed to taxation "on the compromise basis that Mr. Lloyd and Dr. King had felt was fair." The day concluded with a dinner sponsored by Prince Albert. "We are quite astonished at Dr. Tannahill's positive and energetic support. Mary MacIsaac said she could scarcely believe it."[37] The *Prince Albert Daily Herald* added its strong editorial support, November 10, 1948.

The proposed financing formula was turned down by the rural municipalities at a Regional Library Committee meeting of May 27. Gilroy proposed retaining the one quarter mill but omitting the per capita grant, with the province assuming that burden for a total additional cost, should all RMs join, of $7,000 a year.[38] Cabinet responded positively with a proposal to pay 25% of urban costs and 50% of rural costs,[39] an acceptable formula.

The travelling continued. And the good stories:

Did I tell you what happened at the Tisdale Town Council meeting? They weakened, I think, in spite of the opposition from the Superintendent of Schools and the Secretary of the Library Board. As our supporters kept coming into the Council Chamber, the Mayor took a huge bite from his outsize cigar and shouted, "We're surrounded."[40]

Gilroy was told that the only way to talk to the people of Porcupine Plain was to go during the bonspiel when everyone would be in town. "The Bonspiel Banquet dinner in Porcupine Plain was quite good – over 150 people were there. I can't say I think books are in the running with curling, but that may be too much to expect."[41] The weather remained ferocious. "Thirty below today. I'm sitting in front of the hotel's Quebec heater, and even a fur coat and my huge boots are comfortable inside. The bedrooms have to be felt to be believed."[42]

NORTH CENTRAL REGIONAL LIBRARY, 1950-1965

It wasn't easy to start that first region. Municipalities weren't joining and the objective of 40,000 people as the official goal kept receding. When the North Central Regional Library was officially established, April 5, 1950, it had fewer than 25,000 people represented, the great majority of whom were from Prince Albert. But a choice had to be made by government, to start now or risk that the regional idea might die aborning. Mary MacIsaac, in one of her many letters to Lloyd or Douglas, said the CCF government must launch at least one regional library, and no one could be a better advocate than Marion Gilroy, "a girl of such vision, ability, industry [and] personality.... I have never seen her so discouraged as now. She has almost sweated blood trying to sell her idea to reeves and councillors, most of whom have no conception of the need of books."[43] Lloyd had agreed to the smaller number of 20,000 people for the region at a meeting with Gilroy, May 13, 1949.[44] A SLAC meeting May 30, 1949 passed this motion: "That we proceed to establish a restricted Regional Library unit along the lines suggested by Miss Gilroy in her report."

By March 1950, the region would represent only 22,000 people, barely over half the required number. Besides Prince Albert, the RMs of St. Louis and Prince Albert, the villages of Leask and Weldon formed the unit. Mayor Cuelenaere was "ready to go to Melfort to meet the council there...Mr. McCarthy, Chairman of the Melfort Board, feels that Mayor Cuelenaere can counteract the sniping that

Recent photo of the Prince Albert Club building where the North Central Regional Library began in the basement.

persists in Melfort."[45] One sniper was a Mr. Glazier, superintendent of schools and anti-CCF, who insisted that he did not believe the government would pay its share of the regional library.[46] Melfort did join. Politics was the problem at Kinistino, one of the most positive communities in 1948, but now one of the hardest to attract. Gladys Estok noted, "Mr. Wooland said frankly he thought it was all politics – that the terrible CCF government was trying to force something else on them! (Council are all strong Liberals)."[47]

The first order of business was organizing the new library unit. The regional headquarters were in the basement of a building Prince Albert had bought from the province, known as the old Natural Resources Building, though it had earlier housed the Prince Albert Club. When provincial offices later vacated the upper floors, the Prince Albert Library would move into the building as well. The region received the dollar per capita grant for the first book stock – $24,695 – and a small increase later when Domremy joined the region that year where, as a CBC report said, "One minute after Miss Gilroy and her assistant arrived from Prince Albert with four hun-

TONIGHT

10.15 p.m.

OVER

C K B I

GEORGE **H**
FURNEAUX
OF NIPAWIN

will speak on

"A REGION
LIBRARY F
THIS ARE

One of a series c
given Monday and
nesday.

Arranged for
North Saskatch
Regional Libr
Committee

The importance
of radio.

TONIGHT

10.15 p.m.

C K B I

•

D. J. McCarthy

Chairman of the Melfort
Library' Board, will speak on

A Regional Library
For Northern
Saskatchewan

dred new books, a young lad borrowed a book on baseball, another was away with Roger Tory Peterson's *Field Guide to Western Birds.* The primary teacher latched on to *The Cock, The Mouse,* and *The Little Red Hen,* while another teacher took Scott's *Last Expedition* to read to her class."[48]

There was a staff of three: Grace Campbell from Prince Edward Island, where she had a two-year leave; Marion Gilroy; and a secretary, Mrs. Wood, from the Saskatoon Public Library. Shelves were ready in June, in an unheated basement. Grace Campbell recalls dismantling the Prince Albert Library "and only 90 books in the children's department were worth keeping, and the rest, well, they were junked."[49] That basement was cold so they started a fire in the fireplace only to smoke out the second floor. "A representative appeared at the top of the stairs and said we were a menace to the people above us and we'd have to move out." Gilroy went to Cuelenaere, who said to them they had "two of the best librarians in Canada working there," and the other occupants could move out.

There were painful moments. Because Canwood had joined but not the RM, "One little girl [from the RM] picked out a picture book but she couldn't take it home." She didn't have five dollars from her mom to join, said Campbell, "but Grace Crooks and I put in the five dollars, but don't tell anyone." Campbell recalls one fellow in the Prince Albert RM saying, "The kids wouldn't have time to do their chores if they were reading books all the time." It wasn't always an easy job. When levies went up a woman phoned from Hudson Bay saying the mayor wouldn't pay anymore. "He paid for golf so he thought people who read should pay too." After helping to open another library, Campbell drove 200 miles, the road under construction, "got to Hudson Bay at dark, found my hotel, was late to the meeting, brought my display and gave a little talk. The mayor changed his mind and wrote a cheque on the spot." Voluntary help was necessary, and forthcoming. One of those volunteers was Melana Street of Forest Gate, an eighty-year-old spending the winter in Prince Albert. "She offered her services because she is a reader who believes that books are essential to living and that a 'little help is worth a lot of pity.'"[50]

"The careful selection, checking of prices, ordering, classification and processing the initial book stock requires time." When the Melfort library was to move into new quarters, in September, Gilroy and Campbell took a small collection of 400 to 500 children's books and reference books to the event. "It meant marking and packing books far into the night." A guest at the event, Elizabeth Morton, secretary of the CLA, reported on it. She drove to Melfort in Marion

Prince Albert, May 1951, Mrs. Melena Street, Forest Gate, Grace Campbell, Regional Librarian

Story Hour, Prince Albert, with Grace Crooks. Karen Labuik is the second girl on the bench.

Gilroy's car – "a large Ford. I was interested in the extra kit and dungarees carried in the back in case Miss Gilroy had to do mechanical tinkering en route.... A board member named Anderson, brought me a bouquet of sweet peas."[51] As for the distance from Prince Albert to Melfort, "It is as if Toronto had a branch in London or Ottawa was a branch of Montreal."[52] She enjoyed the board chair McCarthy's welcome to the public: "This is your library."

By 1952, the only new participant was Shellbrook, and that because the Home and School Association had raised the $225 "and presented it to the town on consideration that in future the town would pay the grant to the library." (I visited a spacious and bright Shellbrook Library in July 2003 and saw, as a sign of the times, eight computers.) In 1952 the branch libraries were located in Halliwell's Hardware Store in Shellbrook, Graham's General Store in Beatty, a room in the Catholic rectory in Bellevue, the North Star Lumber Company back office in Domremy, the Co-op store in Hagan, the Municipal Office in Hoey, the basement of the school in Leask, Ole Berg's store in Northern Light, Miss A. Daniel's store in Weldon. All the librarians in these communities were volunteers. In Prince Albert one of the basic volunteer groups, the Victoria and Albert chapter of the IODE, furnished the audio-visual room, while the Prince Albert and District Film Council met the cost of the librarian. Grace Crooks, a children's librarian from Montreal, joined the staff, as did Yvette Kagis, a graduate of the University of Latvia. Government support showed itself in a provision of $5,000 towards the purchase of a book van, one of the best investments ever for successful library service. Yet inflation was eating into the 50 cents per capita annual grant, so that "it now [provided] only about half the service it would have, had we escaped inflation."[53]

The CCF government did respond to the region's needs. There was a one-time-only grant of $4,000 in 1953, as well as the bookmobile grant. In 1954 the initial book-stock grant was raised from $1.00 to $1.50 per capita, and in 1957 the yearly government grant was raised from 50 to 75 cents per capita. In part those increases responded to the pressures of inflation in book prices.

A report on regions by Gilroy in 1956 showed the success of the North Central region, about 12,000 more books borrowed than in the previous year, but there were difficulties too. Salaries were low – an offer of $3,500 for a children's librarian was matched plus another $1,000 by the Regina Public Library. It remained difficult to attract RMs, which argued "that the tax on land is already prohibitively high, that the school tax is so high they can not also afford a tax for libraries, that present tax collections are falling behind since the difficulties in marketing wheat, that road construction takes all available funds, and this year that the severe August frosts did so much damage that the farmer's position is more precarious than ever." More money was needed, and Gilroy suggested $1.50 per capita for either a new region or another municipality joining an existing region, while annual grants should be $1.00 per person. She also suggested for each new region the provision of a bookmobile and a regional headquarters building.[54] There was also by 1958 inadequate accommodation: a staff of twelve worked in a space occupied by six in 1951.[55]

In 1958 SLAC decided Gilroy should leave North Central, so it could stand on its own, and she could assist other regions to organize. She was of critical importance to West Central (Wheatland), attending all its meetings, according to Provincial Library annual reports. She worked in Southeast, did preliminary work in what became Lakeland, and travelled the province. She resigned in July 1963 to take up a teaching job.

There were important new people running the region. Grace Campbell became the Prince Albert and regional librarian in 1955 and stayed for eighteen years, until 1973. She had a BA from Acadia, had worked to help establish the Prince Edward Island regional library, completed a Bachelor of Library Science at McGill and was convinced to come west by both Marions, Gilroy and Sherman, the latter a member of Prince Albert city council from 1949-1982, and chair of the North Central region from 1951, when Cuelenaere resigned, until 1982, when she was not reappointed by council because of a strike from April to November 15, 1982, at both Wapiti and the John Cuelenaere Library. Sherman was involved in a series of other activities as well, serving as chair of the Regional Board of Health and of the Regional Hospital Council, and on the boards of Victoria Union Hospital and the Anti-tuberculosis League. She began library work when she went to the P.A. Library and found no children's books. "'Something had to be done about that,' she said, and she brought it up at the University Women's Club, where Betty Davis sold her on the Regional Library movement."[56]

In 1959 Mary MacIsaac was advocating the need of regional headquarters, as was Woodrow Lloyd to his colleagues. "One of my own disappointments in the budget is that we have been unable to advance the cause of regional libraries by doing something substantial and concrete about providing regional headquarter facilities." Such an act, he said, would have enthusiastic acceptance by many, including the women's section of the Saskatchewan Farmers Union.[57] Partly because of the new grants the general acceptance of the regional library began to gain momentum, with 36 participating communities by 1960. An important pamphlet shows the extraordinary growth of the North Central Library, with 28,000 people in 1953, 54,000 in 1960, and 80,000 by 1965, with circulation increasing from 67,000 to 413,000 in those years. In Tisdale, whose population rose by 700 over the same period, circulation rose from 1,400 in 1953 before it joined the region, to 18,000 in 1960 and 28,000 in 1965. There are also statistics of bookmobile service in towns in the West Central Region in 1964-65. In Lucky Lake (population 450): stop 1, 87 books; stop 8, 258 books. Figures are similar for Handel and Zealandia. Regional library service had proven itself.

BOOKS FOR BEAVER RIVER

The first film about regional service in Saskatchewan, was begun June 5, 1961, and had its premiere October 1, in the Orpheum Theatre in Prince Albert before 300 people. The filmmaker for the NFB, Donald Ginsberg, has a lovely account, as an English-born film-maker who knew nothing of regional libraries. First came the title: *Regional Libraries* – dull; *Books for Amberley* – too British; *Books for White Fox; Books for Beaver River* – accepted. His star was Marion Gilroy. "Admittedly she had to be coaxed, cajoled, swayed and

NFB crew shooting a scene in *Books for Beaver River*. On the left, D. Ginsberg, director, then E. Boyko, cameraman (Saskatchewan Government photo)

pushed into playing the part" and he wasn't sure she would appear, but she did, and away they went. "Apart from appearing in the film, she also took it upon herself to act for the crew as water-carrier, tea-maker and coffee-brewer (for the uninitiated who hadn't been introduced to the delicacies of tea)." Ginsberg then listed things he liked, including Waskesiu, the towns they filmed in, Birch Hills, Shipman, Shellbrook, Melfort, and Rayside School. "Never did I dream that children could be so good, look so photogenic and act as if a film unit came around to photograph them every day of the week." The other major performances were by Zack Cennon of CKBI-TV and a boy, Beattie Ramsey of Regina, who wanted to find a book on stars, and did, when the regional library came to Beaver River. There's an account of a day's filming in the *Western Producer,* July 13, 1961.

HEADQUARTERS, 1962, AND WAPITI, TWENTY-FIFTH ANNIVERSARY

The long-awaited headquarters opened Saturday, October 20, 1962, with Premier Lloyd, education minister Ole Turnbull, and public works minister W. G. Davis in attendance, as well as Sherman, Campbell, Morton and a who's who of Prince Albert. The government had decided to fund regional headquarters so that first building seemed to presage more as other regions were created, though others would renovate existing buildings, and only one, Southeastern, would receive a grant for renovating a space. The money was placed in the Provincial Library budget, $144,000 (plus $13,900 for furniture and equipment) according to a government file that gives an insider look at the government's budgeting process, and at items removed to lower the cost. "Both the Department of Public Works and the Provincial Library suggested certain economies."[58] Cabinet did not accept all proposed reductions, so the art budget remained, for instance. At the entrance to the building that October day in 1962 was, and still is, a wrought-iron work by a young Otto Rogers. (When I visited Wapiti in 2003 I thought of it as a tree of knowledge set now under a tree of nature.) Although the government process was complex, the library and architect decided on the needs.

Premier W. S. Lloyd and Alderman Marion Sherman, Chairman of the Board, marking the opening of the new regional headquarters, Prince Albert

When North Central celebrated its twenty-fifth anniversary, it changed its name to Wapiti (Algonquin for elk). Marion Sherman said it took too long to write North Central Regional Library. That's also when the library commissioned Max Braithwaite to write the history of Wapiti, *Like Being a Millionaire,* which is frustrating because he has great material he hasn't footnoted and I haven't found, but it is a book I've come to value the more I use and borrow from it. He heard stories from people who were there at the beginning, and always writes with spirit. It's a lovely book and fitting memorial to the first regional library on the prairies.[59]

Chapter Six

Wheatland
1959-2000

1959-60

THE STORY OF THE ORIGIN OF WEST CENTRAL OR Wheatland region has twice been told, by Rusty Macdonald in the opening chapter of *Don't Cry Baby... We'll Be Back*, 1987 and by Wheatland itself in its tenth anniversary publication, *Wheatland Regional Library, 1967-1977,* but it's so good a story I have to tell it too. It has such a modest beginning in such a modest place, Stranraer, 30 kilometres northwest of Rosetown, with a population in 1959 of 105. Mrs. J.B. Stephenson tells the story of its origins at a Stranraer Home and School Association meeting in the spring of 1959 with libraries a major topic. "I stressed the wonderful potential of Regional Libraries."[1] The next meeting, of the Women's Missionary Society, at the home of Helen McCuaig, who would remain involved for years, was on the topic of how to help young people; Stephenson again explained the values of regional libraries, and later contacted Provincial Librarian Mary Donaldson who said Marion Gilroy would attend a meeting as soon as possible. At the next Home and School meeting, Stephenson talked of libraries, a woman from Plenty took literature home and it was her husband, A.E. Nell, who would become the first chair of the West Central organizing committee. A Stranraer committee of three women was formed and they delivered literature to and canvassed local residents. Stranraer's council endorsed the project, making it the first community in the area to support the regional library. One of the attractive themes of Wheatland is how the small taught the large.

Gilroy spoke at a meeting at Stranraer on November 25, 1959, with representatives of a number of Home and School Associations present. The motion to organize the west central area into a regional library was approved at that meeting, as was the direction to organize the region in one year – in fact, it would take seven. The first officers included Nell, a banker from Plenty as president, McCuaig as vice-president, plus Stephenson, a Mrs. Wiens representing Herschel, and a new but important recruit, Jean Kallio of Lucky Lake – she and her husband Willard would be key figures for many years. The committee had a representative from Rosetown but vacancies to fill from all the other larger centres in the area. "Credit for the very thorough planning and capable handling of the meeting is given by the whole committee to Mrs. J.B. Stephenson of Stranraer whose vision and enthusiasm has set us off with a good start."[2]

The committee defined its region as the Alberta border to the west; the South Saskatchewan River to the south and east; and the North Saskatchewan and RMS 411, 410, 409, 408 to the north, with Unity the northernmost town. The region stopped short of Saskatoon. What is remarkable about West Central is its lack of any city. It had a series of largish towns (again from a 1959 document): Eston 1,600, Rosetown 2,500, Kindersley 2,577, Kerrobert 1,100, Wilkie 1,870, Unity 1,750. That's the fact that made organizing more difficult, and unique in Saskatchewan regional libraries.

The second progress meeting, held at Plenty, January 20, 1960, was attended by 125 people representing 13 RMS, eight towns, and 15 villages, as well as representatives from Home and School Associations – the basic early organizing group, plus people from library boards and municipal councils. There were questions: costs, number of books, exchanges, paying librarians, housing of libraries, function of a library board.[3] Though the meeting was well attended, many who wanted to couldn't get there. "Some of our country roads are already impassable. For myself I am practically snow bound now."[4] The writer said the Beechy Home and School Association was behind the library scheme and working for it.

There were a variety of statements of library principle that first year. Nell responded to the concern that people were losing control over local affairs. A community, the president said, made no commitment to government, only to other municipalities which agreed on a common cause and then elected a library board "answering directly to the Councils that appointed them."[5] Such a sense of local control remained an especially strong feature of Wheatland. The executive had decided the taxation rate would be 75 cents per capita per year and, Nell said, "We doubt that you could spend 75 cents per person per year better than for services provided by a Regional Library."[6] A brief by Stephenson and McCuaig to the RM of Mountain View council claimed that people in a rural municipality could get books "as handy as they get their mail and their groceries." "Today we cannot be satisfied with partial library service by mail. Branches of regional public libraries give small communities and rural areas comprehensive service no small public library can give which has no link up with a regional system."[7] These are central ideas defining the regional idea, that on the one hand it is a superior service to travelling and public information libraries, and on the other hand superior to any local independent library, like the one at Biggar which rejected overtures on the assumption that it was doing fine by itself. Yet Kerrobert was so library conscious, with a mayor and councillor on the library board, that it passed a motion in favour of the region without a petition. One of the great figures in West Central, Muriel Maclean, was and would remain the central library force in that town, and in some years the Kerrobert documents, including book purchasing, make up half the Wheatland files, which are excellent.

Meanwhile back in Stranraer, Stephenson and McCuaig were on the move, in Handel, Rowena, RM of Mountain View, Hershel, and so on. In the April 1970 Wheatland newsletter *Harvestings,* Helen McCuaig talked of their perigrinations, as old ball-playing friends. "Mrs. Stephenson and I, being housewives, with no children at home, therefore, having free time and not much danger of being fired if we weren't home to prepare every meal, decided we would do a little promoting on our own." They didn't get many invitations so "we struck out to visit the Mayors, Reeves, Councillors and Library Boards in many towns and villages." They had many rejections, one reeve saying the Public Information Library in Regina was adequate (though it would be withdrawn five years later), another that their own library was sufficient, another that they had to build sidewalks. "In almost every place we went to, we finally found someone who was interested in what we had to tell them. Sometimes we knocked on half a dozen doors before finding that person, but we left literature in every town and municipality we visited. I don't know if we did any actual good but we had a ball doing it." Baseball friends all those years ago and still on the road.

At the first annual meeting of the region, in Kindersley October 5, 1960, the news was good and bad – letters of approval from Kerrobert and Rosetown, from Plenty, Ruthilda and Stranraer, from RMS 317, 318, 319 – close to Stranraer, for a total population of 6, 600. That's the good news and the bad news at the same time. A start had been made but, after a year, the success was but modest.

1962-66

By 1962 eight RMs, eight villages, but still only two towns had joined the proposed region. Nell had been transferred to another bank and the presidency fell to Helen McCuaig, then Jean Kallio, then Muriel MacLean, who had hoped a man would take the job – "we function better with a man at the helm"[8] – but took the position. *Books for Beaver River* became a popular film at meetings. On February 9, 1963 the committee wrote O.A. Turnbull, minister in charge of libraries, with an important request. The committee had signed up only 12,636 people by then. "We ask you to give thoughtful consideration to our request that the Government purchase and equip a bookmobile to show people in our West Central area...how varied, attractive, and useful a collection of books can be." Though the letter doesn't say so, there must have been many areas of the province that had never seen or used a proper library.

An undated internal government memo on bookmobile service for Wheatland is well-informed, for instance on the list of obstacles faced by Wheatland:

1. Sparse population and very large area.
2. Large number of units – urban and rural – required to provide a population large enough to provide up-to-date library service.
3. Uncertainly about the future of rural municipalities and the villages.
4. Objection to paying even a small additional amount from taxes to support a free public library over a wide area.
5. Self-satisfaction in some centres with the limited service some of their small public libraries offer (Biggar, Eston and possibly Kindersley), especially on the part of their library boards.[9]

Within a month the government had purchased a demonstration bookmobile, first used in West Central. There were meetings both of the executive and a users committee to plan the service, a fine example of central funding and local control. People were delighted with the driver, Wayne Morgan, "who would work Saturday evenings or any time,"[10] for "he's saving his money to go to art school. He has a sleeping bag and can sleep in the 'bile if he's not near accommodation."[11] He would indeed drive from 54 to 68 hours a week at the beginning of the service. The bookmobile was the first to work through the winter on the prairies (Wapiti brought its into Prince Albert for the winter), but bookmobiles were now better and school buses drove through the region in winter. It was used as part of a plan to sign up Kindersley, along with a letter explaining the virtues of regional service (the campaign failed). Although the bookmobile had already been in service since the spring, the official opening was held at Stranraer, September 28, 1964 with addresses by Liberal Education Minister George Trapp (the Liberals had won the 1964 election), and Wheat Pool President C.W. Gibbings to over 200 people in the crowded community hall. Gibbings said that libraries would help quell the unrest of the day, that people should welcome automation, and that a regional library "was not a cost, it was an instrument that would pay the area back several times over."[12]

In 1964 one dark event occurred, the resignation of Marion Gilroy. "On my return," wrote Muriel MacLean, "I found the dreaded letter from Miss Donaldson...telling me that she had received Marion's resignation, which will be effective July 31st. Do you think the West Central Committee can survive this mortal blow." While at the Winnipeg Conference, Gilroy had learned that her sister was ill, so "accepted the offer of the teaching job in a BC Library School so that she could be near her sister. But I'm just sick about it."[13]

The bookmobile thrived. There was a driver, a library assistant and volunteers at every stop, 27 stops every two weeks, with 18,000 books in the collection, 1,600 on the bookmobile. It was a service limited to two years. "One little boy asked if the bookmobile went to Calgary. He was going there on holidays and wanted to read all the time." People came from a wide area to use the service, whether their unit of government had supported the service or not. At the Outlook stop people came from four other villages to borrow books. "In one village I was told it was a red letter day when the bookmobile came.

Rosetown library

In another they told that the day the bookmobile comes is one of the busiest days in the stores."[14]

A population of over 17,000 had joined by February 1964, including Wilkie, Unity, and Eston among the towns, plus 17 RMs, and 12 villages. By that year every region in the province was being organized.

On June 11, 1966, with a total population of 36,000, the organizational meeting for the region took place at the Saskatoon Public Library. Wilfred Kallio was voted chair. The draft agreement between the municipalities and the region was debated, amended and passed. The executive was to consist of three members representing towns, three representing RMs, and one representing villages. Then a name had to be chosen, from this list of nominees: Wheatbelt, Wild Goose, Eagle Hills, Centennial, Two Rivers, Wesak, Wheatland. The choice was finally between Wild Goose and Wheatland, the latter winning 26 to 15. Next the delegates had to choose a headquarters, between three proposals – Unity, Rosetown, Saskatoon – each defended in detail, though Unity was unlikely because it was at the northern edge of the region. Rosetown defenders made a good case for its central location, but the vote was Saskatoon 25, Rosetown 14, Unity 1.

It had taken almost seven years but Wheatland had become the second regional library to begin organization and the third formed, after Southeast, which had the benefit of two cities, Weyburn and Estevan. But the modest beginnings by the women of Stranraer had come to fruition.

WHEATLAND, 1966-1972

One of the first problems facing the new Wheatland library region was where to put the first branches. North Central had begun so modestly that the process was chronological and orderly. All the other regions began with many communities, 53 in the case of Wheatland, including eight new communities without libraries in 1965 and 12 in 1966. The executive created two preliminary documents, one dividing the region into major communities, the other into wider units, planning to decide which community could serve which area. Chronology was also important. Yet many communities, even those that joined last, like Biggar, already had libraries. The annual report of 1967, with Elizabeth Harbord as first regional librarian, showed a remarkable achievement, 20 branch libraries opened in the first year; headquarters set up (in rented quarters in the Saskatoon Public Library's main branch); a staff hired; 130,000 books catalogued; a system of exchanges between branches begun, as well as a request system (or interlibrary loan); bylaws adopted, including a no-fines policy. At a February 10, 1968, meeting, Provincial Librarian Harry Newsom said, "no regional library in the entire country had developed 20 branches in the first partial year of operation."

It was also in 1967 that the Library Inquiry Committee (which will have its own analysis), suggested various boundary changes, the most important of which was adding to Wheatland the largest unassigned area, from Saskatoon east to Lanigan and Nokomis, which roughly doubled its population base. By the February 10, 1968 meeting, Watrous and Manitou Beach had joined the region. An important committee was struck at that meeting, "to look into the matter of service to small libraries," which reported a year later with these principles accepted: that if a town or village requests a library the surrounding RM has to be a member too; that no branch be set up in a community of under 100 people; that as soon as possible local library boards pay their staff – but that item was defeated. In fact Wheatland was the only region that did not pay branch librarians, though it would in time offer incentives for local boards based on hours of opening.

There was an important external report on Wheatland, requested by the region, so the Provincial Library made a report entitled "Survey of Operations of Wheatland" in 1968. It said one half the population (46,000) had joined Wheatland, and one half hadn't, but as the non-joiners were mostly in the eastern half of the region, and in less-populated areas near the Alberta border, the facts were not as black as they might seem. Every new member meant a new book grant and local and government revenue, so new members were important for economics of scale. There were 32 recommendations in the report. The review team visited headquarters a number of times and ten of 25 branches. The population base was at an even greater hazard because Unity, Wilkie, and the northern RMs were proposed by the Library Inquiry Committee for Lakeland Region. The survey suggested service should be extended to areas of low population, for instance Alsask and Eatonia, especially since direct mailing to the region would be withdrawn in April 1969. There were a series of recommendations on central office and branches meant to simplify and clarify procedures. The report said Wheatland should find its own independent headquarters as soon as possible, and that an assistant regional librarian be hired (two years later Bruce Cameron was hired, and he would become regional librarian when Harbord resigned).

In book stock the team recommended more popular literature, including fiction. "There is much fiction which tells us more about the human situation than many purely informational works. Nor should the recreational aspect be denied. It is, quite justifiably, a major element in most people's lives" (p. 20). The block system of book replacement, which Wheatland pioneered in Saskatchewan, placed a burden on local branch librarians, often working alone, to withdraw 300 to 400 books every three weeks.

The most interesting part of the report is a result of the branch interviews. "There is no doubt whatsoever that outright opposition to the whole concept of regional libraries does exist in certain places" (p. 22), sometimes as open hostility, sometimes as non-co-operation, usually in places that had library service before the region began. The report suggests that anyone opposed to the regional idea ought not to be employed, yet the Regional Library Board "has no real influence whatsoever over the composition of Branch Library staffs because it has no responsibility for payment." "Nor is the Board entitled to assume that they are prepared to go on being volunteers forever." (p. 23)

At the February 20, 1971, Annual Meeting there was an even worse example of a non-functioning branch. When various people visited the branch, town not mentioned, they couldn't find the librarian, even during the hours when the branch was officially open. In another case a branch librarian had resigned and headquarters only discovered that when the bookmobile driver made his next visit. The regional librarian suggested such problems would be overcome if headquarters paid branch librarians directly.

A 1970 Wheatland report discussed the principle of paying branch staff; at $1.25 an hour, the total for 24 branches was $30,000, for 47 branches, $52,000, which would mean a cost increase of 50 cents per capita. The report then suggested more modest schemes: $10,000 for honorariums, or paying selected branches, at $18,000; letting the local group pay the first $500 and the region the rest. At the time, the total paid by some local branches was $9,000. To pay superannuation on that figure would be $900.

Key to all expenditures was money, the province increasing the per capita grant from a dollar to $1.10, and a year later $1.20. At the October 24, 1970, meeting, delegates talked (ten pages in the amazingly detailed minutes) of the new local levy since the first five-year agreement was about to end. The proposal was to add 25 cents. Some said their municipality would withdraw, others that it would pass without difficulty. Delegates refused chairman Kallio's suggestion of a sliding scale, towns paying more than RMs, on the basis that they had superior service; the towns pointed out that they provided library space on their own. Delegates were to take back to their municipalities the suggested 25-cent increase, and when the board met next that was reduced to 15 cents. Wheatland became the only region without a sliding scale of municipal levies, in which the large paid most, the small least.

There were a number of changes made to the library in 1971, by new regional librarian Bruce Cameron, including book purchases in part from remainder houses and second-hand dealers, and reorganizing space into work areas. Block exchanges at branches occurred now every five weeks, "so that one thirteenth of the collection is exchanged every five weeks."[15] Paperbacks were exchanged every three months. Some branches had opened paperback exchange depots on their own, which were apparently successful. A new system of paperback circulation being tested at Rosetown and Kenaston did away

with the circulation cards, meaning there was only a due-date slip
and no record of the borrower's name. It was an honour system that
would drastically cut processing costs and would become the norm
for circulating paperbacks. There was a concomitant book-selection
policy "to purchase more in accordance with the tastes of the public
rather than strictly in accordance with standards of book selection
common in most libraries. This means that such books as the Hardy
Boys, and Nancy Drew mystery series, and Harlequin romances have
been introduced in the collection."[16] New revolving stacks were purchased for paperbacks and librarians were told to jumble up books so
readers would poke through them to find what they might want.

There's an attractive story on how one town, Allan, joined the
region. Marilyn Boechler taught in Allan for many years and saw
major changes – rural electrification, SaskTel service, grid roads, the
consolidated schools – which led, she said, to a change in teaching,
from a single text to a variety of books, and the need for a school
library. When potash came in the '60s there was a sewer and water
program. The potash workers came from across the country and
asked where the library was. "There was a whole change of needs."
Boechler had earlier purchased a card from the Saskatoon Public
Library, but after Wheatland began, a group of local residents,
mostly women and using the Home and School Association, began
to campaign for a library. Council said no, it had other uses for taxes.
"Well, you don't know what you've never had," Boechler declared.
"So we decided we needed someone to run for council, and I ran,
and was elected. I was the first woman on that council." She brought
forward the issue of library service. "I wasn't going to sit idly."
Council finally agreed, and after the RM of Lost River joined, Allan
got its branch library, originally in the showroom of a former garage,
then as part of the town office. The promise of volunteer labour led
to hours of volunteer work by many. One more library.[17]

1972 is a good cross-section year for progress at Wheatland,
according to the annual report. Bookmobile service was started, after
consultations with Ian Holder, regional librarian of Parkland, which
had pioneered new bookmobile service. Staff moved into new headquarters, which meant new arrangements for processing materials.

Waldheim Branch Library, train station before *(right)* and after *(above)*.

"Processing follows a logical assembly-line design, enabling employees to laminate, cut and cover 1 book per minute, stamp and glue 2 books per minute, type book cards at the rate of 1 set per minute, and accession at the rate of 1 book every two minutes. In a typical day it is possible to stamp and glue 960 hardback books, laminate 600 book jackets, type 700 book cards, and accession of 265 sets of catalogue cards and books." By bulk purchasing and efficient processing, book costs, said assistant chief librarian Susan Cross, went down from an average of $6.95 in 1970 to $4.55 in 1972. The book-purchasing budget remained high, $40,000 out of a total budget of $140,000. An audio cassette program had also moved through the region.

There was news that the northwest corner of Wheatland would be transferred to Parkland. No region had benefited more from redistribution than Wheatland, gaining an eastern area and some jurisdictions originally organized by Palliser. When Kenaston joined Wheatland, it expected to receive a branch without joining a lineup. A representative from Kenaston, at the February 7, 1970, meeting, said she thought the agreement had just been transferred when the boundaries were changed. Humboldt looked like a natural for Wheatland but was already in North Central. "Mr. Kallio stated that Humboldt is not willing to join Wheatland, because they are being serviced by the North Central Regional Library which is paying their branch librarian."[18]

The serious boundary conflicts by 1975 were in response to the

A Wheatland logo

Library Inquiry Commission boundaries. Wheatland had organized RMs, villages and towns, now awarded to Lakeland, before the new act came into place, and before their area had doubled, so especially Unity and Wilkie had been crucial to early West Central. On January 29, 1975, Wheatland had made a motion to retain RMs 378, 379, 380 and 381 as well as Landis in the Wheatland boundaries, and to transfer RMs 382, 408, 409, 410, and 411 to Parkland, as well as the towns of Wilkie and Unity if agreeable to the towns and their autonomous local library boards. A Regional Boundaries Committee had already been set up, under the chairmanship of Carol Copeland, a Saskatoon library trustee. Both Unity and Wilkie, as well as Landis, wrote of their preference to stay in Wheatland and a letter written by Ed Tchorzewski, minister-in-charge-of-libraries (the NDP had won the election of 1971), included the motion that Wilkie, Unity, Adanac, Landis and the four RMs, 378, 379, 380, and 381 remain in Wheatland, a major victory, with both the towns citing excellent service from Wheatland.

There was one later dispute, in 1997, when Hague, Rosthern, and the RM of Rosthern wanted to join Wapiti. The stated reason for the dispute was the desire of Hague to have better library service, a branch rather than bookmobile service. Rosthern voted in effect to support Hague. Both sides played hardball, though an early offer to have an Owl's Roost Library in Hague wasn't responded to. The first part of a withdrawal was voluntary consensus, but as Wheatland requested $50,000 from Wapiti for the transfer and was offered $10,000, that process failed. The next step was an arbitration process, but before that started a new library act intervened to slow the process once again. Mediation by the provincial librarian failed. Before arbitration, the matter was settled when Wheatland offered Hague a full library branch, with 3,000 books (Rosthern had 6,000). The branch was furnished by Wheatland which had agreed, said the Hague town administrator, to pay the librarian. With Hague agreeing to this arrangement, the other two municipalities withdrew their notices of withdrawal. When the Hague branch was opened in June 2000, it was the first fully automated branch in the system.[19]

Chapter Seven

Southeast
1958 to 1992

W HILE WEST CENTRAL, OR WHEATLAND, BEGAN TO organize before Southeast, the latter became the second region to be inaugurated. It had two false starts, and then two separate regional organizations, Qu'Appelle and Southeast, which ultimately joined together to form the Southeast Regional Library. The first tentative beginning was that of Agnes Weweler; the second, begun in 1958, centred on Estevan and Weyburn, was described in some detail in the August 21, 1958, *Weyburn Review.* It celebrated ten years work by Marion Gilroy, and at least one of the supporters of a region, the Weyburn librarian Mrs. A. Griffin, must have been in contact with Gilroy on that first 1946 tour. Other supporters included Weyburn alderman Jim Campbell, also in touch with Gilroy, the Chamber of Commerce, the Carlyle and the Soo Line Homemakers, and the Weyburn Film Council. In her report to the Library Advisory Council (SLAC) meeting of October 17, 1959, Donalda Putnam, of the Provincial Library, mentioned the activity in the area earlier in the year, "so that, at one time, it seemed our main worry would be a duel between Weyburn and Estevan for the honour of serving as headquarters," but "there has been no word from either city for two months or more."

By 1962 both Qu'Appelle, with 13,800 people agreeing to a region, and Southeast had begun the final continuous push towards a region in the area. In the Southeast, Ida Petterson, an Estevan councillor, called a meeting in January 1962 at which a steering committee was formed with Mr. Art Forgay from Estevan as chair, and J.S. Porter from Weyburn as secretary, and representatives from Carnduff, Alida, Halbrite, Alameda, Brownhead, and Roche Percee.[1] That same year Qu'Appelle also created a steering committee with Irwin Feather from Grenfell as chair and with representatives from Broadview, Moosomin, Whitewood, and Fort Qu'Appelle.

Both regions continued their organizing, Qu'Appelle signing up communities, South-East educating more generally, to councils, Rotary Clubs, Chambers of Commerce, Home and School Associations, and the like. At the March 27, 1965, SLAC meeting, Porter informed the committee "there has been progress since Christmas when he started attending council meetings, usually accompanied by an extension librarian." That was Barbara Kincaid of the Provincial Library. "One of the biggest stumbling blocks is the good service given by the Public Information Library Division," which was more ammunition for withdrawing that service from established regions. Porter said visiting councils in January and for six months afterward "turned out to be a good time because councils are at full strength,"[2] before summer holidays, harvest, and council elections, which "almost preclude the rest of the year." In 1964 the Qu'Appelle Valley Regional Library recognized the difficulty of not having a large population centre, and asked the minister if they could set up a region with only 20,000 people and so asked for a special grant of $30,000 because the campaign was progressing so slowly; "much of the region has no experience of adequate library service, or of any library at all."[3] As late as March 1965 it was making the same pitch, now with 25,000 people[4] – the same number North Central began with. By June 1965, both regions agreed to join forces and on August 16 the delegates from participating councils met at Government House in Regina for the organizational meeting. James Porter was elected chair pro tem and presided over the meeting. The 43 delegates debated and passed the agreement between the region and the municipalities, with the help of Marion Sherman from North Central. They decided on a small executive of seven: two representatives from the cities, two from the towns, two from the rural municipalities, and one from the villages. Then came the discussion on naming the region, from this list: the Jubilee Region, Qu'Appelle Souris, Border, Southeastern, Wheat Land, Southeastern Jubilee, Number 2, Southeastern Saskatchewan. In the debate that followed, Qu'Appelle Souris and Southeastern Saskatchewan received strong support, the latter winning with two-thirds support. There may later have been some unease over the name, however, because in 1968 Provincial Archivist Allan Turner suggested other names, including Qu'Appelle Souris, Qu'Appelle Boundary, Pipestone (after the creek), Calumet, a native name for tobacco and peace pipe, Macoun for the explorer, or Douglas, after Tommy.[5] But Southeastern it remained. The process of choosing a headquarters followed a procedure begun by Provincial Librarian Mary Donaldson after the June 12 amalgamation meeting when she sent questionnaires to all towns and cities with a population over 1,000 as possible headquarters. There were cases made by Broadview, Carnduff (but no building ready), Estevan (with four possible locations for headquarters), Grenfell, Moosomin, Radville (but no suitable space), Weyburn (with three highways and both railroads and space available at the Saskatchewan Hospital). Later in the meeting there was a motion in favour of Weyburn, made by representatives from Spy Hill and the RM of Minta; the motion passed. Porter was elected president while Feather was on the executive.

Agreements were signed between 56 municipalities with a total population of 55,710, with hopes for more before December 31, 1962, so that the region could be formed by January 1963. The book grant would be $83,565, and Barbara Kincaid would be on loan to the region until it could hire professional staff, again after the North Central model.[6] There were 65 participating councils; 25 RMs, 22 towns, 21 villages, and the cities of Weyburn and Estevan. The RMs included Brokenshell whose representative was Mrs. Henry Nelson of Trossachs. (Agnes Weweler had taken a position earlier in the Moose Jaw public school system.) The boundaries were the

American border to the south, the Manitoba border to the east, as far north as Esterhazy on the east and Southey on the west, as far west as Ogema and Bengough, and surrounding Regina on three sides. The total area was 25,000 square miles with a population of 138,000. When the Library Inquiry Committee made its final report, Southeast lost all the area north of the Qu'Appelle River, a substantial loss in population, which it had already begun to service.

Southeast Opening. *(l to r)* Honourable G. J. Trapp, Minister in Charge of Libraries; Miss Mary E. Donaldson, Provincial Librarian; Mr. James S. Porter, Chairman; and Miss Barbara Kincaid, Acting Librarian

The region began operations January 1, 1966, "1966 and all that" as one librarian said. Headquarters were in a renovated Stores Warehouse Building at the Saskatchewan Hospital, which cost $43,000 for total renovations and furnishings, and which opened for business June 1, the regional workers beginning business at the Weyburn Public Library. The best guide to that year are three librarian reports, for April, September 17, and October 2 in the Southeastern archives. In the first we learn that 72 cartons of books had arrived, that 13 more had arrived the previous day, 37 parcels from England awaited completed custom forms, and that more orders were being made. Time was also spent preparing lists for branch libraries, planning the new headquarters, holding a workshop for trustees. By September, $84,763.53 worth of books had been ordered, with an average of 2,000 books processed each month, though a slowdown in catalogue cards from the Provincial Library had limited the process. There were nine staff members, and much student help in July and August. The first branch, Regina Beach, was opened in July, Minister George Trapp doing the honours.

By October, a branch was opening every week – Broadview, Kipling, Alameda, Carnduff, Lake Alma, though the statistics for that first year also include Grenfell, Moosomin, Ogema, Oxbow, Pangman, Radville, Spy Hill, and Trossachs, communities that already had libraries. Two forms of important programming had begun, a puppet show created through the Weyburn Recreation Centre, and a travelling art collection courtesy of the Saskatchewan Arts Board and arranged by Lea Collins. "During the coming year the Arts Board will be purchasing about 75 paintings and prints to be lent to the region for four years."[7]

By the September 23, 1967 librarian's report, 33 branches were open, with Fort Qu'Appelle opening the next week, while 11 branches were still uncertain – for instance the one in the village of McTaggart, which was being moved because of a new highway. Exchanges had begun: Weyburn and Estevan received 40 books a week, Esterhazy 30, Grenfell and others 20, Carnduff and others 15, Bengough and others 10. The book stock was limited and Barbara Kincaid said it would take ten years to arrive at the service goal of two books per capita. A problem with one branch shows the degree to which smaller communities depended on one or two people. Lake Alma couldn't open its library that year. "The strongest supporter of the library, Mr. Hoveland, the Lutheran pastor, has been transferred and Mr. Hoimyr, our trustee, is in the process of arranging to move from town. Consequently our local librarian has had no support and, living out of town herself, is unable to guarantee the library hours." If the branch couldn't open a minimum of six hours a week the books would be withdrawn, as indeed they subsequently were.

There was a different problem at Ogema, "whose library, located on the main street, is frequently used for teas, bake and rummage sales." On Saturday afternoon, the library's best day, it was open 3 to 5, hours when teas were also served. "Consequently, there is a desk at or near the door to collect the admission fee, there are no chairs in the library section, the study table becomes a bazaar table and the sound rises in intensity."[8] Requests for books, or interlibrary loans, were up, from five to ten a day the previous year to 50 or 60 a day that year. Two new book projects were completed, a display on Saskatchewan history sent to 24 branches, often used as part of a community's Jubilee Celebration. The Soo Line Homemakers' Club, one of the supporters of Agnes Weweler's initiative 20 years earlier, donated money for the region to buy a collection of books of interest to homemakers, and they were on display. The region also purchased a backup book for loan of every book on display. Fourteen branches had accepted an offer by the Saskatchewan Arts Board to have talks by visual artists. Indeed this early interest in the visual arts would remain a strong interest for Southeast. The limited book stock was nowhere more clearly evident than in the limitation of children's borrowing to one book, and many of the picture books were already in need of repair. Still, schools were being visited and story hours becoming common.

One of the chief problems of the new region was the dilemma of paying branch librarians. When additional monies came to the region in 1968, it planned to buy more books and to "proceed to paying branch librarians."[9] A Provincial Library Survey in 1969, said, "It cannot be stressed too highly that some form of payment be instituted for branch librarians" (p. 7) even if one cost of that change is "minimal staffing at headquarters" (p. 9). The Annual Report of 1969 said that while the matter had concerned the executive and personnel committee, "the Executive of 1970 are recommending no action until at least 1971," and the chair J.S. Porter asked these questions: what would be the cost? what salary scale used? what relation with libraries that are already paying librarians? what programs would be curtailed? and what would the levy be? At the 1972 annual meeting, one trustee said, "it was a choice between buying books or paying librarians." In the March 1972 internal newsletter, *Library Bindings,* Betty Coldwell, librarian for Ongre, talked about payment there. She was also a trustee and went to council for payment to librarians. "But there was always one more road to build, one more culvert to put in, more machinery to pay for...so there was no money for librarians." The previous year she'd asked for $50 a month, to be divided among three librarians, but they had to settle for $25, not even enough to pay expenses for the two who lived ten miles from town. She was embarrassed asking for money for herself and became a trustee only. She concluded, "Could we have some discussion in this magazine regarding pay for librarians?" By 1973 the groundwork was laid for paying librarians and the next year the region was paying a new minimum wage of $2.50 an hour, for a total of $98,133, while headquarters' staff was paid $104,490. Branch salaries were partly paid for by an increased levy of 25 cents per capita. By 1976, when branch salaries might reach $140,000, there was an additional increase of 10% for RMs, 15% for villages and towns, 25% for cities.

Southeast did get advice and assistance from other regions. At an October 26, 1968 meeting, George Anderson, who was born and had taught in the southeast and who was now a school principal in Melfort and a trustee for the North Central Region, spoke in considerable detail on the responsibility of being a trustee in terms of his experience at North Central. His region had moved, for instance, from volunteer librarians – the only way they could have begun – to a system of paying branch librarians. They started, he said, with a levy of 25 cents that was too low and yet were caught in a five-year fixed budget. When communities, seeing how good the regional libraries were, joined in numbers, the region was in debt for eight years. They went to one-year budgeting and increased levies; municipalities quibbled, but in a showdown – either pay or the regional library would fail – they paid. "We were preparing to say we would have to fold up and quit" – but they paid. Anderson had made it clear how difficult and rewarding it could be as a trustee.

The region received advice from Wheatland and Parkland, too. Advised by Provincial Librarian Harry Newsom to use the block system for supplying branches, two librarians from the region visited Wheatland, which had pioneered the system in Saskatchewan. "In it most of the collection is divided into small blocks balanced in selection,"[10] and a block is sent to a branch, re-collected, and sent to another branch. The advantage was in time saved – checking out a block instead of each individual book. The limitation was that some blocks might not suit all libraries, but Regional Librarian Hilda

Collins was in favour of trying it because it would move books faster to branches. (Collins was the first permanent regional librarian at Southeast, after Barbara Kincaid and an acting regional librarian Carl Wickland. She had come from California for three years before retirement, and would be replaced by Michael Keaschuk, then Karl Wahl. Keaschuk, after a position at Kamloops, became regional librarian at Chinook in 1975, a position he still holds). John Holter of Parkland talked to the February 19, 1972 meeting on bookmobile service in his region. The executive had placed bookmobile service as its first priority, but work on rebuilding the interior finishing of a school bus had not been completed on time. It was in operation in March 1973 and by year end it was serving 13 communities which had no library service earlier, with a circulation of 18,000 books, six new stops in 1964, up to the maximum of 22 stops by 1975, serving a population of 9,400. Revenue from participating municipalities was $9,400. Provincial grants covered book stock and salary and a grant of eight dollars per capita, as well as an operating grant for each bookmobile of five thousand dollars.

One of the special programs at Southeast was the promotion of the visual arts in early years, likely as a result of that first set of paintings and prints from the Saskatchewan Arts Board. In the 1968 Annual Report, Hilda Collins wrote, "The paintings from the Saskatchewan Arts Board have been popular and add to the attractiveness and interest of our Branch Libraries; for even when a painting is in a style which is not pleasing or is new to one, still it is important to see and know what artists are doing now." There had been a recent exchange of paintings. By 1970 that program, which had been offered for four years, came to an end, and in the annual report, the board had decided "to ask every Trustee and Branch Librarian to contact artists in their community and ask if they would be willing to lend us some of their pictures for one year. The response was overwhelming; we now have 84 pictures by local artists." And two of them sold! In 1972 several art events occurred. Alameda had a Tom Thomson evening, that included the NFB film *West Wind*, while two women reviewed books including an early one on Thomson's mysterious death. Manor expressed appreciation for the paintings and their periodic change. At Bengough children were encouraged to bring paintings to feature in the entranceway. There were two travelling shows from the MacKenzie Art Gallery in Regina, a Canadian Art Exhibit at Estevan, sponsored by the IODE, and a Saskatchewan show at Weyburn. There are other notes of arts shows in *Library Bindings* down the years, at Broadview, Windhorst, Lumsden, Stoughton, always shows of local artists.

A cross-section of Southeast is given in the 1969 Survey of the Southeastern Regional Library, and it made some of the same recommendations as did the Wheatland survey. Having lost the area north of the Qu'Appelle River, it became even more important to sign up new communities. At that point the region served 67,221 out of a possible 108,059 people. The region should provide more popular reading: "Consideration should...be given to the purchase of *many more* paperbacks, more fiction, and more material of a light popular nature as much of the rural population of Saskatchewan is not yet book-oriented" (p. 4). The report recommended payment to branch librarians and that more responsibility be given them. There were recommendations meant to simplify and speed up procedures, including buying a photocopying machine, making greater use of the Provincial Library cataloguing service, making a central file using copying, reorganizing headquarters and the like. There were two difficulties. "It was discovered by the survey team that some people had become completely alienated from the library because of strongly worded letters arriving after books had been returned" (p. 13). There was still one wrinkle in regional service being provided by libraries already in existence. "Some branches at the moment have two different checking out systems – one for their own collection and one for the regional library collection" (p. 17). The copy of the report I photocopied had marginalia – "now in effect," "in process," for many of the recommendations.

There were good years and bad years to come, with the mid '80s bad years, Lorne Hepworth of the Conservatives cutting the budget in 1987 by 11.6%, which the region only learned about in the fall when the budget year was partly over. There were cuts in branch hours, capital equipment, publicity, programs. In 1992, the NDP, inheriting a record debt, cut grants by 5%. That year the region was reduced to one bookmobile – the second had been added in 1978 – so 10 stops were cut and two branches closed to become bookmobile stops. Two clerical positions at headquarters were cut. Local levies had gone up. In 1981 municipalities paid $177,792 compared to the provincial grant of $423,081. By 1992 the local levies paid $565,874, the province $602,513. By 2002 municipal grants at $905,558 outstripped government grants at $724,026 and the off-loading of province to region was growing more and more stringent. In 2002 Isabelle Butters, chair for 15 years, gave her last report. Population in the region had declined by 3.64% in the last five years, which would affect government grants, and municipalities didn't want fee increases. So the board "has made the difficult decisions to squeeze headquarters operations, contract our branch services, and reduce support for Board members." As well she wrote, "the government's regional library pool, out of which Southeast Regional Library receives its provincial funding, has grown by only 1.6% over the last eleven years," further weakening headquarters and thereby the whole system. Municipal grants were up dramatically, from $216, 192 in 1982 to $511,686 in 1991 to $905,558 in 2002, a remarkable increase.

The story of the 1990s is automation. In 1982-3 microfiche readers and machines had ended the life of the card catalogue. By 1992, headquarters, Estevan and Weyburn began automation, though it took time for the system to work. Branches were barcoded in 1994-95. The Canada-Saskatchewan Infrastructure grant was important, both to automation and to the building of a handsome new regional office, next door to the Weyburn Public Library and in a design that incorporated both (architect for the Weyburn Library was Izumi Arnot, for the Regional Building, McGinn and Associates.) The Regional Library opened November 16, 1999. By 1996, 27 branches were automated, and e-mail reduced interlibrary loan request time to four days. By 1998 Southeast declared itself the most automated area in the province. To spend time in any regional headquarters today is to see most library workers in front of their computer screens.

It all began at Trossachs, which had an early branch for itself and its RM. By 1987 its circulation had dropped from 2,186 to 1,608 in one year. The branch was closed in 1990, and Trossachs added to the bookmobile route. Then in the budget squeeze of 1992, it lost even its bookmobile stop. Like so many small rural communities in Saskatchewan, Trossachs was shrinking, not growing. Out of the small came the large and the small declined.

Chapter Eight

Library Inquiry Report of 1967
Public Library Acts of 1953 and 1969

I N 1966, WITH ONE REGIONAL LIBRARY ACTIVE FOR 16 years and two others about to begin service, a library inquiry committee was set up by the Thatcher government to give it and the library community direction for the future.

The Library Inquiry Committee was established by a June 29, 1966, Order in Council and began its work almost at once, with one delay, the death of the first chair and appointment of a second chair, Judge John H. Maher of North Battleford, who along with W.A. Riddell of Regina College and Rusty Macdonald, a Saskatoon library trustee, made up the committee, notable because there was no professional librarian on it, though first Donalda Putnam and then Harry Newsom of the Provincial Library were non-voting members. The committee was efficient. It held hearings in what would become the seven regions in the south, at Prince Albert, North Battleford, Kindersley and Biggar, Swift Current, Yorkton, Weyburn, and at Saskatoon and Regina, between October 4 and November 24, 1966. Response was overwhelming, with 25 briefs and 10 letters from Saskatoon, 11 briefs and 53 letters from Prince Albert, 8 briefs and 10 letters from North Battleford, and so on. The committee made a brief interim report December 16, dealing primarily with the

Provincial Library, recommending that the salary of the provincial librarian be competitive, that the grant be increased and staff added. As well the committee recommended that both establishment and operating grants for regions be increased. The government responded with a $225,000 increase to the Provincial Library for 1967-68.

The final report, August 15, 1967, contained twelve chapters, the last a summary of recommendations. Although the librarians at the time were not all that enthusiastic, anyone reading it now can realize that it was the blueprint for the present system, and the government did listen to it. A virtue of the document is its general clarity and its recommendation for clarity in the system. Thus, "The aims and objectives of every library, no matter how large or small, must be clearly set down on paper and reviewed from time to time" (p. 7). The system as a whole should be a co-operative system with a clear hierarchical (my word) governing structure, the Provincial Library at the centre, then the two resource centres, Regina and Saskatoon, then the regional headquarters, and service in all municipalities. "Administration is centralized; public service decentralized" (p. 15).

Chapter Three describes current library service in the province, which it both praises and says is entirely inadequate. "The most important single action in the improvement of library services was the creation, in 1953, of the Provincial Library" (p. 14). The CCF is not referred to, nor is the work of Gilroy. Regina and Saskatoon "are especially bright spots" in the province, with strong civic support. There are 63 public libraries and 15 community libraries operating independently. "None can provide adequate service," the committee wrote. "Just as the educational service of the one-room school became entirely inadequate...now the local library, existing as a single unit, can no longer provide the informational services demanded by space-age man" (p. 11). The committee had the North Central Region as a model, as well as the new Wheatland and Southeast regions, and recommended the principles that had already become central to the one-library system: reciprocal lending rights, ILLO between libraries, standard and measurable library service for all communities, a central Provincial Library to coordinate and lead in the development of the system and provide direct service where needed. The words repeated throughout the report are "co-opera-tion" and "coordination." No one left behind. No library an island.

There is a detailed chapter on the Provincial Library, with 22 rec-ommendations under a series of headings, a clear blueprint down to how it should be organized. The committee's absolute commitment to the Provincial Library is everywhere evident. Either add staff and money or "Saskatchewan might as well close shop now and go out of the library business" (p. 22). Harry Newsom, provincial librarian, was an advisor to the committee from November on.

There's a chapter on regional and municipal libraries, Regina and Saskatoon the only municipalities that had a sufficient population to create strong libraries, which the committee thought should be resource libraries for the province and funded by the province for that service (a provision honoured more in the negative than the pos-itive). Of the elaborate proposals on regions here are a selection. There should be payment for local librarians, either by the munici-pality or the region, but the committee was not optimistic. "To encourage fifty or more municipalities to agree to raise the library appropriation even the nominal sum of ten cents per capita is an almost impossible undertaking" (p. 32). The committee would be proved wrong. The provincial librarian should "take an active role" in establishing regions initially, which was to be the case. The report suggests resource centres in regions, a concept slow to develop but important. Financing should be shared by the region and the provin-cial government. It recommends seven regions, the headquarters mir-rored in the consultation process. The population quota for a region should be 40,000, and by 1976 "additional legislation should ensure that regional library service be mandatory for all settled areas in the province" (p. 37). (That finally happened in the 1996 act.) Lloydminster should be treated as a special case because of its trans-border nature. "It is therefore recommended that a special grant structure be set up for the City of Lloydminster so that it may serve the surrounding area and yet not take part in a regional library, if that is advisable" (p. 37). It would take 15 years before Lloydminster was integrated into the Lakeland region. Dates are recommended for the creation of the four remaining regions, only one of which, Parkland,

1968, met the date; Palliser, 1983, was put off seven years, while both Southwest and Northwest were delayed for two years.

There's a chapter on provincial government support for libraries, which suggests for the cities five dollars local and two dollars provincial, per capita; for the regions a higher provincial contribution; including establishment grants of $1.50 per capita and $15,000 for equipment; an annual grant of 75 cents per capita; a staff grant of $25,000; and an incentive grant that gave 10 cents for each 10-cent increase in local levies. As well government should provide for regional headquarters.

The black mark against libraries in Saskatchewan was lack of professional staff, a lack many saw as a crisis. Some proposed a new library school at the University of Saskatchewan, and a library technician's course at the Saskatchewan Institute for Applied Arts and Sciences. There was hope because the University of Alberta was to open a library school in 1968 (and it became indeed a major source for Saskatchewan librarians). Kelsey Institute in Saskatoon began a library technician's course in 1968 as well. When graduates from Alberta began to come to Saskatchewan there were twenty-two- and twenty-three-year-olds in charge of some regions; Patricia Cuts, John Edgar, or a shade older, Michael Keaschuk; while Laureen Marchand was in charge of a city, and Don Meadows of the Provincial Library. The system was new, a *tabula rasa,* and many of the librarians were as young as the system.

The committee recommended library legislation to embody the principles of the report, including replacing the Saskatchewan Library Advisory Council with the Library Development Board (no reasons given for the change). Surveys of local systems by the Provincial Library should help to evaluate service. There were recommendations on automation and the computer, for cataloguing, for instance. The document has an appendix on who presented briefs and letters, and then brief abstracts of submissions: "Libraries are not luxuries in the modern world but are part of the essential services needed in our communities large and small." (RM of Moose Range, No. 486): "The Council of the town of Carrot River heartily endorses the Regional Library program as the answer for providing

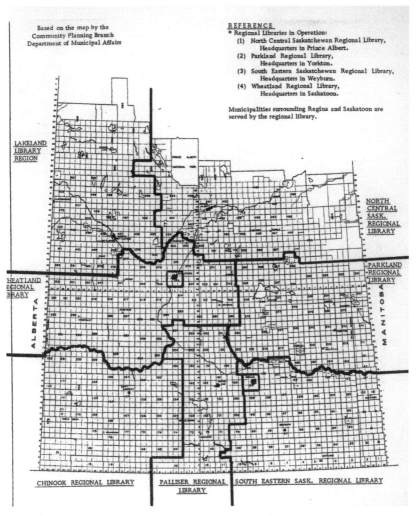

Regions, as defined in the Library Inquiry Report.

adequate library service for smaller centres." "The regional library has a value our tax dollar can scarcely purchase elsewhere – the most service for the least cost of any public enterprise" (Wheatland Regional Library Steering Committee). There follows a list of every municipality in the south of the province, its population, library service, and assessment, as organized by proposed regions, followed by current government expenditures on libraries, and a table of what the government should spend on libraries over almost 20 years, from the $639,000 in 1967-68 to two million dollars in 1977-78 and five million by 1984-85. The report was the rational basis for the Saskatchewan one-library system.

The Library Inquiry Committee Report was embodied in the 1969 Public Library Act.

That 1969 act replaced an equally revolutionary one, that of 1953. It had established in legislation the new world of post-war library service, enshrining the library world that already existed. The Provincial Library was to subsume all the previous government services, the Travelling Libraries, the Public Information Library, and the Regional Libraries Division. One of the small recommendations, repeated in 1969, for the provincial librarian "to keep and maintain a record of all libraries to which this act applies" (Part I, 5), has meant this book is more full than it might have been because of those splendid files.

The 1953 section on public libraries was traditional, most of it taken from the first 1906 act. (From the 1940 act, provisions for pensions were added.) Grants to libraries in 1953 went up from $200 to $400 matching materials grant, a decent amount for smaller libraries but a derisory amount for Regina and Saskatoon (sometimes less than 1% of expenditures and less than the Education and Hospitalization tax paid to the government).[1] The 1953 Act changed the name Mechanics' and Literary Institutes to Community Libraries but they were virtually the same, except they could now receive up to $150 annually, depending on the number of paid members. There were provisions to transfer a community to a public library.

The other new section, IV, on regional libraries, legislated the reality of North Central, allowing any municipality to associate with other municipalities to form a region, allowing municipalities to raise special levies, and the provincial government to fund regional libraries. The act also enshrined the Library Advisory Council, which had been in existence for seven years. It was the act that caught up with reality.

The 1969 Act responded to the Library Inquiry Committee, often expanding on sections of the 1953 Act. The section on the Provincial Library is much expanded, including a list of twelve responsibilities, worth presenting here because so much of Saskatchewan library service in the future lies within them. The Provincial Library was to be a coordinating agency, a promoting agency (for all libraries in the province), a provider of services to remote areas (for example the north), a provider of advisory services to public libraries, and provider of resource collections, of bibliographic services, of ILLO services. It should administer the certification of librarians, conduct surveys of libraries, co-operate with just about everyone. The new Saskatchewan Library Development Board (SLDB) was legislated.

The new item under Municipal Libraries was clause 25 on Regina and Saskatoon, designating them general libraries, resource centres, and advanced reference centres. They would remain independent libraries, part of the provincial system but outside any region. There was still a section on Community Libraries but the key clauses were those that allowed a transfer of property to a public library. Both Local Improvement Districts and Indian bands could join regions, the Indian band defined as a municipality for the Act; there were regulations for the Regional Library Board and Executive – in neither case was a limited term set. Standard library hours and local services would be established by the local and regional boards together, while both boards attended "to the welfare of branch librarians" (pp. 61 ff).

The government also published regulations to the Act on April 25, 1969, less than a month after the legislature passed it, the regulations expanding on a number of areas. The Saskatchewan Library Development Board had two major duties, to make recommendations to the minister and to work with the provincial librarian in establishing "a province-wide library service." It had nineteen specific duties. There were details on what a public library annual report should contain, details on how rare it would be to set up a new Community Library, a section on the legal steps to set up a region – and the need for a population of 40,000 to begin a region. Boundaries were established, a map included. The Provincial Library would be responsible for services in the north – north of Lakeland and North Central. The north had received no mention in the Inquiry Report. The regulations for municipal withdrawal from a

Provincial Library Advisory Board members were honoured for their contribution to the library system. Each member was presented with a memento to mark the occasion by Leah Seibold, Provincial Librarian. *(from left)* Leah Siebold; Thomas Boyd, North Battleford; Leola Moore, Swift Current; Ken Pragnell, Moose Jaw; Isabelle Butters, Weyburn; Viktor Fast, Nipawin; Jean Pask, Esterhazy; Rolland Pinsonneault, Regina; and Carol Copeland, Saskatoon. Three members were unable to attend: Morris Anderson, Regina; Louise Shelly, La Ronge; and Vic Hay, Saskatoon.

region were set – withdrawals to be dated December 31, supported by a resolution of a municipal council. There were regulations on the division of assets after a withdrawal, a clause which fortunately has not been invoked. There are details on what annual budgets should contain, while government grants and local levies would be based on the latest figures from the Saskatchewan Municipal Directory. Provincial support to municipal libraries would be matching grants for materials (as in the 1906 Act) to a maximum of $400. Saskatoon and Regina would receive 20 cents per capita, while for northern libraries the figure would be $1,000. Regions would receive establishment grants of $1.50 per capita, plus an equipment grant of $15,000, and a headquarters grant of $7,500 a year. The annual operating grant would be one dollar per person. Each of these provisions marks an increase over what had been available.

Acts may be slow reading but they are the basis for library service in the province. The important acts are 1906, 1953, 1969, and 1996.

Chapter Nine

Parkland
1956-1982

1956-1968, ORGANIZING

THERE'S A "BRIEF CHRONOLOGICAL HISTORY OF THE Parkland Regional Library, 1956-77" in nine pages and signed by regional librarian Stan Skrzeszewski. It's an excellent document in its own right and has assisted the preparation of this chapter. There was an early attempt, in 1956, to organize a regional library, when 50 people attended a meeting in Yorkton, with Marion Sherman of North Central as guest speaker. There were representatives from Kamsack, Canora, Foam Lake, Wynyard, Lanigan (which would enter Wheatland), Tisdale (which would enter North Central), and two RMs. The chair of the Yorkton Library Board, W.B. O'Regan, became chairman of the organizing committee.[1]

A report of the region in the "Provincial Library Annual Report" for 1968 suggests organizing was ongoing. "The idea was kept bubbling by many groups and individuals, including the Rev. W. Hill of Melville. Meetings were held, councils visited, speakers invited, MLAS informed..." (p. 15).

The first available document dates from 1964, when regional pamphlets were sent to Canora, while Yorkton's regional continuity was already clear: "As you know a regional library has been set up here in Yorkton with membership from the Yorkton Library Board and the University Women's Club."[2] Wynyard was planning a centennial civic centre to include a library (still today an attractive space). In October of the following year, Provincial Librarian Mary Donaldson made a tour of the area and discovered how little people knew of regional service. Canora was interested in a new building and was likely to be positive. Kamsack was willing to discuss the material Donaldson left. Foam Lake was "very handicapped for space," Wadena in the "throes of moving into new space," but they knew little of regional service. The mayor in Wynyard was anxious for books for their new library. No one had done any promotion work in the RMs.[3]

By early 1966 the entire regional committee still came from Yorkton. Geographically, the first region went from Kelvington and Preeceville in the north, to the Manitoba border on the east, with Melville, Bredenbury and Langenburg in the south and Wadena, Wynyard and Lestock in the west, encompassing a total population of 94,700. In May 1966, the first regional library meeting was held, with 28 members present, including representatives from Melville, Langenburg, Kelvington, Preecevelle, Wynyard, Calder, Fenwood, Jedburgh, Lestock, Willow Bunch (which would go to Palliser), and four RMs. The meeting elected a provisional board of 17 members, no more than one person per community, Alderman Don Matheson of Yorkton as chair, Francis Purves of Yorkton Public Library as secretary. By June 16, 1966, the pro tem committee examined, amended and passed the Agreement that would be signed by communities and the region, heard a talk from Mr. Kipling of North Central and from Mary Donaldson, and agreed on a tax levy formula: cities, $1.00; towns over 800, $.75; smaller towns and villages, $.60; rural municipalities, $.50; with an average overall of $.80. The chairman and vice-chairman, Matheson of Yorkton and George Artemenko of Melville, were asked to appoint an executive of seven. At a December 8, 1967, meeting, the new provincial librarian, Harry Newsom, introduced himself, advised the meeting that 40,000 was the minimum number for a region and that RMs must be signed up, and offered provincial library assistance on staff requirements and book service. Five towns offered to contact RMs in their areas, while the committee planned to approach government for formal certification. By December 29, 1966, as part of a presentation to the premier, the region had signed up 28,754, including Yorkton (12,500), Melville (5,400), Kamsack (3,200), Wynyard (2,400), and Wadena, Langenburg, Saltcoats, two villages and one RM, with another 12,000 agreeing to a region if it began July 1, 1967. The committee had also presented a brief to the Library Inquiry Committee meeting in Yorkton November 21.

Three communities had offered to house the headquarters, Wynyard, Yorkton and Melville. There was manoeuvring from some Melville people, including Liberal MLA Wilf Gardiner. Harry Newsom quoted the Libraries Act which said, "the regional library board shall designate the headquarters of the regional library, subject to the approval of the Minister." Premier Thatcher agreed that the region should make the choice, asked Minister George Trapp to see if a decision on headquarters could be make quickly. Trapp was certain Yorkton would be chosen.[4]

A June 6, 1967, meeting learned of contacts in the region, with Elfros, Balcarres, and Churchbridge all positive, and with 30,704 people represented by signed agreements. A regional library board was created, of twelve members, with Artemenko elected chairman, a seven-member executive then chosen, representing Melville, Yorkton, Wadena, Kamsack, Langenburg, RM 181, and Lestock. In a secret ballot on headquarters, Yorkton won ten to one over Melville, with Artemenko of Melville then congratulating Yorkton, one of those sweet moments when potential conflict disappears. Melville's disadvantages were two, a smaller population and a location at the southern edge of the region.

At a meeting October 24, 1967, Newsom outlined the steps that needed to be taken, which included an offer of assistance from the Provincial Library, which would place books in the region while Newsom offered to meet with municipal councils (and four meetings were organized, in Kamsack, Wadena, Balcarres, Churchbridge, and their surrounding areas), while the librarian in charge of Indian and

Métis people, David Sparvier, would contact Indian bands. Clearly Newsom, new to the province, was going to do what he could to make Parkland a success. The Wadena meeting included B. C. McNamee, secretary treasurer of Kelvington and my wife's father, V.W. Loucks of Invermay, connected to the family in more complex ways, and a Mr. Psovsky of Margo, a family next-cabin-over at the lake. This is, after all, a history of Saskatchewan.

Newsom reported on the meetings at a December 8, 1967, executive meeting: bad weather but good progress at Wadena; the town, two RMs and a reserve at Kamsack and good progress; "no progress at Balcarres due to poor mail service." He'd return to Balcarres, Canora, and Wadena. "Mr. Newsom stated that he planned to spend more time with councils and particularly in the Watson area."[5] In January he visited Lestock, Wynyard, and Foam Lake. In February and March Newsom sent out four form letters: one to councils which had agreed to participate in Parkland, a second to municipalities which were likely committed, a third to those which were not committed, a fourth to RMs which had not been contacted lately.

The March executive meeting took the decision to make the opening possible: forming sub-committees on building and equipment, finance and personnel, liaison and public relations. They had a building in mind and a committee, including Newsom, to finalize an agreement. The executive committee then gave Newsom power to order equipment, hire staff, and "to formulate a policy re salaries for branch librarians and the hours of opening for branch libraries," all recommendations to be made to an executive meeting in early June.[6] By February 1978, 31,099 people were represented by signed agreements, with 43,769 probable and 47,758 a possible figure. There's an interesting letter of March 11, 1968, by Newsom, explaining the procedure to add an Indian band to the region, in this case the Cote band, that included a request by the band to Ottawa to receive the current federal grant of $1.00 per capita, stating that David Sparvier would visit both Kamsack and the chief and look for a librarian.[7]

The executive meeting of March 29, 1968, grew even closer to the real thing, a building to be leased, at 92 Myrtle Avenue, a former turkey hatchery. Newsom was to be regional librarian until July 1,

1968, Francis Purves to be hired on an hourly rate, creating a regional staff of two. A tentative budget was accepted, based on a population of 50,000, which was Newsom's projection; banking was arranged; Robert's Rules of Order accepted – all those (if you're a meeting addict) delicious motions to begin the new world, administrative as all get-out, but how else can you begin a new world that's going to last? Newsom formulated all these regulations in a nine-page memo of April 4. There was an equally interesting memo sent by Newsom to Rusty Macdonald, chair of the SLDB, suggesting who he give credit to at the first Regional Board meeting: Mayor William Fichtner of Yorkton, "for his work and vision in working for this for years – who kept this library development in front of the government," George Artemenko, Al Bailey, Don Matheson, and the city clerk of Yorkton, T. F. Tille, "who has taken such a personal interest and made funds, time and space available, co-operated in every possible way," a hero known only from this memo, as well as praise for the library boards of Yorkton, Melville, Canora, Wadena, Kamsack, Kelvington, Invermay, and Watson, "who had the vision and understanding to back this development. (Rusty this is very important)."[8] Knowing Rusty, he'd have done a fine job.

PARKLAND, 1968-78

The first annual Parkland meeting, May 4, 1968, with twenty-two members and twenty-six observers, received a lovely message from Wheatland: "Welcome to the club, book on turkey hatching available through inter-library loan. Agriculture our specialty. Forwarding *Library Birth Without Fear* by Harry Dauntless." The meeting heard a long presentation by dauntless Harry Newsom, reported in minute detail, explaining the virtues of the regional system, that towns would have access to books across the continent, that together they win and that the Provincial Library would offer assistance. Libraries from Southeastern, like Spy Hill, were represented by observers at the meeting; they could join Parkland, since the boundary changes detailed in the Library Inquiry Report of 1967. Newsom was tempo-

May 4, 1968, opening of Parkland. Standing, board chair George Artemenko, seated, Harry Newsom.

rary regional librarian until July 1, when another employee of the Provincial Library, Don Meadows, would replace him. Mayor Fichtner was thanked more than once for his early work. The chairman, George Artemenko, also said, "The steering committee had meetings with the late Mary Donaldson who gave considerable assistance, but since Mr. Newsom arrived, the ball really got rolling."[9]

Reporting for the budget committee, Newsom made this point: "The Executive and I believe that the region should pay the local librarian salaries from the very beginning. Many of the problems encountered in other regions stem from the fact that you cannot expect the same degree of responsibility from a volunteer."[10]

Meadows began work as Parkland's first regional librarian July 1, and though it was originally planned that a new librarian would be on the job by January 1, 1969, he stayed for almost two years. In an interview Meadows said "I'd hit the road by 5:30 or 6 a.m. Monday morning and get back Friday night at 8:00, for a year and a half, 1,000 miles a week," and eighteen-hour days, signing municipalities to the new agreement. His first staff member, Purves, "was a lovely lady who knew everything." On the road Meadows, whose first job had been selling pharmaceuticals, was "still selling," signing agreements. "I thought I was hot on the library trail." He was travelling one day with Artemenko, "a fine, fine fellow," and they visited an RM council, all men as always. "I launched into my song and dance. The reeve and the secretary treasurer were nodding heads, a good sign. Then this guy with a tan that stopped at his cap, and in a double-breasted suit, stood up – he was a small guy – reached over, his finger under my nose and said, 'Listen meester, I'm telling you books is bullsheet.' Then his friend stood up, 'Dat's right. My friend is right. Dat's where kids got those ideas.' George said to me, quiet, 'I think we have to leave now before he starts complaining about your face.'"[11] Fourteen years later Meadows got a phone call saying the RM had joined the region.

By July the existing libraries came under regional jurisdiction, then in the fall ten new libraries were established: September 9, Langenburg; September 28, Saltcoats; October 1, Lestock; October 4, Churchbridge; October 10, Southey; October 21, Jedburgh; October 22, Elfros; November 1, Veregin; November 19, Quill Lake; December 9, Calder; – while the next year six more branches were established, including two that had been in Southeast, Spy Hill and Esterhazy, and the first reserve, Gordon band, with Cote band joining the following year. The official opening was November 2, 1968. There's an interesting statistic in the 1968 Annual Report. For the first six months of 1968 the ten established libraries on their own circulated 72,000 books, then for six months in the region circulated they 90,000 books, almost the entire increase was in juvenile circulation. To give a quick sense of how rapidly Parkland progressed over its first decade, the book collection went from 20,000 in 1968 to 100,000 in 1974, then to 151,000 in 1978. Items circulated rose from 176,000 in 1968, to 393,000 in 1974, then to 563,000 in 1978, while ILLO rose from 594 in 1968 to over 12,000 in 1974 and to over 26,000 in 1978, the amazing progress typical of regional libraries. Meadows said in the 1969 Annual Report, "Many people are using libraries for the first time in their lives, and they are finding it an exhilarating experience."

There were other stories in the 1970s, a response to an increase in minimum wage, problems with the first union contract in 1976, a major levy increase in 1977-78, a statement on universal participation, some information on service to Indian bands.

A 1972 letter to the minister prompted by the increase in the minimum wage, opened with a preamble in favour of the government's stated purpose of improving the quality of life in rural

Saskatchewan, then noted that the increased cost in Parkland would amount to $8,733. The book budget was already low at $20,000 and there was a budgetary deficit for 1972 of $8,877, partly because of a heavy financial commitment for the bookmobile. Parkland was requesting a 15-cent increase, to cover the wage increase with a bit left over for books.[12]

Arriving at the first union contract was a protracted and sometimes acrimonious process. The union was unhappy that management had the Yorkton city solicitor replacing the trustee committee, negotiations breaking down as a result. Inflationary times didn't help. The 1976 Annual Report includes this statement in the regional librarian's report: "Negotiations between CUPE Local 1904 and the Parkland Regional Library Board dragged on until mid-December. Due to the tensions and hard feelings generated by these prolonged negotiations, the relationship between board and staff was not as productive as it should have been and more could have been accomplished had the relationship been better." The negotiations had a second serious cost: "The long negotiations were partly responsible for a high staff turnover rate, especially among the senior staff."

The levy increase in 1977 also caused some tension. The large increase was defended by regional librarian Stan Skrzeszewski – two minimum wage raises since 1975, plus rising costs for books, the wage settlements of 30%, and the need for a new bookmobile. Rates would rise to $3.00 for Yorkton, $2.50 for Melville, $1.70 for towns of over 800, $1.20 for villages, $1.00 for RMs, all per capita.[13] Parkland had relatively low levies, five regions having higher ones.

The increase had been prepared for by dire warnings from Skrzeszewski, who suggested a $100,000 deficit for 1976, with inflation rising faster than grants; the region encouraged a massive letter-writing campaign to Education Minister Ed Tchorzewski. Yet in the summer of 1976 they ran a series of ads on their solvency: "THE PARKLAND REGIONAL LIBRARY is pleased to announce that it has finished 1975 with an estimated *surplus of $2,000.*"[14]

In the 1975 Annual Report, the regional librarian was already supporting universal participation, with a preamble on why it was needed:

Having a village with a library in a non-participating rural municipality means that the rest of the Region has to subsidize that particular library. Also, leaving municipalities free to withdraw because they are dissatisfied with the service means that a lot of energy is spent convincing municipalities to participate rather than improving services. Hopefully 100% participation in the Regional Library System will help us to overcome this difficulty.

There's a photograph of the truck-trailer bookmobile unit in the Regina *Leader-Post,* February 14, 1977. In 1979, according to the annual report, the region ordered a second bookmobile, "a sixty-six passenger school bus appropriately modified." It was called, in what is clearly a press release, "The first paperback bookmobile in the prairies," which would also carry a book collection on "Native culture, arts and history" and had a native operator, Biran Akan of the Muskowken band. It would serve nineteen stops including six reserves.[15]

In 1981 there's a detailed account of bookmobile 1, which travelled 1,067 miles on a three-week run, at 4.5 miles per gallon (bookmobile 2 at 7.7 miles per gallon). Bookmobile 1 had 19 stops in 1980, served about 11,192 people in villages, with a circulation of 61,731. "In 1981 it will receive $17,626.28 in municipal levies, a Bookmobile grant of $8,000, and an Equalization Grant of 11,192 x 2.20 = $24,622.40, for a total of $50,248.68."[16] The next year, Skrzeszewski wrote the provincial librarian on the cost of bookmobile service so it would be given greater credit than that proposed in the new grant formula. The total costs came to $96,490 for the two units, with salaries of $57,900, and no income listed. They were in the process "of outfitting a new bus unit and the total cost will be about $22,000, not including the book stock."[17] There was even a detailed 1983 schedule of stops, while that new bookmobile, replacing the tractor-trailer unit, was a 1982 Bluebird bus.

Annual reports list the winning and losing of customers. Successful stops, like Raymore in 1982 and Jansen in 1984, became branch libraries. In general by 1984, "The population in most of the villages we serve is either decreasing or holding steady." In 1985 new electrical outlets at schools made a difference, circulation up by 145% at Abernethy, up 257% at Gordon Reserve. A switch earlier from gasoline to propane on Bookmobile 1 saved about 15 cents a litre but the bus had less power and there weren't many propane filling stations in the region. In 1988, Endeavour, at a circulation of 6,448, led all the rest, with six communities over 3,000, Bulyea, Dunleath, Rama, Margo, Rhein, Goodeve, and Willowbrook, with two reserves, Gordon's and Poorman, doing well, while at the bottom end were Veregin, 195; Daystar, 74; Fishing Lake, 74. A detailed bookmobile report is included in the 1989 Annual Report. There were still 42 stops but circulation was down 10%. A school closure in Stenen affected that stop, while in Grayson "a class with a very large proportion of young female readers – traditionally an avid group of readers – graduated to a class outside the region." If a new RM joined, circulation went up, as it had at Sheho. Paperbacks were in demand. Bookmobile 1 circulated 40% paperbacks while bookmobile 2 was entirely paperbacks, and its circulation breakdown was 40% easy to read, 27% adult fiction, 16% adult non-fiction, 14% junior fiction, 3% magazines. The bookmobiles visited small communities, usually between 25 and 300 people, and the bookmobile operators had an excellent knowledge of the region.

The library moved in 1975. "We started that year in an ex-turkey-hatchery; at the end of the year we found ourselves in an ex-drug-store."[18] Yorkton Public Library had its own physical drawbacks, limited space and extreme heat, "especially during summer months, when the temperatures regularly remained over 90° Fahrenheit."[19]

INDIAN BANDS, 1973-82

By 1973 eight Indian bands had become members of Parkland, while five others hadn't joined.[20] The Cote band, the largest with a population of 1,224, was reluctant to sign the agreement again because of dissatisfactions:

1. The service we expected just wasn't brought into the community.
2. It was noted the only time we did get someone was when the money was due.
3. We had problems getting a person in becoming a librarian.
4. Lack of training and inexperience in this type of work.

Finally, "we do hope that you will look into improving this very worthwhile service."[21]

That same year the regional librarian wrote Don Meadows, now Provincial Librarian, saying that two bands still owed levies for 1972-73. An earlier election of the Fishing Lake band was being disputed so no one could sign the agreement. The agent of Indian Affairs at Yorkton thought Keeseekoose band might pay its levy out of welfare funds, and said, "He is hopeful that next year's grant can be paid directly to us through Indian Affairs Office in Yorkton," in effect to bypass the band, which is what happened.[22] The 1974 Annual Report had the region serving seven bands. The branches in Cote and Gordon had closed while the latter had quit the region, which had a good arrangement with a school at Keeseekoose and was trying a similar arrangement at Peepeekisis. In 1978, 15 communities joined the region, including five Indian bands: Gordon, Little Black Bear, Okanese, Poorman, and Star Blanket.

In 1981 John Murray of the Provincial Library had two concerns with Parkland's band policy: "That the regional library not encourage payment direct from DIAND [the Department of Indian Affairs and Northern Development] because it undercut the independence and responsibility of the band. (John recognizes, however, that this had always been the case in Parkland, unlike other regions who received payment from the bands.) That the agreement did not allow a branch library to be established, and this may be interpreted as being discriminatory. If the region does not possess the personnel or financial resources, it may decide not to offer branch services. However, to preclude such might be inadvisable."[23]

The actual contracts between region and municipalities was the same for an Indian band (Cote, 1969), an RM (Elfros, 1968), and a town (Foam Lake, 1967), according to files at the Provincial Library.

PARKLAND, 1980s

1980 can serve as a useful cross-section year for Parkland. According to the Annual Report that year, circulation of 739,569 items was an increase of 17% over the previous year. Four new communities and an Indian band joined the region while new libraries were opened in Lake Lenore and Annaheim, with Sturgis and Quill Lake moving into larger and better quarters. Paperbacks were on the rise and now made up a third of all circulation. Two small studies that year proved their popularity. Programming for Saskatchewan Library Week included a poetry competition, with over 300 entries, while visitors included Maria Campbell, to Gordon Reserve and Yorkton, as well Stephen Scriver and Geoffrey Ursell. 1980 was the province's seventy-fifth birthday and Homecoming parades in nine towns used the region's Book Worm float, while ten other libraries entered their own floats. The Yorkton Library began its Saskatchewan history collection. By that year the new bookmobile brought service to thirteen new communities including those six reserves, and Preeceville joined Parkland, the last town in Saskatchewan to join a region. They'd also made an agreement to provide service to the Parkland Community College.[24]

The process of provincial automation was underway, with the Provincial Library, and Regina and Saskatoon public libraries joining together in a non-profit corporation to purchase automated library services. Regional libraries would continue to receive catalogue cards though they would now be produced by the UTLAS (University of Toronto Library Automation System) computers.

There was one other letter to Shillington, minister of libraries, from Skrzeszewski, congratulating him for supporting universal participation of all municipalities in his speech at the recent SLA Convention, especially since the Saskatchewan Association of Rural Municipalities and Saskatchewan Urban Municipalities Association didn't currently support such legislation.[25]

Financial statistics for that year compared the seven regions. Parkland had the third highest municipal levies, after Wapiti and Palliser, and the second highest provincial grant, after Wapiti; while for those levies that were comparable across the province, Parkland had the second lowest levy for villages, with Wheatland lower, and the third lowest levy for RMs, with Chinook and Wheatland lower.

Theodore, near Yorkton, gave a notice of withdrawal for December 31, 1981. Skrzeszeweski replied that a withdrawal notice must be presented two years in advance, and that, more generally, "I cannot understand why a Council would voluntarily cut services to their own community and therefore reduce the number of people coming to their town at a time when most communities are fighting tooth and nail to retain as many services as possible."[26] The mayor, Carl Dusty, said it was expensive for bookmobile service, over $800 and rising to $900 the following year. Theodore people had borrowed 4,818 books during the last year, the fifth best bookmobile stop in Parkland. "However, the village council feels the high number of books is only being taken out by a small proportion of residents."[27] Yet by 1984 Theodore had opened a new library as part of a new municipal building, two years under construction, designed by an alderman, built by Theodore taxpayers, which was usual, municipalities responsible for headquarters according to legislation.

Levy increases were passed by a large majority in 1981 and prepared for by the regional librarian through a series of letters to municipalities explaining how much each paid and the cost of providing that service – though not including either headquarter costs or provincial grants. The figures show which communities paid their own way and which needed the heaviest subsidies. A large community like Kamsack, including a RM and a village, roughly paid for itself – library costs at $9,348.65 and levies at $8,493.25. Watson's cost were $5,346.60, its levy $2,844.23. Town levies, now at $2.44 per capita, would rise to $2.78 in 1982, $3.22 in 1983, and $3.80 in 1984 (and in the next round of increases $3.99 in 1985, $4.18 in 1986, $4.37 in 1987). Costs at Elfros were $2,706.17 while levies were $1,750.17, paid mostly by the RM, and its levies would rise to $2.47 by 1984. Finally, the RM of Stanley, near Melville and with three bookmobile stops, cost $8,200 and returned in levies $2,332.91; like Elfros its levy would rise from $1.58 in 1981 to $2.47 in 1984 (and $2.72 in 1985, $2.79 in 1986, $3.21 in 1987). These are the most detailed accounts on costs and levies I have found.

Kamsack librarian Carl Eggenschwiler, *(left)* one of the key local librarians in Parkland

Step one in the new technology came to Parkland by 1982 when 38 branches had microfiche as a way to give more power to people in smaller places. 1985 saw the purchase of an electronic typewriter with memory, the conversion of Telex to Envoy for ILLO to save money, plus the beginning of plans to transfer the main catalogue to machine-readable format.

There were five resource libraries in the region by 1984, with Esterhazy and Canora joining Melville, Kamsack, and Wynyard. Canora and Saltcoats opened new libraries that year; Melville doubled the size of its library. Kelliher and Bredenbury were in new facilities, with Jansen and the RM of Prairie Rose due to open shortly. By that year there were 54 branches (with branch 52 at Theodore, branch 53 at Englefeld, branch 54 at Jansen), 41 bookmobile stops and ten book deposits. A going concern.

Chapter Ten

Chinook
1961-1997

Organizing in South West, or Chinook, began May 2, 1961, at Lancer, at a Home and School Association meeting. Later, at an October 11, 1962, annual meeting of the Lancer Library Committee, Marion Gilroy and *Books for Beaver River* were featured while the RM of Miry Creek, like Stranraer before it, became the first municipality to pass a motion in favour of a new region. The Sceptre Home and School had sent out letters to 96 RM councils, and received nine replies.[1] Jean Murch from Miry Creek, one of the most important trustees in the region, gave a talk in 1967 explaining to delegates at an annual meeting the early history of South West, including those 1961 and 1962 meetings. Donalda Putnam from the Provincial Library said, "Please don't be discouraged – you are our first ray of hope in your part of the country." At a Home and School regional meeting in Swift Current October 21, 1964, the regional steering committee was formed, with Arnold Zabel chairman. Zabel and the secretary, Mrs. N. Sillerud, both of Swift Current, were informed by Elspeth Miller of the Provincial Library that they'd need to wait for the tabling of the Library Inquiry Committee Report to learn of grant levels and ground rules. "Although no official

announcement has been made it seems almost certain that the
Government is prepared to establish one library per year for the
next five years,"[2] an optimistic projection whose most accurate
word is "seems." Wheatland, Parkland and South Central had
already met quotas, said Miller, who hoped the delay would not
depress South West. By March 1967 South West had signed 25,000
people, from eight RMs, two towns, (Cabri and Maple Creek), several villages, and the one city, Swift Current. The total population
of the region in 1967 was 74,266. The Provincial Library gave
organizing assistance and in June and July 1967 met with councils
in Leader, Burstall, Swift Current, Gull Lake, Eastend, and
Shaunavon and set up a booth at the Swift Current Exhibition and
Stampede. The area had been doing its own organizing too,
including an April 19, 1965, half-hour telecast on CJFB-TV.

The area was especially deficient in library service and a brief to
the Liberal minister in charge of libraries, J.C. McIsaac, March 28,
1968, said there was no library service for the 32,000 people in RMs,
only 3% service in villages and 37% in towns – in many ways as
bleak a picture as in the 1930s. Murch attended that meeting with
sixteen other people, led by Mayor Dahl of Swift Current. A SUMA
meeting in Regina helped swell the ranks. McIsaac offered "every
consideration" but that led to no action. Premier Ross Thatcher
said there was not enough money.[3] One village, Kincaid, explained
its dilemma. When it applied to be a member of South Central
(Moose Jaw) it formed a small library of its own, based on gifts of
books, mostly fiction. "I would say that from our population of 350
there are 25 participating families. Interest is lagging as most of our
readers have read all of our books."[4] Now, the writer says, the village has been placed in the Swift Current area, and she wonders
when things will get better. Provincial Librarian Harry Newsom
replied that the Swift Current region would likely be a reality
before the Moose Jaw region and the organizing meeting for South
West was set for November 4, 1967. There was a preliminary
meeting of the steering committee on September 20, the Library
Inquiry Report now available, as was Newsom, promising assis-

tance from the Provincial Library staff. The meeting agreed on a nine-member executive: two from towns, one from villages, two from RMs, two from the city, two members at large. A September 26, 1967, document has check marks for all participants, from Frontier to RM 932.

At that organizing meeting November 4, 1967 in Swift Current, attended by 25 voting delegates and 37 observers, the name Chinook was chosen (no alternatives listed), the draft agreement was passed, Swift Current chosen as headquarters, an executive elected (chairman Robert Lodge from Swift Current, vice-chairman Murch, while two others elected would be important later for the region, – Phoebe Bunnel from Swift Current and Dorothy Sanderson from Vanguard). As well, a decision was taken to approach government for enabling legislation.[5]

Then they waited. In the spring of 1968 Newsom wrote to McIsaac expressing his own choice for the order of creating new regional libraries. Palliser was chronologically ahead of Chinook by seven months, but Chinook should come first "because only 14,000 persons out of the proposed total are *now* getting reasonably good library service."[6] He asked if North West, when it would be organized, should also be considered ahead of Moose Jaw. Palliser was dropping down the pecking order. Newsom added that the Provincial Library could do two regions next year, if one were Moose Jaw, because it would be easy to develop. Later, the Library Development Board would accept Newsom's advice.

The region divided itself into five areas for organizational purposes. Chinook ran from the US border on the south to the South Saskatchewan River for most of the north, to the Alberta border on the west, while the communities on the east, from north to south, were Central Butte, Chaplin, Gravelbourg, and Glenworth. The region hoped for a 1969 opening but Thatcher said, "I would rather doubt whether our finances will permit us to bite off another one until 1970."[7] The news from McIsaac was no better a year later and Chinook had to wait until 1971 to become a legal entity.

2. CHINOOK 1970s

Chinook finally held its organizational meeting April 24, 1971, when it represented 23,328 persons. Books were being bought, and shelves to sit them on, and furniture for staff to sit on once they were hired, so the region could begin operations in the middle of May. The first regional librarian was Keith Turnbull, seconded from the Provincial Library, assisted by a newcomer to Saskatchewan, Patricia Cuts, and John Rafter, who would later succeed Turnbull, for about a year. An executive was elected, with Lodge as chairman and Murch as vice-chairman. (When Lodge took a job out of the region in 1973, Murch succeeded him as chair.) By August 7 the participating municipalities represented 34,750 people, just over half the population. The region bought a used bookmobile from Regina, for $1,000 plus $1,300 for repairs, plus the lease of a truck to pull it.

By the end of 1971, according to the first annual report, Chinook was providing service to the seven branches already established: Swift Current, Cabri, Leader, Maple Creek, Eastend, Shaunavon, and

Official Opening, Chinook, 1971. From left to right, Keith Turnbull, Don Meadows, Gordon MacMurchy, Minister in Charge of Libraries, Jean Murch, Dr. Robert Lodge.

Kincaid, and had opened eight new libraries, in Vanguard, Ponteix, Morse, Hodgeville, Gull Lake, Abbey, Stewart Valley and Frontier, while the bookmobile visited ten other communities. The official opening took place November 24, 1971, Minister Gordon Mac-Murchy in attendance. The region now served 39,853 people.

Pat Cavill (formerly Pat Cuts) told me a moving story of library service. "One Friday night I was going to Swift Current in driving rain. I was going to a meeting. I was young, it was a Friday night. There was this truck in front of me throwing up water. I passed it and it was the bookmobile. I got all tearful. Here he was on his Friday night bringing books to people." Her drive from Regina to Swift Current every week for a year changed her. "I saw the land change all the time. It became my imaginative home."[8]

A small event in 1972 can show how close to the bone finances in Chinook were. An increase in the provincial minimum wage, combined with a new regulation that all part-time staff had to be paid for a minimum of three hours, plus a small decline in population added up this way: minimum wage increase $2,710, plus a grant and levy loss due to population loss (940 out of 48,000) $2,071.70, for a total of $4,781.90, which sounds small but levies were fixed. There was a meeting of the executive in January of 1973 that was concerned with shaving costs in a number of ways; a branch supervisor position replaced by a technician, volunteers asked to assist with bookmobile stops, delegate costs to be the responsibility of the local municipalities (not unique to Chinook), while out-of-region fees should increase (again, true of all regions).

There had been a small conflict with Swift Current in 1972, because fewer books were put into the branch than when it was independent. Recommendations for solutions were made by Turnbull, who laid blame all around, with the local board for not complaining earlier, with the branch librarian for not making needs known, with the regional librarian for not seeing the problem. "The purpose is not to lay blame on anyone," he said, after he'd done it. One hundred novels were put in the branch at once, the number of blocks would be increased, and the region said it would grant Swift Current between three and four thousand dollars for the librarian to order her own books. Library hours would be increased so children bused into the city could use the library, though it remained in cramped quarters. All would be well "if things are not allowed to deteriorate because of inaction on the part of the local library board,"[9] Turnbull wrote.

By 1973 the region served 85% of the population while circulation had doubled from 35,000 to 70,000; ILLO use had also doubled as patrons became familiar with it. The provincial government had increased its per capita grant from $1.20 to $1.60, which meant service in the region was adequate. There were only two more branches to be set up, at Burstall and Gravelbourg. The bookmobile was on its last legs and a new one needed to be purchased. There were paid, not volunteer, people at bookmobile stops, who promoted the stop, collected overdues and helped with ILLO. When Phoebe Bunnel requested ILLO on playing cards, "she received 17 books from 10 libraries in three different countries," including the New York Public Library, the Library of Congress and the National Central Library in London, England. That's service.[10] The books most people wanted were those on Western Canada, followed by Canadian authors in general, while the main damage to books "was caused by dropping books into the bathtub," said John Edgar (regional librarian); the second cause – books being chewed by hungry puppies."[11] In 1971 the Swift Current Public Library moved into its present quarters in the R.C. Dahl Memorial Building.

The Annual Meeting of February 1974 passed a motion to increase levies by 20% and they then rose substantially over the next three years, so that the Swift Current levy increased from $2.25 in 1976, to $2.70 in 1977, and $3.25 in 1978; while towns over 700 increased from $1.30 in 1976, to $1.55 in 1977, to $1.85 in 1987; towns under 700 and villages went from $1.00 to $1.50 while RMs rose only from $.90 to $1.00. The region was without bookmobile service for a year. The original bookmobile had been in an accident in 1973 that rendered it useless. The new bookmobile was purchased with the assistance of the new $10,000 capital grant from the government, whose grants in other areas rose as well, establishment grants from $1.75 per capita to $4.00, operating grants from $1.50 to $2.50 – great support in inflationary times.

A special meeting of the executive dealt with a troubling matter, the resignation of the branch supervisor and the regional librarian, John Edgar, though he would stay another six months to take the region through its next budget. Mike Keaschuk, hired as regional librarian the next May, remains in that post today. That loss of staff was one reason the region wanted the Provincial Library to survey the region, which it did between November 18 and December 31, 1974, with the region receiving the report in March 1975. The survey team was Keith Turnbull, chair, plus Don Meadows, Juliette Henley, and Bob Ivanochko.

The main conclusions of the survey were dire. "The Chinook Regional Library has suffered from poor funding, resulting in serious problems in almost every area of work" (p. 1). "The physical working conditions are bad, wages have been poor, and the number of staff inadequate to do the work" (p. 2), both at headquarters and at the branches, where librarians worked extra hours for no pay. There were no written bylaws for the region; no hiring policy; no statement on wages, benefits, and responsibilities for employees; and no pension plan; while job descriptions were sketchy, especially for senior staff. Nor was there a written policy on the purchase of materials. There needed to be more staff training, better communication between the region and Swift Current. A second branch supervisor should be hired.

The headquarters building "provides a cluttered, noisy and depressing environment for the staff" (p. 12) – the work-area floor was painted concrete, "cold, cracked, always dusty." The noise was terrible, ceiling heaters "combined with the roar of the photocopier, rattle of the typewriters and chairs moving over concrete," and so on. "Cold and drafty areas in the workroom vary from day to day depending on the direction of the wind" (p. 13), plus diesel fumes, and mice and crickets in the fall. (Two years later there were European Chicken Fleas.) A terrible building. Other smaller suggestions: a monthly newsletter for branch librarians, another technician and clerical worker, improved paperback deposits. The report on Swift Current was more positive, and regional service to it, though more Canadian materials should be purchased to meet demands, and it should have control of its materials budget, which should be set at least at $10,000.

Thirteen branch libraries were visited by the team and all suffered "from an extreme shortage of materials" (p. 36).

> Local libraries and local boards feel the need for improvements in the following areas of materials: Canadian history and literature and history (especially Western Canadian or Saskatchewan history); repair manuals, especially small gas motors, car repair, outboard motors, carpentry, electrical wiring, snowmobile manuals, motorcycle repairs, plumbing, truck and tractor manuals, veterinary medicine manuals, basic first aid, and medical manuals, Canadian directories and almanacs; best sellers of lasting value. (p. 38)

There were no catalogues in some branches, like Cabri. Hours of opening at nine to twelve hours, six in Vanguard, were inadequate.

By 1975, according to the Annual Report, the region had responded to several of the survey's recommendations – two branch librarians had been hired; the region had joined a superannuation plan; had increased salaries, created a policy on holidays and vacation leave; it had also presented to the board proposed bylaws and a statement of policy. "Each Board member received a copy of the Survey Report in March 1975. Many of the recommendations have been acted upon. However, if there are some areas of concern, we hope that you would bring these up at this annual meeting." By the following year a branch manual had been completed, while a new bookmobile, custom-built by Ken Sawby of Maple Creek, was on the road by August, 1976. The province continued to fund regional libraries handsomely, with a 26.3% increase. The region began one new service, in November 1976, a paperbacks-by-mail service to communities served by the bookmobile as well as to handicapped people and the aged.

Money. Keaschuk explained the region's financial position in a 1977 letter to Minister Don Faris, on the costs of an increase in minimum wage (supported), on new postal rates, on the loss of 10% population according to 1977 figures, and on a 20% levy increase after the three-year agreement was up.[12] Swift Current celebrated its sixtieth anniversary in 1978, and, led by Alderman Wilson, rejected any levy increase beyond 7% so the city would not in future be surprised by sudden large budget demands. (Chinook's levy increase for 1979 had been 18%.) At the annual meeting, February 24, 1978, a motion on levies read in part: "The municipal levies shall be limited to not more than a 7% increase over previous year commencing January, 1980." The minutes also included the region's weighting factor for levies, with RMS at 1, villages at 1.5, towns at 1.85, city at 3.25.

The terrible headquarters building came front and centre because a five-year lease was to expire December 31, 1979. The annual headquarters grant from the government, $22,000, paid for the annual rent of $14,400 plus improvements "for quarters which are dreadfully inadequate," Keaschuk wrote."[13] In his report on the building Keaschuk suggested three options: the government financing a new headquarters (cost $300,000); the region constructing a new facility (the mortgage, $38,000, was well beyond the designated grant), or buying the present property, at $120,000, plus an adjoining lot to bring the property up to the 75-foot frontage required by new Swift Current zoning regulations. In fact the headquarters building was grandfathered in as an existing use.

Meadows explained to Minister Ned Shillington what the government had done in the past for regional headquarters and detailed the state of headquarters buildings in all the regions. "A precedent of sorts was established by the construction of the Wapiti H.Q. building in Prince Albert by the Dept. of Government Services and the renovation of the Warehouse building in Weyburn (again Government Services) for the Southeast Region."[14] Meadows pointed out that no region could finance its own building, even over twenty years, without dipping into operating grants. He then reported on the status of headquarters buildings: Wapiti good, Parkland adequate with a new combined headquarters with Yorkton Public Library in the future, Weyburn fine, Wheatland had acquired its own building, using "accumulated establishment grants (not illegal, but inadvisable) and H.Q. capital and operating grants to finance the purchase and construction." There were two very poor headquarters buildings, at Swift Current – "present building is drafty, poorly constructed and badly designed" –

and at Moose Jaw, the worst of all regional headquarters, in an old building, with poor heat, restricted access, and so on.

Chinook was given the preference over Palliser, partly because it spoke up first and because a decision had to be made by the end of the year. After that January 5 letter, there was an elaborate correspondence between Shillington, Meadows, and Government Services until the following November when a requirement study for a building was complete.[15] Subsequently the executive met with the minister November 1 and with the SLDB on November 23-24. The following day Chinook approved the purchase of its present building which, according to the Annual Report of 1979, cost $100,000 with a 20-year mortgage at 14% or a rate of $12,000 a month, roughly within the limits of the provincial grant for headquarters, which did increase year by year.

CHINOOK, 1980s

One of the positive themes for Chinook in the 1980s was a program for writers-in-residence and authors visiting branches. By 1980, a Southwest Saskatchewan Writers Project, the work of a partnership between Chinook, the Cypress Hills Community College and the Swift Current Allied Arts Council, had created four objectives: a writer-in-residence, public readings by writers, a week-long writing project, and the publication of a book to celebrate local writers. By the end of that year three writers had read during Saskatchewan Library Week; Lorna Uher (Crozier) became writer-in-residence; and a week-long workshop was held in Ponteix at the end of October, featuring Uher, Howie White, Jack Hodgins, Patrick Lane, and Lois Simmie. Rick Hillis became the second writer-in-residence in 1986 and he oversaw the publication of two editions of *Premium Swift Review,* collections of local writing. Rod McIntyre was writer-in-residence in the mid-nineties.

By 1980 money had become the root of all tension, when a new three-year cycle began with a 16.02% levy increase approved at Chinook's fall meeting and opposed by Swift Current representa-

Bank of Montreal (1912), now the Battleford Library

CNR Station (1910), now the Big River Library

CNR Station (1912), now the Blaine Lake Library

CNR Station (1924), now the Eatonia Library and Community Centre

Bank of Commerce (circa 1908), now the Elbow Library and Town Hall

CPR Station (1938), former Meath Park Library

Carnegie Library (1916), North Battleford, now the Allen Sapp Gallery

Men's Club (1912), former Prince Albert Library

Elementary School (1913), Pennant, now the Town Office and Chinook Regional Library

Town Hall (1906), Qu'Appelle, now the Town Hall and Regional Library

Albert Library (1927), Regina

Connaught Library (1930), Regina

Imperial Bank of Canada (1903), now the Rosthern Library and Town Office

United Church (1911), Stenen, originally the Crystal Lake Library

CNR Station (1909), now the Waldheim Library

Stone School (1903), now the Yellow Grass Library

All photos courtesy Saskatchewan Heritage Foundation, by Frank Korvemaker, except Rosthern, by Bob Burke, and Big River, by Garth Pugh

tives. There was much heat. A Swift Current alderman said the "city will have to look for alternatives," to which a board member from Leader said it was like "putting a gun to the delegate's head."[16] In response to Alderman Wilson's comment "that politics were being played against the city," Keaschuk said he had not been lobbying to have rural Chinook banding together against Swift Current. By December 2, 1980, Swift Current passed a motion to withdraw from Chinook on January 1, 1982, wanting, according to Wilson, "a fixed per capita rate."[17] Then came the discussion about how much Swift Current would gain from the region and what it would lose. Keaschuk said the increase amounted to 37 cents a person in the city, while its contribution to the region did not cover salaries at the city branch. The region received 75% of its budget from the province, only 25% from levies, so if the city left the region it would not be eligible for provincial grants. Swift Current did recognize the advantage of the region, and stated that its withdrawal was strategic, to make the government pay attention to city needs.

There was some local opposition to the council move. The Swift Current Library Board regretted the city's decision and offered to act as an arbitrator.[18] When a number of women's groups protested the withdrawal, aldermen Wilson and Whitehead addressed the visitors for almost an hour on their side of the issue and said the letters received contained "a certain amount of hysteria,"[19] which inspired strong rebuttals, and outrage at "hysteria" being used as a term to attack women's points of view. Chinook said it could go it alone without Swift Current. One board member said the 16% increase was a result of the 7% cap promoted by Swift Current for the previous two years.

Two years later, at a December 20, 1982 meeting, Swift Current both rescinded its motion of withdrawal and then passed another notice of withdrawal for December 31, 1984. It's rare to find a comic meeting but that one will serve. First you say you're in, then you're out, so what're gonna be? It was said by council to be another bargaining chip with the provincial government to give it time to create new legislation that would respond to the small urban libraries, whose needs were increased autonomy, a mechanism for resolving disputes, increased city representation on regional boards, and the need for resource centres in regions. In 1989 Swift Current again rescinded its motion of withdrawal.

Provincial Librarian Leah Siebold wrote a briefing note to Pat Smith, minister in charge of libraries, explaining the Swift Current situation, which included evaluations of three trustees, two bad, Murch – "the strongest advocate on the board for the status quo" (and who was honoured with a life membership in SLTA in 1986) and Leola Moore, who "views proposed changes as unnecessary accommodations of city's demands," and one good, Elma Janke, "conciliatory, would like to resolve problems, promote change." The issue was Swift Current's notice of withdrawal, its second, and that "the other cities (except Regina and Saskatoon) have expressed the same concerns and have threatened to withdraw in unison from the regional libraries, if their demands are not met." Siebold talked of revision to legislation: equitable city representation on regional executives (to a maximum of 40% a city); local levies receiving "the separate approval of any municipality which contributes over 25% of the local revenues, or that a special agreement be prepared with the municipalities concerned" (supported by all the cities and many regions, though not Chinook). This provision, she said, "does not give Swift Current power over the region, as Chinook claims, it only requires Swift Current's approval for what the city contributes." There was also a proposal for mediation/arbitration supported by many regions (not Chinook) and all the cities. Regional resource centres were to be defined by legislation though they were already a fact in some regions (not Chinook). Chinook received the highest per capita grant from the province because of its sparse population, 72% from the province, yet she noted, "Chinook has shown little inclination to communicate with Swift Current City Council; they resent the negative publicity of 3-4 years ago."[20] The region would not have seen this document and so could not respond to its charges.

By 1983 levy increases were modest, under 6%, and technology had arrived, in the form of microfiche readers, a kind of halfway house on the way to computers, and a technology some found at odds with human happiness. There was a new bookmobile on the road in 1982, at a cost of $40,000, a converted Blue Bird bus which was more flexible on highways and which Keaschuk thought one of his important achievements.

The story of the last half of the '80s is automation and the effects of sharply reduced provincial funding. In 1986, the region's fifteenth birthday, automation began at headquarters with a book control system. A clerk was hired to assist with RECON, that is converting previous records to machine-readable format, preparing to transfer records to UTLAS. When the provincial cuts of 1987 were made, Chinook lost 11.71% of its funding, resulting in a $65,000 deficit, which was covered by reserves, by laying off the automation clerk, by reducing the materials budget from $159,000 to $120,000 (then to $105,000 in 1989). That reduced materials budget meant circulation fell for the first time in Chinook's history, from 541,362 to 501,000 in 1988 to 475,613 in 1989. According to Keaschuk in the 1989 Annual Report, "For many years our system has circulated more books per capita than any other region in the province. We lost that distinction the year our materials budget plummeted." Automation got back on track, with an automated ILLO program as well as a book label program. There was a 5% levy increase approved for 1989, but that would raise a little over $10,000, while Keaschuk pointed out that to make up the loss of provincial income, levies would have had to rise by 32%.[21] Black days for libraries.

CHINOOK, 1990s

There were three dates in the '90s important to automation at Chinook: the closure of the card catalogue, July 1, 1991; the transfer from the region's Mandarin software to the provincial standard Dynix, May 26, 1997 (and Swift Current, July 9, 1997); and the spread of computers to fifteen communities in 1999. Y2K (Yorkton to Kamsack according to Brent Butt) passed invisibly.

Circulation declined through the 1990s, from 426,555 in 1990 to a low of 347,147 in 2000 (then an improvement for the next two years). The materials budget went from a low of $105,421 in 1989, increasing every year but one, 1992, when the NDP reduced funding by 5%, to reach a high of over $200,000 in 2001, though of course the dollar had declined and book prices risen.

The decade would not be complete without a notice of withdrawal from the Swift Current council, made December 19, 1990, for 1992. A Swift Current alderman said in effect it was again a rhetorical gesture. "All it did was give notice of intent. It gave the city more time to study the problem, to get more information."[22] The chair of the Swift Current Library Board, Dick Hopley, said, "when that transition is complete, however, the city would find itself with a $200,000 system to run on a $7,000 provincial grant."[23] Swift Current rescinded its motion of withdrawal September 21, 1992.

The Region initiated co-operation with schools and by 1993 seven schools were receiving the Region's microfiche catalogue. A "Born to Read" program was begun in 1994, as a family literacy program coordinated by the Cypress Hills Regional College with co-operation from Community Health, the Southwest Reading Council, and the Chinook Regional Library. Babies born in the College region in 1994 received a gift package containing a book bag, board book, T-shirt, and information pamphlets."[24] That's starting young.

1997 was the watershed year for the bookmobile, which made its final run September 12 that year, to Bracken and Orkney. The region replaced that service in two ways, with a twenty-four-hour 1-800 number on its Reader Request Line, up by September 22, and with new corner libraries, which were popular paperback deposits of 650 to 750 volumes. Nine corner libraries were established by the end of the year: in Cadillac in the Community Hall, in Bracken and in Hazemore in senior citizens' centres, in Aneroid at Judy's Place (café), in Lancer in the museum, in Shamrock in the RM office, in Success in an empty house, in Golden Prairie in the post office, in Rush Lake in the RM office – all the communities had less than 100 people.[25] The black news for the region and the main cause of reduced circulation was the decline of population in the southwest area of Saskatchewan, down 25% from the year the region began.[26]

Chapter Eleven

Lakeland
1962-1999

ORGANIZING, 1962-73

L AKELAND BEGAN ORGANIZING A BIT LATER THAN other regions, with an original meeting in 1962 but the real beginning in 1964, a pro tem regional board formed in 1968, the region funded in 1972. John Welykochy was the first and active president, Tom Boyd the chairman pro tem and first chair, Sonia Curry secretary, and Patricia Cuts from the Provincial Library first regional librarian when branches began to open starting July 1, 1972.

In 1964, there were enquiries from Goodsoil, Loon Lake, and Battleford, the latter an especially interesting account since it gave a brief recent history of its Community Library: in 1958, 1960, and 1962, its annual expenses were as high as $327 a year, as low as $198. It was open four hours a week, with circulation about 3,000, with between 110 to 130 books purchased a year, membership at about 100 – "about 5% of the population of the town."[1] A Battleford meeting, with 90 people present, was addressed by Provincial Librarian Mary Donaldson, and it voted in favour of a regional library based partly on statistics for North Central.

A May 23, 1964 meeting heard about North Central, this time from Ralph Megill of Tisdale bringing news of success, and of how to manage a region. There was a question-and-answer session, then updates on organizing in the region, C.R. Penner saying Borden was ready to join, while North Battleford Mayor Roy Dean (who I saw playing ball for the North Battleford Beavers when I was a kid) said that the 1964 meeting was more favourable than the 1962 meeting and it was time to set up a steering committee. That was done, the meeting then electing as chairman Welykochy of North Battleford who represented the Battleford Central Council of Home and School Associations.

A November 25, 1965, meeting at North Battleford showed just how much organizing Welykochy had done, speaking at Home and School meetings in Cut Knife, Lone Rock, St. Walburg, Rockhaven, Mayfair, Turtleford, Cochin, Lashburn, as well as councils at Battleford and North Battleford (both offering support). Penner had canvassed door-to-door in Borden, while Mrs. Lake had worked Highway 26: Edam, Turtleford, and Mervin. Mrs. Mary Froese reported that a local committee had formed in the Mayfair-Mullinger area, supported by the ten teachers in the school. A delegation from West Central, including Jean and Willard Kallio, was present and the steering committee passed a motion that RMS 408, 409, 410, and 411 should be in the West Central region.

By November 1965 a report on regional development by Donaldson showed North West representing 14,176 people, including North Battleford at over 12,000. Meanwhile West Central had 28,197, South West 18,805, South Central 39,340 (but asked to reach 50,000), while East Central was Yorkton only. Donaldson said, "there has been little obvious activity [in North West] though the possibility of combining with the West Central committee is being explored."[2]

A steering committee meeting on March 5, 1966, gave an update on organizing, mostly business as usual. Welykochy understood the difficulties of organizing libraries. "We must be realistic and meet our strong competition; Regional Parks, Centennial Projects, Nursing Homes, Senior Citizens Homes, Water and Sewer Projects, Grid Roads, Recreational Facilities...just to mention a few."[3] It was clear that against all those important projects library supporters would have to work hard to get on the agendas of town and RM councils.

By June the potential amalgamation with West Central was off. "Mr. Welykochy reported that in a telephone conversation with Mr. Kallio he stated that we had not yet held a meeting to discuss the matter, and Mr. Kallio had apparently inferred that we were not interested and had made plans to proceed without regard to this committee's program."[4] Wheatland was ready to organize that year. Penner had bad news from RMs he'd visited, and said, "The women have to push the men to get full participation." Welykochy had spoken at Cut Knife, Rabbit Lake, Waseca, Borden, Maidstone, Lashburn, Maymont, Spiritwood, and the RM of Mayfield. There were 18,000 signed up, three other libraries under construction, the provincial bookmobile to appear at fairs at Turtleford and Radisson, but the Provincial Library organizing would likely slow down awaiting the report of the Library Inquiry Committee. A sad letter that summer said there were only five libraries left in the region, at North Battleford, Lloydminister, Meadow Lake, Mervin, and Lashburn, while community libraries had closed down at Battleford, Maidstone, Pierceland, and Richard.[5]

In 1967, Welykochy moved out of the region and was replaced by Penner. That fall, on November 7, provincial librarian Harry Newsom addressed a special meeting that led to a new organizing drive, the new chair Penner off to contact Hafford, Krydor, Redberry, Radisson, Borden, and Great Bend, while Froese would contact Meadow Lake, Glaslyn, Parkdale, Medstead, RM of Medstead, Rabbit Lake, Round Hill, and Meeting Lake, with seven other people taking on similar travels. Personal contact was the way North West was organized. Newsom offered to help where necessary.

By April, 1968, councils representing 27,000 people had joined. The steering committee examined a draft agreement, assumed that headquarters would be in North Battleford, and adopted a levy structure: North Battleford $1.50, Lloydminister $1.25, towns and villages 75 cents, RMs 60 cents, Indian bands ten cents plus one dollar as a federal grant, which was the federal Indian Affairs Branch formula in 1967. There were 35 members at that April 24 meeting.

By November 16, 1968 there was a pro tem board for Lakeland with its chair, Tom Boyd, and secretary, Sonia Curry, the North

Battleford librarian, the only holdovers from earlier executives. The choice of a name was made at that meeting. Other names considered included Poundmaker, Kewatin, and Kewatinook.[6]

By April 30, 1969, municipalities representing 45,000 people had joined and Lakeland was ready to go. The board planned to present a brief to the premier in the fall while in the meantime pro tem committee members would contact their MLAs. Should all those borderline communities designated for Lakeland join the region – they were already in one of the existing regions (North Central or Wheatland) – the 45,000 figure would rise to 55,000. The committee also recognized the difficulties posed by the government's deferment of Chinook as a region since it meant an even greater delay for Lakeland.

Recognizing the need to provide some library service in the interim, the Development Branch of the Provincial Library established small rotating book collections at Borden, Macklin (which chose North Central over Wheatland), Turtleford, and St. Walburg. According to the assistant provincial librarian, Mr. Needham, "discouragement of the population of this district was so great that unless some drastic steps were taken...there existed a grave danger of people losing interest in...regional libraries." These new libraries would form a core and "would greatly assist in the rapid development of the regional library," which turned out to be the case.[7] When Maymont and Cut Knife were ready they would be added by the Provincial Library, as would Radisson, to discourage it from entering the great embrace of Wheatland. If Loon Lake and Meadow Lake requested service it would be given to them as well, but no others could be added because that was all the Provincial Library was prepared to do for Lakeland.

On April 12 Don Meadows told the Lakeland executive that the region would become a reality the following year. The executive postponed meetings with the government until after the June 1971 election, won by the Blakeney NDP, so they planned a November meeting with the new minister of libraries, Gordon MacMurchy.

The Lakeland Region was born July 1, 1972, when eight of the nine existing branches joined (North Battleford, St. Walburg,

Borden, Turtleford, Maymont, Macklin, Cut Knife, and Lashburn) with other branches being set up after August 21 (Loon Lake, Neilburg, Radisson, Hafford, Marsden, Battleford, Denzil, Pierceland, and Goodsoil). The official opening was November 15, 1972, with Patricia Cuts of the Provincial Library as the first regional librarian. She quit her job at the Provincial Library to remain as Lakeland's regional librarian (after her stint at Chinook). According to the Annual Report of 1973 there were also branches at Glaslyn, Meadow Lake and Maidstone, with four more opened in 1973, at Mervin, Onion Lake, Thunderchild, and Paynton.

Cuts in the May 1973 issue of *Quill and Quire* had her own version of early days at Lakeland, a four-day bulk-book-buying spree in Toronto with the assistance of Keith Turnbull of the Provincial Library, finding headquarters with the help of Boyd and others – looking at half a bowling alley, the old bus depot, the basement of a discount store, the premises of a farm equipment dealer, until Boyd, vice-principal of the North Battleford Comprehensive High School, found them unused space at the school, 3,000 square feet of it with a power-operated door so any vehicle could be unloaded indoors. "We were ecstatic!" June 1, 1972, was opening day for the region and Cuts had to train nine people on the spot. On July 17 they set up the first branch at St. Walburg, and then averaged a branch a week until November.

What joy it must have been, after all the travails, to create a new world with such speed.

Cuts said in the *Quill and Quire* article that they used 200 people as the basis for a branch. Each municipality housed the library and paid maintenance, while Lakeland provided books, supplies, and paid the local librarian. Such a small branch "would contain 800 books in the rotating collection and a basic reference collection of about 80 volumes." Programming was difficult because most libraries were so small. Books in French, Ukrainian, and German were in demand, with a small Ukrainian collection already in Hafford.

It was an extraordinary achievement in a year, but at the end there was no money left to buy books, the 1973 book budget spent by May, in five new branches. Staff, without books to process, spent time cataloguing already existing branch collections. The executive decided to spend part of the 1974 book budget in 1973. There was a 10% per capita grant added by the province to honour the former premier and minister in charge of libraries, Woodrow Lloyd, "a fitting tribute to this great man," and it meant an extra $4,382.90. Newsletters were set up at once, the *Standard* for trustees and *Reflections* for branch librarians.

The best account of tough economic times for the new region was a letter from the Lakeland executive to Minister MacMurchy, in June of 1973, on the costs of setting up a new branch library, in this case at Paynton. The municipal levies for six months was $244.75, at half the 75 cents a year. Government grants, for both establishing and operating, amounted to $1,492.50 (with $363 of that to be paid to the local librarian). A book collection for Paynton would cost about $6,000, yet the region had only $1,374 to work with. The letter concluded by asking for a special grant of $20,000, which was not forthcoming.[8]

CONFLICT WITH NORTH BATTLEFORD, 1975-79

The beginning of the painful battle between Palliser and North Battleford began modestly enough. In October and November of 1975, Cuts sent two packets of information to the North Battleford city commissioner at his request, the information including provincial grants and levies from 1972 (six months) to 1974, the provincial government paying about two to one, as well as the book stock and budget spent on the North Battleford Public Library. That led to a report of complaints written by board members Ariel Sallows and Jake Amos to the city commissioner. The complaints were: North Battleford had inadequate representation on the Regional Board – three of 67, though it had 23% of the region's population; the levies were unjust, North Battleford paying 50% of the levies raised; RMs not in the region were using the North Battleford library; staff hadn't been increased in three years. What should happen? A resolution to the problems and fuller autonomy for the North Battleford library. Finally, the report suggested giving notice of withdrawal to the region.[9]

The notice of withdrawal was passed a week later, enumerating the grievances. Chairman Boyd of North Battleford hadn't been aware of the notice of withdrawal. "I got hold of Mr. Boyd shortly after our conversation," Cuts wrote. "As I suspected he had no knowledge of city council's decision and was absolutely shaken."[10]

Provincial Librarian Meadows replied quite critically to the decision, saying Sallow and Amos had not contacted the regional library authorities before they made their report, that its point on finances was false since the North Battleford financial contribution had not increased since 1972 (and it received 29% of the total book budget and 42% of the total paid to branch libraries). As well, "Local board autonomy now includes the right to hire and fire [a false point, as it would turn out] and to order books and supplies."[11] Meadows did support increased North Battleford representation on the board, but thought representation on the executive fair. There was a meeting between Meadows and North Battleford on January 9 and a phone conversation with the mayor four days later; Meadows then wrote a letter of reconciliation.

A new problem surfaced later that year, a request by new members of the North Battleford board for a survey of the library: there might be difficulties with the librarian, Sonia Curry. Cuts was concerned about incompatibility with the region. "Since we have recently spent some time examining our acquisitions procedures and refining them, it has become obvious that Mrs. Curry's will have to drastically change."[12] Cuts said in a 2003 interview, "She [Curry] was so difficult I made decisions and let her fuss. I'd do it differently now." A request from North Battleford's legal counsel and board member Sallows that North Battleford become an independent board like Saskatoon and Regina was turned down by the minister of libraries, Ed Tchorzewski. He referred to the 1967 Library Inquiry Report and the 1969 Act. "The government is, therefore, not prepared to fund a number of small municipal libraries, an act which would see the demise of a system second to none in Canada."[13]

In October, Lorna Gaudet, a new patron, wrote a scathing letter about management of the North Battleford library. She and her husband had moved from "the fine service of Saskatoon" to the letdown of the North Battleford library, where she encountered:

1. An unlisted phone number
2. An unwieldy library card
3. An enormously time-consuming check-out system which left staff with no time for more useful endeavours
4. An incredible book stamping process of putting date out – not due date – on books borrowed
5. Most of the books in the library on a seven-day loan period
6. Hours surely not set to accommodate the reading public
7. But the most distinguished aspect of my new home's library was the atmosphere. To enter the library was to have mistaken one's way and stumbled into the seats of the mighty. One felt lucky to have escaped with one's life, let alone a book or two. I recall applying for a membership card and finding myself in an inquisition...waving my proof of honesty as a book borrower – my Saskatoon library card.[14]

After the city joined the region there were improvements, more books, ILLO, a phone number, a due date on borrowed books, longer hours (but the library still closed Wednesday when people would be free to use it). Otherwise it was business as usual, including the atmosphere. "I conclude that one must be white and stout-hearted to use this public library facility," Gaudet wrote. "And the situation will not improve for the better until the Chief Librarian is retired from her firmly misguided control of a library built to serve all the people in the region."

There was some common ground reached in December 1976 by the Lakeland executive and a new regional librarian, Catherine O'Neill, who had been the region's first branch librarian. The executive agreed to lobby for changes in legislation to permit more North Battleford representation on the board and to present proposed levy changes to the board. The matter of non-participating RMs using the North Battleford library was a matter for the North Battleford board to decide, but the executive would offer assistance, if necessary.

The Survey of the North Battleford Branch, Lakeland Library Region, dated April 1977, was an exhaustive 77-page document, the survey itself conducted in the week of January 24, 1977 by three senior members of the Provincial Library, Keith Turnbull as chair, along with John Rafter and Don Meadows. When the region was organized, they said, it focused on those communities which had no libraries, but it did not use the "qualified experienced director and staff" at North Battleford, nor was the North Battleford board adequately consulted. One result was the limited knowledge by North Battleford staff of the region's structure. Then the survey turned to weaknesses of North Battleford. "Many aspects of the North Battleford Branch's direct service are provided using outmoded techniques and methods which are entirely at odds with Regional and Provincial policy" (p. 11). There were problems with the collection, only seven of 59 notable children's books for 1985 in the library, while weeding had been neglected so that there were many old worn-out books, including children's "Easy" books and children's reference books. "Many popular, practical and adult non-fiction titles were shelved behind the circulation desk away from the view of the public" (p. 20). In serious ways North Battleford did not belong to the Saskatchewan one-library system, since patrons had to return books to North Battleford and "the patron's library card is filed back into the file of library cards" (p.33) so North Battleford patrons could not use the Saskatchewan system, nor would North Battleford accept other library cards. Patrons with overdue books were phoned or mailed a notice in week one, with an overdue notice sent for the following six weeks. The library "occasionally contacts the RCMP to take further action to insure the return of the books" (p. 34). After six months the patron's name was entered into the "black book,"which also included names of those who had not paid overdue fines. Not surprisingly, much staff time was spent on checking books out and in keeping records. The survey team suggested a photocharge system, implemented at Saskatoon and Regina, as well as a smaller, wallet-size library card. There should be systematic programming though space limited it. Recommendations included joint meetings between city and region, both boards and librarians, on a series of points, including work flow charts, the visit of North Battleford staff to other branches in the region and elsewhere, the improvement of space at the North Battleford library. The ball was in North Battleford's court but the game should be played by both region and city.

There was a joint meeting May 31, 1977 between the two boards and librarians with four recommendations approved.

It didn't work out.

The regional librarian, O'Neill, wrote an extensive report critical of Curry. Since the Provincial Library survey there had been improvements, she wrote. The circulation system had been streamlined, "thanks to the hard work of the headquarters' staff who typed thousands of new library cards." The Lakeland card had been adopted and ILLO altered since the technician attended a provincial workshop, but other matters, O'Neill wrote, hadn't changed. The region was routing review media to North Battleford to assist with book selection but Curry had complained about how time-consuming book selection was. Not enough children's books were being ordered; no weeding had been done. The popular books were still behind the desk. The North Battleford staff, she wrote, "suffers from a complete ignorance of the provincial library system," of their own library, and from low morale. There is "a never ending stream of complaints we receive directly from our borrowers and indirectly from other city residents." Conclusion: "there is only one solution to the problem and that is the dismissal of the North Battleford librarian as soon as possible."[15]

The Lakeland executive, under Chairman Nick Gabruch of Paynton, reported on difficulties with North Battleford, repeating many of the points in the survey, including North Battleford's refusal to honour Saskatchewan-wide borrowing privileges, not even recognizing the Lakeland card. "The North Battleford librarian has actually refused to register an individual because 'he looked like a transient.' The prospective user was of Native ancestry." (p. 2) Then the usual complaints, including not accepting an offer from Lakeland for a librarian to work Saturdays. There was a litany of meetings missed, twice back in 1974 when North Battleford did not accept an invitation, once later when Lakeland wasn't informed of a meeting. Letters of complaint about North Battleford were sent in November 1976 but minutes show no action taken, not even discussion. After that May 31, 1977 joint meeting, attempts at change "met with frustrating results." "The North Battleford librarian could not take direction from the Regional Librarian" (p. 12). All those points led to the decision to fire Curry.

There were attempts by North Battleford and its library board to have the decision overturned, including an appeal to the minister of education on the basis that "a democratic injustice has been done to the North Battleford Library by Lakeland's unilateral action in dismissing her."[16] But neither the minister, Don Faris, nor North Battleford NDP MLA Eiling Kramer, felt they could intervene because the region had acted legally according to section 96 of the Public Libraries Act of 1969. Attempts by the North Battleford representatives on the executive to change the decision were defeated on votes of five to two (Amos and McDonald of North Battleford in the minority). At an executive meeting August 23, 1977, North Battleford said its notice of withdrawal stood, while counsel was present to answer questions about the dismissal. According to regional policy, Curry was given only six months dismissal pay. At the same meeting O'Neill was given the power to advertise for a new branch librarian for North Battleford, even though the city had given a notice to withdraw from the region by 1979. Sallows, who had for forty-two years been a local trustee, was distressed by the decision. "She [Curry] has been the chief architect of the city's library for the past 31 years."[17]

There were then two reactions to that harsh action. Curry took her case to court with mixed results.[18] An editorial in the *North Battleford News Optimist* said, "Lakeland's action was like the government firing the Leader of the Opposition."[19] The second action was a motion by North Battleford December 28, 1977 to withdraw from the region.

The next librarian at North Battleford, Laureen Marchand, started about a year later, October, 1978. She'd just graduated from library school, "green as a pea," and chose North Battleford over two other job offers because she'd be "running my own library."[20] She found "that nothing had changed for decades." Part of the problem with the library was the building itself, the Carnegie Library, handsome outwardly and with two high-ceilinged wings, but with inadequate space for books. Weeding was crucial. "It felt like when books in an area completed their space, apparently ordering stopped." In the Science section "the most recent books were 1971, 1972." Marchand explained to the board the need and standards for weeding, and began the process. For programming there were three spaces that could be used, "bleacher-like steps in the basement for children's hour," plus an open space in the Children's area where chairs could be placed for programs, as well as the boardroom. Programs were much increased. Yet all was not smooth sailing. "The staff felt very uncertain," and the board meetings were uncomfortable; some Board members who had supported Curry "hated me," Marchand said, and perhaps the new things she'd learned to do at library school.

Marchand was only at North Battleford for a year and a half. She applied for the regional job after Catherine O'Neill left, didn't get the appointment, reportedly was told she lost it because of a North Battleford trustee on the hiring committee. She went to Regina Public Library and for years now she has been part-time or full-time at the Saskatoon Public Library.

There is a document dated a year and a half later, April 27, 1979, which is in one way the happy ending to the story, as O'Neill and Marchand co-authored in thirteen pages a record of the new degree of rapport between the two sides.

The region had supplied more books to North Battleford, which had become the resource centre for the region. Weeding was now ongoing, those titles shelved out of sight were now in the stacks. A part-time staff person had been added. The Lakeland card had been adopted. A photocharger system was being investigated. The file of library cards had been eliminated, except for those who still preferred it. Overdues received only two notices. ILLO procedures had improved, the staff member in charge having attended provincial workshops. Space had been rearranged and programming was more effective and constant. Staff had more time to do reference work and programming. Communications between the librarians was ongoing; they met every two weeks to plan region-wide events. The improved communication extended to the regional and city boards, with the exchange of minutes, with joint meetings, and agreement on roles. The North Battleford staff now understood the regional system. Sweetness and light prevailed. Meanwhile North Battleford Council had established a reserve for a new library (by 1979 $100,000) yet had still not rescinded its notice of withdrawal: "the continuous improvement in the services offered and the relationship between North Battleford library and the people it serves is the most effective campaign possible."[21]

LAKELAND, 1982-86

The third regional librarian was Joylene Campbell, now provincial librarian, and she remembers her days at Lakeland, where she discovered, as her mother had told her, that "working for a board was very, very difficult." She was there for seven years, starting in 1980. When she arrived, the region, desperate for money, raised the levies and

Recent photo of North Battleford Library, officially opened February 28, 1987

received withdrawal notices from twenty of the municipalities. She "worked hard all the time," talking to library boards and councils. At Meadow Lake both she and the local board made presentations to a council that had given notice of withdrawal. "I said, your representative hasn't attended any meetings," only to discover that the recalcitrant board member was the mayor, who she says was beaten in the next election partly because he hadn't supported the library. She got the withdrawals withdrawn, her most exciting experience. She also said she learned to "pick your battles." She expected opposition on a new materials selection policy but it was accepted by all – North Battleford had recently received a donation of books by a religious group and was pleased with a policy that would deal with that thorny issue. The battle Campbell withdrew from was over the colour of the new bookmobile. She proposed blue and white but the executive chose red because that was the colour of the Wheatland bookmobile. She liked being regional librarian. She liked the closeness to people and rural communities. (She'd been born and brought up in Netherhill close to Kindersley.)[22]

There are a series of statistical profiles of Lakeland completed by Campbell or by the Provincial Library. First, from 1973 to 1982, Lakeland showed growth in its materials budget from $37,000 in 1973 to $60,000 in 1977 to $121,000 in 1982, while costs rose from $99,000 to $263,000 to $441,000 over those ten years. The percentage spent on materials was highest in 1974, at 28%; lowest in 1977 at 15%; and stood at 18.7% in 1981. Staff as a percentage of operating expenditures began at 62% and a decade later was 61.5%, so it was a constant. Circulation per capita rose from 1.8 in 1972 to 6.1 in 1977, up to 6.9 in 1981, a good indication of growth in that decade. The North Battleford branch circulation was 34.9% of the region in 1976, 28% in 1981.[23] There's an update on these statistics in the 1987 Annual Report. Circulation rose every year from 1983 to 1986, from 462,332 to 571,983, then with the addition of Lloydminister to the region, jumped to 697, 969 in 1987. Circulation per capita, at 6.9 in 1981, had reached 10 by 1987.

There was also an interesting comparison between Lakeland and the other regions and cities for 1981. That year Lakeland had the smallest population of any region, 57,784 (the loss of municipalities to adjoining regions was clearly a serious blow). The other low-population regions were Chinook, 60,365, and Palliser, 61,842. Lakeland was second last among regions in provincial grants but highest in grants per capita, at $7.71. Other regional per capita grants were as follows: Palliser $5.79, Wapiti $4.88, Lakeland $3.44, Chinook $2.59, Southeast $2.30, Wheatland $2.00. The two major cities were entirely unlike the regions in funding patterns, receiving the smallest per capita grants, Saskatoon at $2.68, Regina at $2.40, while their local tax base per capita was very high, Saskatoon at $22.17, Regina at $27.69, for years one of the highest rates in Canada. It's clear the two cities were in their own way subsidizing the regions, a decision they had consciously taken. Wheatland's low rate was partly a result of not paying salaries to branch librarians. Provincial funding was a high percentage in five regions: Wheatland 75.67%, Chinook 74.20%, Lakeland 69.13%, Southeast 68.36%, Parkland 68.13%, then a much lower share for those two regions with large cities: Palliser at 54.33%, Wapiti at 50.70%.[24]

There are three 1984 events worth reporting on. A questionnaire was sent to local library boards and branch librarians to gather opinions on Lakeland's service. Some answers gave a clear indication of preferences while others were relatively inconclusive. The part of the collection that had improved in the last three years was clearly adult paperbacks (24 said yes, compared to 9 affirmatives for juvenile paperbacks). The improvement had increased circulation (unanimous). As for adult needs, 15 respondents suggested top-ten best-selling lists, 6 adult non-fiction hardcovers). There was less clear advice on juvenile materials, though children's cassettes (7 requests) was the first priority. On the whole, the respondents were pleased with publicity and general service from headquarters. The greatest strength was ILLO (identified by 24); the greatest weakness the time it took to get requests filled (p.13). Again, when asked what the branches could do to improve service there was no clear advice. Seven recommended better book collection, 6 more branch hours, and 6 large-print paperbacks.

Also in 1984 the trustees had begun a letter-writing campaign across the regions asking government for increased grants. The assis-

tant provincial librarian wrote a stock letter to assist the minister
with her response, telling her the SLTA was promoting the letter-
writing campaign, and that Lakeland received 67.6% of their operating revenue from the province. She advised the minister, Patricia
Smith of the Conservatives, to explain increases over the last few
years to Lakeland, and drafted a letter for her. The minister wrote
that between 1979-80 and 1981-82 the average increase was 8.2%,
while the consumer price index rose by nearly 11%. The NDP is not
mentioned by name. "My government in the past two years, 1982-83
and 1983-84, increased grants by an average of almost 10%, while the
consumer price index for the same two years ending March 31, 1984,
will likely be slightly over the six percent mark."[25] The letter-writing
campaign was a year or two early. The financial world for libraries
was about to get bleak, and the advice by Leah Siebold of the
Provincial Library may have assisted the government to come to its
decision a year later that it need provide no additional grants to
regional libraries.

That year Lakeland learned how the new grant structure worked
for it (I've not found the equivalent statement for other regions). The
categories were three: density, service support, and service points.
Lakeland had a lower density of population than average; its service
support per capita was above average; it had more service points per
capita than average – its final factor was 1.183 which translated into a
41-cent per capita increase, from $8.56 to $8.97, times a population
of 61,114 for a grant of $548,192.58.[26]

There was a second survey two years later, in 1986, this time of
staff. Forty-six responded, showing considerable satisfaction with the
region (27 to 4); with the staff (28 to 2); with the adult book collection (25 to 3); with co-operation among branches (33 to 4); with co-
operation within the library system (33 to 1). The staff were negative
on funding (28 to 5), on the audio-visual collection (17 to 6), on
wages and benefits (18 to 11). Question three asked if service was adequate for defined groups. Most respondents said service was adequate, except for young adults, with 26 saying the region should do
more, and 17 saying the service was adequate. The service most
approved was adult service, 35 saying adequate, and only 7 suggesting

improvement. Only in one category did any number, 5 respondents, say service should be reduced, and that was for Indian/Native, with 5 others suggesting increased service and 27 deeming it adequate.

When the library staff were asked if budgets were going to be cut and what actions should be considered, 37 suggested reducing the number of duplicate items, 33 reducing the number of magazine subscriptions, 25 said discontinue cassettes, while 22 said discontinue summer reading programs and Saskatchewan Library Week. The region would soon be tested by serious provincial government cuts. When asked about weaknesses in the region, 17 identified funding, 7 identified wages and benefits, while a further question on the most important problems facing Lakeland resulted in 32 saying inadequate funds, 16 saying inadequate hours of operation, and 16 saying inadequate pay. Most librarians felt they were well-informed about Lakeland and its changes, of their own job tasks, of in-service training. There were other questions and answers in this revealing, and positive, insider view of Lakeland and regional library service.

Lakeland was generous in its comments on a possible new equalization formula, saying funding levels to Wapiti and Palliser, two regions with high local levies, needed improving, as well as Southeast which had an inequity in its original grant, while regions which didn't raise adequate local levies should not receive a higher proportion of government monies. Presumably that was a reference to Wheatland, whose local levy was by far the lowest.[27] The new Provincial Librarian, Karen Adams, presented to the minister of libraries basic regional statistics for 1984 which she said supported Lakeland's claims. After no increase that year, both Palliser and Wapiti would receive less than 50% financing from the government. The statistics showed Palliser ($7.56) and Wapiti ($6.97) had the highest local levies, with Wheatland ($2.60) the lowest. Provincial grants per capita ran from a high of $9.73 for Chinook to a low of $6.62 for Southeast. There was no agreement yet in the library community, Adams said, about the "fairest" system but all awaited the report of the local Government Finance Commission and its recommendations.[28]

LLOYDMINSTER

The story special to Lakeland was Lloydminster, the border city which stayed out of the region for fifteen years. In 1968, while Lakeland was being organized, provincial librarian Harry Newsom prepared an agreement between the city and the Provincial Library, which stipulated this role for Lloydminster library, that it be a major resource centre and that it provide library service on both sides of the border. It would receive the usual grants and services, and be responsible for the usual services. There was no mention of a levy. Nothing came of the proposed agreement, however. The Library Inquiry Committee had made Lloydminister a special case.[29]

An important meeting on Lloydminister was held shortly after Lakeland was created, on March 11, 1974, between, among others, NDP Minister Gordon MacMurchy of Saskatchewan and his Conservative Alberta counterpart, Horst Schmid. In the minutes, taken by Keith Turnbull of Saskatchewan, MacMurchy is recorded as saying that under the 1969 regulations, services to Lloydminster would end by April 1, 1974, if no "action was taken." Schmid said Alberta libraries were in a state of transition, while Mayor Robertson of Lloydminster said "the City Council would like to see Lloydminster as the head of a Regional library system as they are unique in their situation." Turnbull noted there was already a headquarters at North Battleford. The meeting decided that representatives from both provinces would negotiate a settlement. The Saskatchewan team, Turnbull and Cuts, prepared their report by June, 1974, which included a series of Lloydminster concerns and which may give a fuller sense of what happened at that March 11 meeting: City Council would prefer Lloydminster to be the headquarters of a region, while the board wanted to provide service in Alberta without prejudice, and was concerned with losing autonomy in a large system; the board also wanted to retain volunteers and found the $2.00 per capita levy too high. The preferred option in the report was the city joining Lakeland under the usual prospects, money in, levy out. No proposal was received from Alberta.

Stalemate.

Lloydminster was receiving provincial library services but that had to come to an end, since they provided no levy, and funding ended in 1975.[30] The Library Development Board (LBD) was kept informed of the story, at meetings June 7, 1974, January 30-31, 1975, where Meadows informed the board that he would soon be meeting with the chairman of the Lloydminister Board; June 21, 1975, where Meadows said the Alberta elections had slowed the process, which were to be handled at the ministerial level. By November 27, 1976, he said discussions were still ongoing, Lloydminister asking for an additional government grant; by May 6, 1977, he noted that an April 26 meeting hadn't taken place and that the Provincial Library planned to take no further initiative unless directed to; while by October, 1977, Meadows said the issue might be raised at a joint ministers' meeting in December.

Lloydminster always had a different view of what happened at that key March 1974 meeting, the chair of the local board asserting in 1976, "It is my understanding that they [the ministers] agreed that a library region would be formed in this area to take care of the complexities of a library operating in two provinces and serving the citizens of both provinces."[31] Schmid's response in March, 1976 to minister Tchorzewski, who had replaced MacMurchy in the education portfolio, roughly supported the Lloydminster proposal, which would include in Saskatchewan 28,000 square miles, 12,000 population, four branches (Marsden, Lashburn, Maidstone, Neilburg) and three bookmobile stops – and an untested administration. Patricia O'Neill protested on behalf of Lakeland, saying services to Lloydminster and its low non-resident fee for adjoining areas had prevented the region from signing three RMs in the area. Lloydminster had its own story of March 11, 1974 and was sticking to it, though there was no evidence in the minutes to prove its assertion.[32] By 1977 Meadows suggested a $1.00 per capita grant, with a change in the act so Lloydminster would be treated like Saskatoon and Regina, while the city would agree to reciprocal borrowing and ILLO procedures. That would take five years to happen.

Funding came in 1983, with about $5,300 in 1984 and $6,154.68 in 1985, modest sums; but provincial grants to cities were always very modest compared to grants to regions. The Provincial Library and Alberta participated in a requested evaluation of the Lloydminister library in 1984, a positive experience. Then in 1985 the story came to an end.

A joint meeting between Lakeland and Lloydminister took place March 25. From Lakeland, Lloydminister wanted cataloguing and access to the union catalogue, ILLO, multilingual materials, and reciprocal borrowing. From Alberta, it wanted talking books and reference collections, and the payment of a professional reference librarian.[33] A second meeting on November 28, 1985 examined a draft agreement in detail. There is a contract in the Provincial Library file on Lloydminster which is not dated but is likely 1986. It enshrined those Saskatchewan values enunciated at that March meeting, including the keystone, reciprocal borrowing. It lists in detail the responsibilities of local and regional librarians and of boards, including close collaboration and a method for the resolution of disputes. The ghost of the North Battleford disputes can be felt in the details of this agreement. Appendix A includes the levy structure; the cities to pay $7.92 per capita in 1986 (the year of this agreement); $8.14 for 1987; $8.38 for 1988 (ratios being RMs 1.6, villages 1.9, towns 2.2, cities 3.2, with Indian bands between RMs and villages).

The official opening of the Lloydminister library as a Lakeland branch took place March 25, 1986, and Lloydminister first appeared in Lakeland's Annual Report for 1987. "Lloydminister orders produced a 25% increase in ordering which created a backlog at Headquarters."[34] The presence of Lloydminster was obvious immediately. It headed a category called Circulation Per Paid Staff Hours at 38.01 (North Battleford at 32.69 and Library on Wheels at 27.29).

LAKELAND, 1987-2002

Statistics first. Circulation for the region broke 700,000 in 1988 and again in 2002. Mostly the region had reached its maturity and circulation remained static, even with declining populations. Levies rose gradually through most of these years. To use RMs as an example, they paid $4.07 per capita in 1987, $4.67 in 1995, $5.68 by 1998 (the one clear increase), and $5.91 by 2001. North Battleford, Lloydminster, and Meadow Lake were resource libraries. North Battleford's highest circulation was 198,000 items in 2002, Lloydminster's highest was 167,000 in 1994, while Meadow Lake reached 70,000 in 1997. Maidstone, Battleford (21,000 by 2002), Turtleford (29,000 in 2001 and 2002), Paradise Hill, and Neilburg were the other communities whose circulation remained over 10,000 for these years.

Automation was incremental, headquarters automating "one function at a time" as the 1988 Annual Report said, with payroll automated in 1997, bestseller lists in 1998, paperbacks in 1999, while Recon was underway in 1991 at headquarters, North Battleford and Lloydminster; Dynix in operation by 1994 at headquarters and North Battleford, so that cataloguing and circulation were automated. The same gradual process of automating was true of the branches as well, Macklin and Denzil receiving grants in 1998, while by the following year, according to the annual report, 24 of 36 branches were automated, and in 2002 the region "was almost fully automated." Bit by bit. The region had made loans for automation available by 2002. The region had benefited, as had the entire province, with the free internet installations provided by the Every Library Connected Project, while 11 communities took advantage of the Gates Foundation gift of computers – Windows *uber alles.* Gateway, "a search engine (software) that will allow patrons to reach all public library catalogues in Saskatchewan simultaneously," was installed that same year. As part of the thirtieth anniversary celebrations, Lakeland created its website.

The region cancelled its bookmobile ("Library on Wheels") in June 1988; two former bookmobile communities became paperback deposits, two became satellite branches, and one joined with a school library. There were two writers-in-residence, Brenda Niskala at North Battleford in 1988, and most importantly, Harry Joseph at Meadow Lake in 1990 – the first Aboriginal storyteller in residence at a public library. A regional library formed on the Alberta side of Lloydminster, in 1989, the Northern Lights Region. There was an additional decentralization of power, in 1999, when branches began to choose their own paperbacks. Because of high mailing costs Lakeland introduced courier service, which proved a convenient and quick way to deliver ILLO and block changes. In 1999, the region moved its offices to a former SaskTel building in downtown North Battleford, one block from the handsome North Battleford Public Library. Old battles had been put to rest, but one service had declined and posed a dilemma, service to Indian bands.

Chapter Twelve

Palliser
1964-1995

1964-1967

THE ORGANIZING OF SOUTH CENTRAL (PALLISER) began in 1964; the two key members at the beginning were Katherine McKinnon, Moose Jaw chief librarian, and Mildred Taylor, chair of the Moose Jaw Board. There was an important meeting in March of that year, with representatives from Assiniboia, Briercrest, Coronach, Craik, Davidson, Hearne, Kenaston, Limerick, Mitchellton, Moose Jaw, Ogema, Woodrow, and four RMs. Ralph Megill from Tisdale, spoke at the meeting, keeping alive the tradition of members of North Central assisting the new regions with their experience and success. Megill talked of grants and levies and the increase his region planned, of 30% or more, to pay salaries to all branch librarians. Tisdale in 1953 had only 2,000 books and an annual circulation of 1,200, he reported. By 1963, as a member of the region, Tisdale had 8,000 books and an annual circulation of 25,000. Other delegates reported on the successes or failures of organizing. Assiniboia was waiting for "leadership from Moose Jaw" and constructing a new library building. Coronach and the local RM had passed motions of support. In Kenaston the Home and School Association, the Homemakers' Association and the Lions

Club were onside. And so on. A motion in favour of forming a steering committee was passed, with Taylor elected chair and directed to choose other members of the committee.[1]

By the end of 1964, Tugaske had planned a library as part of its centennial project. Taylor had chosen her steering committee, from Mitchellton, Hearne, Coronach, Assiniboia, and two members from Davidson. The region had been provisionally divided in three, north to south, for convenience, with Kenaston the most northerly, Mossbank and Spring Valley in central, Assiniboia and Coronach in the south. An agreement with Moose Jaw was reached providing the levy did not exceed $2 per capita. By the spring of 1965, 47% of the population had joined, or 39,340, with 34,500 of that figure from Moose Jaw, while the total population was 86,996. The new region had the most arbitrary of all regional borders, partly because it was organized around Moose Jaw. The southern boundary was the US border; there was a bit of the South Saskatchewan River to the west, a bit of Long Lake to the east, but for the most part it was as arbitrary an area as the province of Saskatchewan and not defined as much by towns as by RMs. On the northeast was Imperial, in the centre Rouleau, in the south Coronach. On the west, Riverhurst and Central Butte were in the centre, with Gravelbourg and Kincaid to the south. Kenaston was the northernmost community in the region, Coronach, the southernmost. Moose Jaw fell roughly in the centre of the area, with Mortlach the only other town on the Trans-Canada. (Kenaston would join Wheatland, however, before Palliser came into existence. The region also lost, said long-time regional librarian Cora Greer, RMs to Chinook and Southeast. To come last meant, like Lakeland, that you lost population.)

Through the advice of Donalda Putnam, Provincial Library supervisor of regional libraries, South Central increased its representation objective to 50,000 (all other regions needed 40,000 to begin) so there would be a greater rural base, though it was recognized early on that the region was "very risky if there is a possibility Moose Jaw were to withdraw."[2]

A meeting on April 20, 1966, featured detailed organizational reports, Central Butte, Mortlach, Kincaid, and RM 75 all saying yes.

They were told two things from the organizing experience of Southeast and West Central: that the best time to visit RM councils was in the first three months of the year, and that "even an average man had a better impact on councils than a very good woman."[3] Councils were likely to be all male.

Demonstration bookmobile service would come to Palliser in 1966 after its run in Chinook, though Palliser was warned of the bookmobile's limitations. It weighed eight tons, so "very few grid roads are up to it in width or firmness. In rain it would bog down completely." Its maximum speed was 40 miles an hour, less in hilly areas. Stops must be at least two or three hours long; the bus must stop where the driver could stay for the night.[4] The bookmobile toured the area from September 27 to October 15, was visited by 2,656 persons, many of them students from schools, though as the books were not available for lending there was some frustration.

By October 28 over 45,000 people had joined the region. At an October meeting, four communities visited by the bookmobile, Elbow, Gravelbourg, Limerick, and the RM of Mazenod, had asked for speakers. Taylor and McKinnon did most of the travelling and talking, at those and in other communities, including Marquis and Riverhurst and two RMs. Palliser received no Provincial Library assistance as other regions had. The region wrote a letter to the Liberal minister in charge of libraries, George Trapp, declaring the 50,000 figure had been reached and asking if he could confirm the grant so they could begin. They received this reply: "I regret we are not in a position to make your region a reality. I assure you, however, that this will be done as soon as it is financially possible."[5]

1973-75, THE REGION BEGINS

There were two openings of Palliser in 1973, the actual opening July 3, and the official opening November 22. The region, the seventh and final one in the south of the province, had a staff of thirteen that first summer, eight permanent staff, four students, and Bob Ivanochko as regional librarian seconded from the Provincial Library until the region chose its own. Early on Ivanochko described the strengths and difficulties of Palliser. It proved easier to organize because the "territory covered [was] small. There are fewer centres with a substantial population and half the population lived in Moose Jaw," so it could operate with fewer branches. Yet other factors, "such as the large staff involved, the union contract covering employees, and the autonomy of the Moose Jaw branch make it more difficult to deal with than other regions."[6] The key to the viability of the region was always Moose Jaw.

The complex relationship between Moose Jaw and Palliser were spelled out in detail by the Provincial Library's Keith Turnbull in the spring of 1973, before Moose Jaw joined. Much of the proposal had to do with balance, for instance that Moose Jaw would become the reference centre of the region, that all material ordering would be done by the region, "but the material selection would be done by the Moose Jaw Public Library staff." Most equipment, with the exception of a photocopy machine, would be at Palliser. On hiring and firing, "The Palliser Regional Library Board [would] hire or fire for a branch library (including Moose Jaw Branch Library) *only* on the recommendation of the Moose Jaw Public Library and her Board." The letter, and all its detail, was helpful but not a contract, and in the disputes to come was not referred to.[7] When Moose Jaw officially joined that summer the region had adequate population. Branches were opened in Assiniboia August 2, then Davidson, then Rockglen — these communities already having local libraries – then Riverhurst (located in the Fred T. Hill Museum), Imperial (in the Community Centre), Mortlach (in the school basement), Craik (in the same room as the school library), Tugaske (in a community building), Holdfast (in the Community Health Building), Elbow (in the Village Office).[8]

The official opening in November was chaired by the board's first chair, J.K. Pragnell of Moose Jaw, with greetings from Moose Jaw Mayor Herb Taylor, from Moose Jaw North MLA Gordon Snyder, from Rusty Macdonald, chair of the Library Development Board, present to see much of that board's early objective completed. The address was given by the Library Minister Gordon MacMurchy, who said of regional development, "this was easier in Saskatchewan than in other provinces because of our Saskatchewan tradition of pulling together."[9]

Moose Jaw was more important to Palliser than any other city to its region. Provincial Librarian Don Meadows told council in February 1973, "there's no doubt about it. There's no way it [the region] could be established without Moose Jaw."[10] One alderman was scared that "once we get in we'll be in a trap and will be faced with something we won't want." He was expressing a lone view at that meeting but his opinion would have greater support in times to come. That

Trail ride, July 17, 1974, starting for Mortlach, with regional librarian Cora Greer and Gordon MacMurchy. Clydesdales in background.

the headquarters would be in Moose Jaw was a selling point. At that November official opening, Moose Jaw represented 31,000 people out of a total population of 48,000 represented by the region at large.

By 1974 there were 17 branches and a new regional librarian, Cora Greer, who had been the first branch supervisor of the region. She says she was hired in this way: "Ken Pragnall came to me with the applications for the job and said, 'which one of these do you want for a boss?' I wrote a letter of application and was hired. When people asked how I could do such a big job, I said, 'I thought about the job in small pieces and later put it all together.'"[11]

There was one great promotional event in 1974, with MacMurchy beginning and ending a journey by Clydesdales and a wagon filled with 300 books and some librarians, on its way down the Trans-Canada Highway from Moose Jaw to Mortlach. Greer said it demonstrated how difficult transportation of books had been in 1920 when Mortlach first formed a community library. Twenty-two representatives from the other regions joined in the festivities, including four arriving in a light aircraft piloted by Wheatland's Bruce Cameron. They began with an early breakfast and joined the trek by wagon or on horseback. MacMurchy, a farmer, said, "I haven't done this for about twenty years." Once the parade reached the Trans-Canada, MacMurchy was driven back to Regina for a meeting, but returned for the last lap into Mortlach, with a new pair of Clydesdales on a 90° Fahrenheit day – in heritage temperatures. The day ended with a beef barbecue in Besant Provincial Park. The Mortlach librarian announced that circulation was 600 a week and interlibrary loan service was catching on. "As the Besant mosquitoes arrived and lightning flashed across the sky, all those present figured it had been quite a day."[12]

When the Provincial Library cancelled its direct mail service in July 1975, Palliser began its own direct mail service to those without close access to a branch. Telex machines were installed in all regional headquarters that year to speed up ILLO service. That summer Greer was assisted by a student working on her Master of Library Science degree, Joylene Campbell, who would become a regional librarian at Lakeland, and later provincial librarian. The importance of Moose Jaw to the region was clear in the contributions that year, Moose Jaw providing $111,000 of the $128,000 total regional contribution (the provincial government contribution was $193,000 plus $10,000 for capital improvements and $7,800 for regional headquarters space.) The original Moose Jaw levy was based on its current expenditures in 1973.

Palliser's problem was inflation. It began last and before it could adequately stock the smaller libraries it walked into high interest rates, so it needed large levy increases just to stand still. In 1975 and 1976, even with large provincial and levy increases, it ran a deficit, and decided to close branches and headquarters, without staff pay, for two weeks over Christmas.

PALLISER AND MOOSE JAW, 1976-81

The first expression of dissatisfaction from Moose Jaw surfaced at a city council meeting in July 1976, when the chair and vice-chair of the

Moose Jaw Library Board said provincial legislation was being prepared to compel all city libraries to remain in their regions. (Such mandatory legislation was finally passed twenty years later in the 1996 Act.) An alderman declared, "the region has attempted to reduce our staff at Moose Jaw Library by one person without consulting us."[13] This was an inflammatory accusation, and as Moose Jaw did have four members on the executive of the region it's hard to imagine these actions could be invisible. Greer presented the region's case a few days later, stating that if Moose Jaw withdrew, Palliser would no longer be viable and that expenditures on the city by the region were approximately $118,210, larger than the levy, "which is $48,689 more than the city's contribution to the region."[14] She also noted that Moose Jaw paid 28.6 % of total revenue, the provincial government 62%, other municipalities 8.8%.[15] The Moose Jaw board, remaining at odds with Palliser, identified a number of issues between the city and region, including this one: "that the chief librarian of the Moose Jaw Public Library is more familiar with the running of the library than one who has no experience in a library such as ours."

Meadows had attended a meeting of the Moose Jaw board to discuss Palliser's removal of a position, from technical services, and "an apparent breakdown in communication between the Palliser Board and the Moose Jaw Board."[16] He suggested a meeting between the two boards with a member of the Provincial Library. Palliser nominated its members but the meeting apparently was not held. Greer says now the technical services position had been cut because Moose Jaw was replicating work done by the region and that "Ida Cooke [Moose Jaw librarian] did what she always had done, whatever Katherine McKinnon had done."[17]

Moose Jaw said it had not made a motion to withdraw from the region but it did want the library legislation amended so it would have the same independent status as Saskatoon and Regina:

This City and per our unconfirmed understanding, other Cities desire to have the same rights as Regina and Saskatoon thus has directed an approach to the Government of Saskatchewan to grant the same rights of exclusion for the

City's Public Library system to all Cities, as granted to the
City of Regina and the City of Saskatoon and further, that
the Saskatchewan Urban Municipalities Association be
requested to explore the substance of the motion on behalf
of the City of Moose Jaw and other interested Cities.[18]

This letter is transcribed exactly, and its message is black – remove all
cities from the regions, an action which could, except for Wheatland,
bring the regions down.

Then came the battle of statistics. Moose Jaw council accepted
Greer's estimate on the city's revenue and expenditures, but there's more
than one way to read statistics. Here's how Moose Jaw showed itself the
victim. Its population of 31,854 was 55.5% of the region, but it received
only 28.6% of revenue. The provincial grant was $4.52 per capita, for a
total of $259,000. The council then assumed expenses on regional head-
quarters, staff and vehicles, were acceptable at $89,000, but "$169,000
is left, or $2.95 per capita, so Moose Jaw should receive $93,000, is only
receiving $48,000, the rest apparently being directed to aid the twenty
(20) branches."[19] When passions run high statistics can become a
weapon, wielded here against small communities in the region, and yet
not contradictory to Greer's case. Incorporated as part of the appendices
were comments by Greer, including this statement: "The Moose Jaw
Public Library Board earlier demanded 58% of the Provincial Grants,
yet it also wants the regional headquarters to act as its agent. This means
Moose Jaw would be receiving service from headquarters which would
be supported by government grants and all other municipalities except
Moose Jaw. Is this fair?"

In 1977 Moose Jaw, "The Friendly City" as its letterhead declares,
had a new method to determine its contribution, based now on
Prince Albert's contribution to its area (in 1977, Prince Albert at 2.5%
of the weighted levy, Moose Jaw at 3.5%). A letter also detailed the
points on which it would agree to stay in the region: that the Moose
Jaw Public Library "shall have autonomy to administer its share of the
Palliser Regional Library budget"; the expenditure "shall not be less
than the City's contribution plus 50% of the Provincial grants"; that
council must approve the per capita grant to the region.[20]

There was a brief conflict over levies in 1978, Moose Jaw Council originally reducing the region's 10% request to 5.4%. The Moose Jaw city treasurer said that "most costs would be eliminated if the Moose Jaw system were autonomous."[21] Council approved the 10% at its next meeting, but the city still wanted greater control over its library. Elmer Laird of Davidson wrote a sharp letter to the *Moose Jaw Times-Herald* on March 29, 1977. His version of the Moose Jaw directive to the region said the city wanted all its own tax money, plus half the provincial grant minus money paid to headquarters and other smaller items. Moose Jaw also wanted, he said, autonomy for its board and the same level of regional service. Because of population, the city had a veto over levy increases (which needed 50% of the municipalities and 50% of the population to pass). Laird suggested leadership and co-operation from Moose Jaw. Perhaps, he wrote, the regional headquarters could be moved to a small community "that has a harmonious rural atmosphere so our regional headquarters staff can escape from the rural-urban split conflict that they have been exposed to for the last five years." Greer agreed that the rural-urban split was real. "The city people said I was on the side of rural people. The rural people said you only see the city side. I thought I must be in the right place."[22]

Then came levy times again, another 25% asked for. Moose Jaw council countered with 20%, the 25% losing on a vote of 5-4, the 20% passing by a vote of 7-2. In a letter, Greer said in the five-year period since 1973 the levies had increased by 12%, in line with inflation. The compromise was a 21% increase, but the following year when the region asked for 25%, Moose Jaw offered 10%. At the fall regional board meeting, Moose Jaw's motion lost on a vote of 20-17. Other motions failed for lack of a seconder and finally a motion passed accepting the 10% increase now with the executive to reconsider the budget for the spring meeting.

And then things got worse.

At a meeting in June, 1979, Moose Jaw Council voted to withdraw from the region, accepting the recommendation of its library board. Alderman Nidesh, a member of the board, led the attack. He said that while relations with the regional library had been good in the past, this year "the Palliser Regional Library executive has seen fit to indicate to us that we're just...puppets of them and they were going to impose on us their will."[23] He added, "we came to the conclusion that we have absolutely no local autonomy...that we're not serving any useful purpose." He suggested fee for service as one way to retain local autonomy. The percentage levies over the past four years were: 1976, 25%; 1977, 10%; 1978, 21%; 1979, 10%. The vote for withdrawal passed by a vote of 10-2, with John Skoberg, former NDP MLA in opposition, and Mayor Taylor in support of the motion.

Because North Battleford had also given notice to withdraw from its region, Lakeland, the cities asked for a special meeting with the Saskatchewan Urban Municipalities Association (SUMA), held in Regina September 17, 1979. The executive director of SUMA said, "A relatively small number of people are in control of the decision-making on the regional board's executive," and many library boards feel "they fly in the face of local autonomy."[24] Moose Jaw's Mayor Herb Taylor said the Public Library Act needed clarification; for instance, did local boards or the regional library have the power to hire and fire? That got to the heart of the explosive situation at Lakeland, where the region had fired the North Battleford librarian. Though she wanted North Battleford in the region, Lakeland librarian Catherine O'Neill said that financially the region would be better off without the city, which was not the case for Palliser. One reality for Moose Jaw and North Battleford was the requirement, under the act, that they would have to finance their own libraries solely out of their own tax base. Only Regina and Saskatoon were independent, but government grants to cities were very modest. The delegates from the cities and towns at the meeting did pass a resolution to confirm their commitment to the regional concept. The SUMA executive planned to meet with Doug MacArthur, minister in charge of libraries (one of five in the years of the Blakeney NDP), partly to talk of escalating costs and reduced provincial grants.

Moose Jaw council upheld its withdrawal notice at a February 2, 1981 meeting, but barely: a tied four-four vote meant a motion to rescind the withdrawal was defeated. Mayor Taylor was now on the side of the region. "If we pull out, Palliser will cease to exist and small libraries would join other regions."[25] Indeed the Library Development Board had discussed the issue of Moose Jaw's withdrawal and passed this motion, moved by Isabelle Butters, a Southeast trustee, seconded by Tom Boyd, a Lakeland trustee:

> In view of the motion of withdrawal of participation of the City of Moose Jaw in the Palliser Regional Library and
>
> Whereas the Palliser Region would be uneconomic without the Moose Jaw population, and in the best interests of the people served;
>
> Be it resolved that the Library Development Board recommend the dissolution of the Palliser Region with the rural population being divided logically between Chinook, Southeast and Wheatland Regions at the end of 1981 when the Moose Jaw withdrawal will become effective.[26]

At an earlier LDB meeting, as regions were being formed, Boyd had suggested that, because of population, only two regions be formed in the south, with some sort of independent status for Moose Jaw. When I asked Cora Greer about that suggestion, she said the difficulty would be the greater distances to travel. The surgery didn't come to pass, as Moose Jaw rescinded its motion of withdrawal in late 1981.

BUSINESS AS USUAL – LATE '70s, EARLY '80s

Annual reports give information on a variety of regional matters in the late '70s, and early '80s. Inflation and less-than-adequate grants meant the 1976 book budget was 14.7% of total expenditures (not the 17.5% recommended by the SLTA) while the following year it dipped to 12%, then rose to 15.4% in 1978. Salaries and benefits made up 77% of the budget. The Books by Mail program increased from 77 users in 1977 to 584 in 1979. In 1978, "I'm a Book Nut" buttons were for sale and the region's fifth anniversary was marked by a bicycle relay carrying ILLO requests from Caronport, Bushell Park and Moose Jaw. In 1980 the region had its first book sale, selling three tons of books at 25 cents a pound. The next year, Library Week included "a men's only night" in Tugaske as a way to increase circulation, "an open house featuring a belly dancer" at Bushell Park, while both Willow Bunch and Rouleau "will take books to the curling rink" during bonspiels. The region moved its office in 1984 to the former South Hills Co-op Store, its present location. By 1985 the region was completing 77% of ILLO requests, while 38% of the population had library cards.

In 1986 it was suspected that the librarian at Mossbank was inflating her statistics by 150%, to keep opening three hours more than was warranted. A three-month study verified the discrepancy. The librarian was fired, but was defended by the union, the matter going to arbitration – which found against the board because the consequences of such an action were not addressed in the branch manual. The librarian was reinstated, then resigned two months later. The arbitration took ten months and cost $8,500.

HARD TIMES, 1983-95

It was in the 1980s, under the Devine Conservative government, that the provincial share of library service sharply declined, and the offloading to municipalities began in earnest. The annual grants to Palliser were:

1983 . . . .$508,978
1984 . . . .$531,975
1985 . . . .$531,975
1986 . . . .$547,072
1987 . . . .$494,980
1988 . . . .$504,989
1989 . . . .$511,354
1990 . . . .$518,649
1994 . . . .$524,126

The value of the 1990 grant reflected in 1983 dollars was only $390,000, the board newsletter reported.[27]

The same kind of point was made in annual reports. In 1988,

Assiniboia Library

Greer said, "in the last five years (1984-88) municipal levies have increased by 22.2% while provincial grants have dropped by 5.1%, resulting in an overall increase of 6.2%. During the same period, the consumer price indices record a 17% increase."

The black year was 1987 when the provincial grant was reduced by 10%, "a devastating year for libraries, the board chair proclaimed."[28] The cuts in 1987 included $24,200 from materials. "Because the library has been unable to buy sufficient copies of popular materials, there have been long waiting lists for many titles – up to 18 months," and no audio-visual materials would be purchased. Staff was cut by 2,866 hours, with reduced hours in branches, half a position lost at headquarters, and the archives department at Moose Jaw closed. The publicity budget was cut in half, maintenance deferred, staff development cut by 40%, reserves inadequate. As well, cuts to the Provincial Library meant a slowdown in ILLO service, and some programs – large print books – were transferred to the regions. The provincial government did respond with a one-time materials budget increase of $39,000, to relieve that problem for the year. Moose Jaw Mayor Scoop Lewry said of the government, "Instead of passing the buck they're passing the bills."[29]

Devastating population statistics were recorded in the November 1994 trustees newsletter *For the Record,* comparing populations between 1958 and 1994. Large centres did alright – Moose Jaw up by 4,000, Assiniboia up from 2,150 to 2,774, Davidson up from 844 to 1,115 – but many towns or villages that had branches showed declines.

Wood Mountain declined from 122 to 46, Tugaske from 261 to 157, Willow Bunch from 711 to 476. Villages in general went down by an average of 33%, including Aylesbury, 165 to 63; Dilke, 190 to 98; Hawarden 204 to 102. Only Pense, as a dormitory town for Regina, increased from 326 to 556. The population decrease in RMS was 56.6% and they all suffered a substantial decline. The terrible depopulation of rural Saskatchewan is clear from these statistics. Think of the new demands on branch libraries with fewer people. But they survived, some of them very well indeed. Circulation went up almost everywhere as these statistics from annual reports show.

	1980	1994
Assiniboia	20,870	39,951
Davidson	21,675	29,356
Bushell Park	16,478	22,115
Rockglen	7,257	19,231
Imperial	6,550	17,783
Mossbank	6,440	15,800
Willow Bunch	6,940	8,864
Wood Mountain	11,074	4,545

There was also the good news, year by year, of towns and villages getting new and better library space. Yet financially the world was bleak, an NDP government continuing to cut or only modestly increase budgets. By 1993, the chair of the Palliser board said that since 1983, "the Provincial grant [had] increased by 2.1%; the City levy [had] increased by 45%; and the rural communities [had] increased their levies by 46.8%." As well, "Headquarters staff reductions over the years [had] resulted in less contact between Headquarters and branch staff." Greer said the region always put "as much money as possible into the branches," so headquarters "suffered."[30]

There were severe cuts again in 1993, 5%, the NDP of Premier Roy Romanow struggling with the deficit, though it never did fund libraries adequately even with a balanced budget. The two-week staff layoff at Christmas was reinstated, but reduced to one week the following two years. The collective agreement for 1991-93 had only a

Moose Jaw Public Library, 1964

signing bonus. Moose Jaw too held the line on increases so cuts there included children's programming and the archives one more time. Cutbacks to the Provincial Library meant more and more ILLO requests were coming back unfilled, a terrible situation for a one library system. By 1995 the provincial grant "was at an all-time low" at 40% of the Palliser total budget.

There were positive signs. One response to chronic underfunding was to create an Adopt-A-Book Program, which generated $25,000 in five years. New facilities for branch libraries continued to be opened and technology had come to Palliser, the telex replaced by Envoy, a faster and more efficient method of transmitting ILLO. By 1986 both Palliser and Moose Jaw were updating their shelf lists to prepare for the new machine age. By 1988 the weeding was complete and the fiche catalogue had come to Palliser and 13 branches. By 1991, the shelf list had been divided in two, those titles purchased between 1980 and 1981 were now on the UTLAS database and so were machine readable, while the pre-1980 titles, a bit over half the collection, were in card format, but a Utah firm had converted the cards to machine-readable form. Both databases were linked and barcodes for the collection produced, on the Dynix computer, and soon rural branches too were being bar-coded. Moose Jaw had the same systems. The following year staff were trained in the brave new world. By 1995, Palliser and Moose Jaw had computer access to the Saskatchewan Union Catalogue through PLEIS

(Province-wide Library Electronic Information System) and through a SaskTel network. Now they needed money to expand internet service to twelve rural libraries over two years.

There was good news for Moose Jaw too, beyond new technological capability. A new library building was needed, so a site was chosen and money made available, but because of pressure from citizens, council held a referendum; in 1992 voters chose renovation and expansion to the original building, a good decision since the original building is so handsome and its site superb.

In 1992, the expansion was complete and a new group, The Friends of the Library, was formed and received charitable status. Within a decade they had raised $600,000 for the library, by semi-annual used books sales, bazaars, bake sales, garage sales, bingos, a silent auction, by selling houseplants, a limited edition plate of the original building, book bags, fridge magnets, anything that worked. It sounds just like Saskatchewan.

Peace and co-operation had come to the region, said Greer, partly because automation held all the parts together.

Moose Jaw Public Library interior, charging desk *(Saskatchewan Government photo)*

Chapter Thirteen

Northern Services
1978-1997

T HERE WERE SEVEN SOUTHERN REGIONS BY 1973 while service to the north – meaning north of Lakeland and Wapiti – was the responsibility of the Provincial Library, 400 miles south of La Ronge in Regina. Long distance library service. The Provincial Library supplied direct service, mostly to teachers, about 30,000 items a year, as well as exchanges with four libraries in the late '70s (La Ronge had incorporated as early as 1972) and 14 book deposits. That information is included in an early, June 28, 1978, report on Northern Library Development. Reports and negotiations filled the 1980s yet it took a decade before independent Northern Library service began. There was a pro tem board by 1979, chaired by Ken Collier, communications at a government level between ministers of Northern Development and libraries. Later the Department of Education would play an important role. A report in 1979 expanded on the first report, five libraries by then (La Ronge, Buffalo Narrows, Pelican Narrows, Sandy Bay, Ile-a-la-Crosse), plus 17 book deposits, and it made a series of recommendations: on audio-visual and art components necessary for a First Nations oral culture; on children's books suitable for those with a low vocabulary level; on the need for a new library act; and for an increase in funding to cover additional cost factors prevalent in the north, "such as greater loss rate of materials (up to 20%), rough handling of materials so that binding and repairs are required, etc."[1] The government did grant $12,000 in 1979 so the pro tem board could continue to meet. The most detailed early report was made July 6, 1981, by Merry Harbottle, the provincial librarian at the time. The total population in the North was roughly 30,000 people in 90,000 square miles. Metis made up 38.5% of the population, and status Indians 35%. The average Metis age was twenty-four; Indian, twenty. It's easy to imagine the importance of children's materials. This was the document that requested government grants rise from a $2,000 matching grant to a $15,000 matching grant. Harbottle also proposed two new positions be created in the North.[2]

There are a number of reports on specific northern libraries, mostly through personal visits by Provincial Library employees. In 1979, John Murray described facilities at a number of northern branches. At Sandy Bay, the library "is housed in a trailer without proper shelving or any of the standard requirements. The library board desperately wishes to proceed with expansion, training, and funding to remain open." The Pelican Narrows library was also in a trailer, shared with the school library. "Originally housed in the band offices the collection was moved because of reports of vandalism." There was a problem in 1981 in Uranium City, with deterioration in the relations between the mayor and the new library board. The mayor didn't want to pay rent to the Department of Northern Saskatchewan for a trailer, and wanted the library moved to a school "which has been condemned by Atomic Energy of Canada due to high radiation levels of which the Board are aware."[3]

Provincial Library staff toured and reported on northern services on November 1983, January, March and November in 1984, and April 1985. They saw good things: Kitsaki School Library, "very good library facility, good book collection; partially trained library staff, Edna Mirasty – 8 months Library Technicians program."[4] Staff on the January 1984 trip liked Beauval: "visited Valley View School; has excellent new library facility...library can be shut off from the rest of the school and has a separate entrance allowing public access." The council wanted to create a public library. Almost all libraries in the north were in schools. On the April 1985 trip the reviewers liked the Pelican Narrows library: "very active. Margaret Brass does the story time in Cree and English." There were dark times too. In 1983, "Most of the people in Pinehouse are unemployed and there is little money. In bad times people barely have enough to eat." In the Turnor Lake book deposit, "some of the books are apparently still in boxes in a washroom." The Sandy Bay library building had been demolished, "no location found for books, which were mostly in boxes in the basement." In January 1984 the reviewers heard from an angry Buffalo Narrows: "they were offended by the suggestion that books sent to the North are never returned; they feel that they are doing a good, responsible job and they are probably right." Stan Skreszweski, flying in a Cessna 185 at 5,500 feet, said, "It's about minus 30-35 degrees Celsius outside. Phyllis and I froze in the airplane, despite the heating system in the plane. You can see your breath. On our way to Sandy Bay I wrapped myself in the engine blanket to keep warm. Even the ink doesn't want to flow from this pen." There was a key recommendation in the November 1983 report: "Because of the lack of money in the North it is very difficult for Northern communities to come up with a matching dollar amount, or to spend the money in advance of receiving a grant from the Provincial Library."

The expanded matching $15,000 grants were first available that year. By 1985 such grants were in their third year. They show how differently some communities were organized. Tawowikamik Library in Pelican Narrows, located in the school, had a handsome circulation of 25,000 items. The town contributed $14,000, the province $15,000, while payments were greatest for books, over $14,000, low for salaries, just under $2,000. La Ronge was also a successful library, though not located in a school. It had 1,000 registered borrowers, was open 30 hours a week, and circulated over 14,000 items. Only $5,000 was spent on books, $14,000 on salaries. La Loche was open only four hours a week, circulating about 5,000 items. The town contributed $6,658, which was the librarian's salary, while the provincial grant was $2,000. In Ile-a-la-Crosse it was the school which contributed the money, $22,000, the province $15,000. Salaries were

$20,387, presumably for a school librarian – the library open 40 hours a week. There's little information in the Creighton report since its town and provincial grants, $5,500 each, were transferred to the Flin Flon Public Library. Each of the five libraries was in some particular way different from the others. There was no single way of doing things in the North.

The problem with the grant structure was the topic of a 1985 paper. According to the 1981 census, there were 12 municipalities with populations of over 500 in the North, as well as four Indian reserves and five Indian bands. "Under the current formula communities have to raise money in order to obtain the matching grant. This means that in communities with little or no revenue, library grants are unavailable." Municipalities had to form library boards, spend one year's operating budget, hire staff, claim a grant and wait a year to receive it. "Beauval, although it has had a fine library facility for the past year, has not been able to apply for a grant and won't get a grant now till 1985 or 1986 at the earliest. Ile-a-la-Crosse has stopped applying for a grant, although they operate a good library in the school, because of the awkward grant structure." Four options were presented, the third favoured, since it recommended a base grant of $4,000 per library plus $2,000 per capita, which would provide $5,000 plus to Beauval and $9,000 plus to La Ronge. Although none would receive the $15,000 possible under the matching grant program, more communities would receive some funding.[5]

Maureen Woods was the Provincial Library representative to the North. In the fall of 1985 she toured northern communities and spent all of 1986 developing concepts with groups; in the fall of 1987 she took her discussion paper to groups and the following autumn moved north to La Ronge and began to develop the system. It was based on two new concepts. First, the Northern Region was organized not as a region proper but as a federation of legally independent library communities combined with central service, originally the Provincial Library but relocated to La Ronge in 1988. Second, many public libraries were housed in schools, a principle that was anathema to most public librarians because school and public libraries served entirely different communities. Woods had "asked an

Indian woman at Montreal Lake if she'd like us to move the library out of the school and she said, 'no, that's the centre of the community. When we die our funeral will be there. When a child marries it will be there. Why would we want a library anywhere else?'"[6] A third point came out of the second principle, on the inclusive nature of membership on the regional board, which was made up of public libraries, special libraries, school libraries, and band-controlled school libraries, a total of 40 members by 1995, for instance. At the end of Wood's June 1989 Report on the Federation of Northern Libraries, she concluded, having interviewed more than 50 groups and many individuals in the north:

> I have never heard anyone say they did not like the idea. On the contrary, people think it's too good to be true. They find it logical, responsible, respectful and reasonable. (No wonder, it's the best of their own thinking.)

Hard, if you were in government, to say no to the document.

The transfer of records from the Provincial Library to the North began in the fall of 1988, with La Ronge the repository, while support for the North would be $200,000 higher than the previous year, according to a September 5, 1988 Lorne Hepworth press release. A Northern board meeting December 9, 1989 created bylaws and an executive structure that mirrored northern realities, with two members each from four geographical regions, north, east, central, west, as well as one representative each from college, public libraries, and schools, with two members from Indian bands. Those two members could be represented in the earlier seven categories, and usually were. In 1980, Audrey Mark replaced Woods as regional librarian, and still remains in that position. In a report to the SLTA in 1990, the region thanked Woods: "Maureen's unflagging vision of a unique library service to the northern half of the province persuaded the agencies who could effect decisions that a northern system is a necessity not a luxury."[7] By then seventy-five percent of ILLO were for schools. Partners were working toward library technician training. The new name, Pahkisimon Nuyʔáh, was chosen during an executive conference call, January 15, 1991, and ratified at the next AGM. Here's how it happened.

> The Executive Committee set about coming up with a name that would be completely different...a name that would be written in both Cree and Dene.... The committee reduced a large list of choices to five names and mailed these five to the rest of the Board which through a mail-in vote chose the word for sunset. As one Board member stated, 'We have terrific sunsets and a terrific library system.' The spelling of the Cree and Dene words were checked with Cree and Dene speakers and dictionaries (where available). Pahkisimon is a Cree word and Nuyʔáh is Dene (the question mark is representative of a glottal stop or pause between the 'e' and 'a').[8]

The system is usually referred to as PNLS (Pahkisimon Nuyʔáh Library System).

There was a logo competition, won by a grade nine girl, Erin Haffermehl of Valley View School in Beauval. The colours were black for tree and book, red for the sun and lettering, orange for clouds. The 1991 AGM that approved the name and logo also passed a belief statement and defined the library technician's course (supported by Northland College, Northern Lights School Division, Saskatchewan Education and PNLS). The meeting also passed a motion to be "registered with Affirmative Action in the Human Rights Commission to promote a native hiring policy," which was granted.

The major program in the north was a Northern Reading Program – "the dominant annual library event in Northern Saskatchewan with excellent support from all participating communities," said the chairperson in the 1992 Annual Report. The mascot for the program was a bookworm – Willy the Iceworm. The champion schools were declared every year. "Beauval Public Library had a very successful Northern Reading Program contest pitting the community against the school. The community won."[9]

An important need for the region was a new headquarters building. Picture it – La Ronge, September, 1999, 8 a.m. A lone

Pahkisimon Nuye?áh Library System (PNLS) Official Opening. Director Audrey Mark chats with Board members and others at the PNLS Official Opening celebrations, March 8, 1991. *From left:* Executive Board members Doreen Morin of Sandy Bay and Rosine Broussie of Black Lake, trustee Caron Dubnick of the Uranium City Advisory Committee with her baby, PNLS Director Audrey Mark, and Lois Jordan, Curriculum Coordinator with the Lac La Ronge Indian Band.

member of the library staff is spotted standing at the front door, waiting. Eventually this person is joined by four other staff members and still they wait.... The problem, the front door won't open. It's stuck.... The solution. Get it fixed. Replace it. The estimated time frame? One month, two tops....Plan A? Use the back door. Plan B?... "Use only the entrance to the College if the cold weather freezes the back door."

Doors were one thing, walls another.

> For ten years our poor mail deliverer can't use the mailroom for over half a year because the cold lifts the back floor up about five inches... Just ask Allyson, our Processor, who constantly has to deal with water-damaged materials, from the leaks in the walls, floors and windows. Just ask Cathy, our circulation clerk, who sometimes has to wear gloves while typing because of the extreme cold in the back half of the building.[10]

A new space was complete within the year, though fundraising and planning had been going on for a number of years. The 2001 Annual Report is full of information on the new building, in Air Ronge, assisted by a major $550,000 grant from the provincial government. My favourite story is the La Ronge Ice Wolves hockey club helping the move from the old to the new place. There were many volunteers. "Many librarians, former librarians and friends came to help us unpack boxes and put them on the shelves."

There's an important "Presentation to the Minister's Committee on Library Services to Aboriginal People" (June 20, 2001) that provides substantial information on the region. There had been an increase in professional staff over the first decade, from one to three professional librarians, from three to seven library technicians – and seven library technicians-in-training, but down from three teacher librarians to one. "In 1990 there was little participation in provincial library associations. In fact there was a time when the board was so angry about the SLTA [presumably about combining school and public libraries], they discussed starting a Northern alternative. Now, Northerners are heads of SLTA, SLA [and serve on other committees]."

Attempts to train technicians haven't worked well. One attempt, where students spent three weeks in class, then two weeks at home, failed because no one looked after the library when they were at class and chaos ensued. Most Northern libraries were run by a single person. A language problem faced Dene speakers most. When a translator left, no one finished the course, which assumed a high literacy level in English. Four students finished a diploma course. A bursary program worked, four having taken advantage of it. More staff were being sponsored to attend conferences.

The presentation also explained geographical reality in the north. To visit libraries "the average [drive] is three to four hours long over gravel roads or poorly maintained highways." Scheduled airline costs were over $500, chartered flights between one and two thousand. "Nearly every trip requires an overnight stay, sometimes in extremely primitive conditions." For the delivery of library materials, "Canada Post is our main and in most cases only means of delivery of materials. Books that are mailed to the east side (Pelican Narrows, Sandy

Bay) go from La Ronge to Regina to Winnipeg to Flin Flon, and are driven down the highway from there."

The central issues, or challenges, facing PNLS were staff training; automation (behind other systems in training); technology (systems that worked in the south didn't always work in the north and it cost money to bring in technicians from the south); delivery service; and money (provincial grants had remained static for a decade and the matching $15,000 grant hadn't increased).

Because most systems were run by a single librarian who might never have been in a real library before, and some didn't even have grade twelve education, says Maureen Woods, "We realized we needed to do something to give respect to the librarian and the library. We phoned a library in advance to see what the key issues were, and then took a package of people and material and did a work bee. We'll stay a week in your hotels, meet council, teachers, the

The Pelican Narrows Public Library Board Trustees and staff from Pelican Narrows attending Tawowikamik Public Library annual general meeting in 2002. *From left,* standing: library administrator Margaret Brass, who has been with the library since 1982, board member Norma Linklater, and Wapanack School library clerk Elizabeth Michel. *Seated:* board members Evelyn McCallum and Rebecca McCallum, public library clerk Marilyn Ballantyne, and chairperson Julianne Custer. Julianne, Rebecca, and Marriette McCallum, who is missing from the photo, have all been library board members for more than 20 years. *Tawowikamik* is Cree for "Place of welcome."

chief, the mayor. The librarians were often badly treated so we had to promote them."[11] The group might file catalogues, do a story hour, a puppet show, exchange books and so on. In 1997 there was an aircraft visit to Stony Rapids, Fond du Lac, and Uranium City for library promotion. In September people created a resource centre at Michel Village, later assisted the librarian at Pinehouse with her fiction collection. The 1999 Annual Report had news of work bees at La Loche, Pinehouse, Buffalo Narrows and Beauval to help with automation, also at Beauval "to help weed, reshelve and reorganize after the fire," and at Deschambault Lake to weed and organize.

The last word on the North will go to a story by Woods paraphrasing a story told by long-time northerner Lois Dalby to a group of fifty or so.

> She said that when she moved to the north there were no services and if she had a question she asked the natural resources officer, and then as time went on they got schools and teachers so she'd have a choice to ask a teacher or principal for information, and then they got health centres, so there were other educated persons to talk to, and then we got libraries and we could go to the library and chose our own information. Now the users are choosers.[12]

That, says Woods, is a microcosm of what librarians do.

Chapter Fourteen

Regina and Saskatoon
1908-2002

REGINA

R EGINA WAS AHEAD OF SASKATOON FOR MANY YEARS, both as a city (2,249 people in 1901 to 113) and as a library system. Regina's first board meeting was March 27, 1908, Saskatoon's December 9, 1912. Regina had a central library building by 1912, Saskatoon by 1929. Later, by statistical measures, they were two of the best libraries in Canada.

Regina began service in three rooms on the second floor of a new city hall, then received the largesse of the Carnegie Foundation for a $50,000 library building, designed by the well-known Regina architectural firm Storey & Von Egmond. The library opened May 11, 1912, then was struck by the June 30 tornado that devastated Regina's downtown. "About two-thirds of the roof was torn off, the parapet largely destroyed" and so on, according to the 1912 Regina Public Library (RPL) Report. Carnegie came to the rescue with an additional $10,000. The Carnegie Library remained the central library in Regina until it was demolished in June, 1961 to make way for the new Central Library, which, with a mezzanine added in 1973, is the Central Library of today. A 1957 Annual Report shows how crowded the original building had become.

Overcrowding had become so acute at the Central Library that drastic measures became imperative. Newspaper reading was discontinued. More serious, the Boys and Girls Department was moved to Connaught Branch to make space for the Catalogue Department.... Meeting rooms available to the public were reduced from three to one. Bound newspaper files and Patent Office Record files have been discarded...additional shelving has been built at Central, some of which admittedly is of more service to tall than short people.

When the new building was opened, circulation doubled in a year and went down at every branch and for every bookmobile.

Regina opened branches early, two wooden structures built by 1913 and often moved, one of them three times and finally called the Prince of Wales. Two permanent brick buildings, Albert in 1927 and Connaught in 1930, both designed by Joseph Warburton, are still part of the Regina system, though Connaught came under threat of closure in 2003. They were designated as heritage buildings in 1984.

Because the need for a new central library occupied board and staff concern, there wasn't another branch opened until 1979, the Regent Park Branch, located in a shopping centre; in 1979 the Glen

Regina Public Library, Carnegie Library.

Children's Story Hour, RPL Central Library, 1913.

Elm Branch was opened in the east end of the city; in 1981 the Sherwood Village Branch; in 1985 the South Albert Branch; and in 1989 the Sunrise Branch in the southeast. In 1995 two new branches opened: the George Bothwell Branch to serve south Regina, replacing the South Albert branch; and the Regent Branch to serve north Regina, replacing the Regent Park Branch. By 1996, "Over 90% of Regina residents [had] a branch within two kilometres of their homes," which was a result of the board's Branch Siting Policy.

New Central Library, Regina, September 19, 1962. *(Photo Department of Industry & Information)*

Mrs. E.N. (Betty) Davis accepting the Canadian Library Trustees Merit Award, CLA Conference, 1968

Land of 16mm film. Mr. R.C. Johnson, Film Librarian, RPL, March 1960.

Regina Public Library Board ready to leave on inspection tour of library properties February 13, 1965. Mr. A.T. Little, Dr. A.E. Perry, Mrs. E.N. Davis, Mr. R.B. Bagshaw, Q.C., Chairman, Miss Marjorie R. Dunlop, Chief Librarian, His Worship, Mayor H.H.P. Baker, ex officio, Mr. G. R. Bothwell. Missing – Mr. J.R.A. Pollard.

Regina Vignettes

1912 "It is appalling to note the tremendous quantity of unworthy and unnecessary books that are year by year unloaded by some publishers." That was Regina's first librarian, J. C. Honeyman.

1914 "A new feature was introduced during this year by which citizens spending summer vacations...could be supplied with reading material for themselves and family."

1955 "A system of pooling many of the adult books was commenced in the fall of 1954 and there are now 37 pools of 20 books each."

1967 Doris Rands, branch librarian at Connaught, said, "Our Beth Hone pot has been used for everything from lilacs to autumn leaves to Mr. Seiferling's begonias, and it has been greatly admired." The following year Connaught featured drama, Byrna Barclay adapting a James Thurber story, the next year adapting one of her own stories as performed with fellow Kinettes; grade five students put on plays for younger children and there were Saturday afternoon drama classes. In 1971 Connaught was developed as a neighborhood library centre.

1969 "Twenty-six cartons of discarded books were sent out to fill requests from country points."

1970 "In 1970 I refereed a hassle between two elderly gentlemen over the ownership of the Regina Leader Post; I awarded a TKO, the paper torn in shreds."

1990 "The Library won the annual award of the Movement for Canadian Literacy for excellence in literacy work."

1996 "Literacy volunteers alone contributed $640,000 worth of time in 1996."

1997 "1997 began with exceptional cold and with a staff complement dislocated by the transfers and bumping that took place as a result of the closure of the Audio-Visual Unit at Central Library on January 1, 1997."[1]

SASKATOON

In 1912, Saskatoon, "the fastest growing city in the world," as it advertised itself, rejected the Carnegie offer of $30,000 for a library, thought inadequate for so splendid a city; burgesses passed a $100,000 money bylaw that same year, but in 1913 took away all the credit so plentiful the year before, and the Library Board chose library number one in the basement of the Oddfellows Hall, a most anticlimactic beginning. The city did approach the Carnegie Trust in 1922 but was told that no further grants were available for library buildings. The library moved in 1923 to a two-storey wooden building, the Great War Veterans' Building, but had to move again when the T.E. Eaton Company planned their store on that site. Finally a permanent brick building was opened in 1929, the library to occupy only the main floor and basement, with the city health department offices on the top floor. As in Regina, there was never enough room. In 1938, "A much-needed cabinet file cannot be purchased because there is no place to put it."

Saskatoon began its branches modestly too, a West Side (or Riversdale) Branch opening in rental quarters in 1928, a South Side (or Broadway) Branch in 1930. Both changed homes in the early '40s,

Interior, Saskatoon main library, 1929.

Frances Morrison with children at story time in the Christopher Robin room, 1948.

the Broadway branch in its third (1941) location the one I visited as a child. A Mayfair branch opened in 1952 in the basement of the Mayfair Community Hall (which had a great sprung dance floor). More bits and pieces were added in the '50s: a larger West Side Branch, a Haultain Branch on the second floor of a commercial building, a modest library in Sutherland, which had just joined Saskatoon. It was all impermanent until 1961 when the J. S. Wood Branch, named after Saskatoon's third chief librarian, was opened in South East Nutana, the fastest-growing part of the city. It was the first permanent library building in Saskatchewan since Regina's Connaught Library in 1930. The important date in Saskatoon's branch development was 1979, when the Carlyle King Branch was opened in the Cosmo Civic Centre as part of Confederation Park Mall, and that would provide the model for all other branches, according to a Long Range Policy adopted by the library board the following year. Branches were to be located in major, or satellite,

Frances Morrison Branch Library brightly lit to welcome patrons.

shopping centres: the Cliff Wright Branch in the Lakewood Civic Centre and the Rusty Macdonald Branch in the Lawson Civic Centre, both in 1989, and the Alice Turner Branch in 1998. As new branches opened, old ones closed. Broadway and Haultain closed when J. S. Wood opened, Riversdale closed when Carlyle King opened, Sutherland closed when the Alice Turner Branch opened. There is only one local library on the Regina model left in Saskatoon, the Mayfair Branch, rebuilt in a permanent home in 1991.

While on the library board I was involved in two of those stories. The board had decided, always on the advice of the head librarian, to close Mayfair, but citizens wanted a meeting, which I chaired, and speaker after speaker was adamant about keeping their library. It was delightful hearing people talk back, and in retrospect the event has even more resonance, the anger and joy of people speaking in public about keeping their library. That's been a pleasure too in the recent Regina public defence of libraries and services. We went back to the board table and gave Mayfair an extension – and the next member of the board came from that area. I was also a member of the Carlyle King branch steering committee, and remember three things. We

Children crowd around Muriel Clancy's desk while she signs out their books from the Christopher Robin Room.

needed another $300,000 for external architecture but there was a set amount of money available and it didn't stretch that far (and there was no money bylaw as there had been for J. S. Wood and Main). The original name presented at a meeting was the overstated Cosmopolitan Cosmoplex. I said, without authority, that if that name were chosen the library would not build a branch there. It became Cosmo Civic Centre (civic because almost all the money was tax money). The library representatives, Frances Morrison and myself, suggested a theatre for the second floor which was added. The Cosmo Civic Centre included, beside the library, a rink, a gymnasium, handball courts, other smaller services, as well as a health centre, including daycare. The building was funded by the province, $912,000; the city, $975,000; the library, $500,000 from capital reserves; and the Bridge City Cosmos, $20,000.[2]

J.S. Wood Branch
Library as it looked
when it opened.
October 24, 1961.
*(Creative Professional
Photographers)*

R. H. Macdonald
checks an item in
card catalogue at
Frances Morrison
Branch prior to
catalogue's official
retirement. March
20, 1984.

Saskatoon Vignettes

1947 "The circulation of the West End Library in particular rose by leaps and bounds, the result for a time the small children's shelves were left bare."

1957 At Riversdale, "One quarter of the adult patrons were Ukrainians," so more books in Ukrainian were brought in.

1962 At J. S. Wood, on "Saturdays well over 200 youngsters crowded the auditorium for their own movie program."

1969 The city accepted the board's proposal of setting aside ⅓ of a mill annually for library expansion.

1984 SPL completed RECON and received "the distinction from UTLAS in 1983 as being the most efficient RECON operation within the UTLAS network of libraries." The process used 50 to 60% of staff time for 2½ years.

1993 The changing of the media guard: the 16mm film collection disbanded while the compact disc collection grew by 67.7%.

1995 "In 1993 an American publication, *Places Rated Almanac*, rated Saskatoon as the reading capital of North America" (out of a list of 343 cities). That led to a reading challenge from Brampton. Saskatoon won, 167,168 to 143,843 for the period October 16 to November 25.

1998 The library decentralized Technical Services to the new Alice Turner Branch. Construction at the branch used an energy efficient module, "the first library in Canada to do so."

1999 Automation uptime was at 99.8% but there were outages. At Cliff Wright "Communication lines to Main were the culprit." One terminal had intermittent failures and was replaced by a new unit. An eight-day interruption to Internet service was traced to a "fault in the TELUS network in the US involving a routing loop in their network." Correction involved four agencies.

There are two sources of statistical information about Regina and Saskatoon – and other urban libraries – *The Dominion Bureau of Statistics* from 1943 to 1968, and CALUPL (Council of Administers of Large Urban Public Libraries) from 1978 to 2002 (the last year available). In that earlier period, 1943 to 1968, Regina was always one of the libraries with a high expenditure per capita, averaging around third in Canadian cities, but by no other measure was either city remarkable. In circulation per capita, though both libraries were rather low in the scale, Saskatoon led Regina from 1945 to 1953, Regina leading from 1956 to 1961, when Saskatoon again had a higher per capita circulation than Regina until 1968.

There's a decade without comparative statistics. By the 1980s Regina was the leading library in Canada on expenditures per capita from 1979 to 1985, and thereafter was second or third. Saskatoon was sixth to ninth on such expenditures in that decade. On circulation per capita Regina was as high as fourth in the same period, but most often about sixth. Saskatoon ranged from fifth to sixteenth. There was a major shift in 1989. That year Saskatoon purchased more materials per capita than any library in Canada, for the first time, and it was also first in overall materials per capita, also for the first time, Regina having led that category in Canada every year from 1979 to 1988. The shift in favour of Saskatoon continued in the '90s, but both libraries remained Canadian leaders. In material added per capita either Saskatoon or Regina was first every year from 1990 to 2000, except for 1991. It's an amazing record. On expenditures per capita, Regina was back in the first by 1997 and has been first or second every year since, even with modest mill rate increases. Saskatoon ranked fourth or sixth through these years, as low as twelfth in 1994. On circulation per capita, however, Saskatoon led Regina every year in that decade, being second in Canada from 1992 to 1998 and third thereafter; Regina fourth, fifth, and down to seventh in 2002.

But the main conclusion is clear. The Regina and Saskatoon public libraries have been for the last twenty-five years among the very best in Canada. It's a tribute to the two library systems and their citizens who have continued handsomely to support their libraries. As the provincial grant for the cities is at best modest, it's clear the two cities can be proud of themselves.

PROGRAMMING

I've emphasized library programs in smaller centres but city programming is amazing. In Saskatoon, according to *Library News,* December 2003-February 2004, there are programs going on all the time, in the main and seven branch libraries. Here's a quick summary: seven programs in Healthy Choices, across the system; Computers for the Totally Terrified and other such programs, six in all, across the system. In January, there were 42 programs at Frances Morrison Library, 16 at Alice Turner, 21 at Carlyle King, 32 at Cliff Wright, 17 at J. S. Wood, 8 at Mayfair, and 17 at Rusty Macdonald. A busy world. Peter Eyvindson was still telling his stories, over the New Year; Public Legal Education Association (PLEA) was still presenting lectures on the law – Wills and Estates, Buying and Selling a Home, Youth Criminals Justice Act, and six more. There were many stories for children – indeed you can book a story hour at the library or have a children's librarian read at a community event. There was a writer's contest for grade seven to twelve students. There were literary events: readings by John Steffler, a Maritimes writer, and Lois Simmie, a local writer, while a video program included "Wendy Lill, Playwright in Parliament." There was a celebration of the fifth anniversary of the most recent branch, the Alice Turner Branch. A library packed with richness.

At RPL, according to @ *the Library,* for January-March, 2003, there were fewer programs per branch but a rich diet nonetheless, including six PLEA programs, information on writer-in-residence Alison Lohans (Regina was the first library in Canada to host a writer-in-residence), a series of programs across three branches, "Dogs and Cats Series" for pet owners, continuing programs on literacy including two tutoring programs. There were programs for children, like "Dragons Den" at Central and four branches at one

end, and programs for seniors at the other, like Friday afternoon programs at Glen Elm. Movies were alive and well: a fundraiser was held
for the RPL Film Theatre and a special series of matinee musicals ran
Wednesdays at the theatre (which screens independent, art, and for-
eign films four evenings a week, and offers free documentaries or specialty films on Wednesday evenings) plus a Sunday film series at
George Bothwell and three feature films at Connaught, including
Monsters Inc. and *Spiderman.*

At Sherwood Village and Sunrise there was An Evening with the
Symphony; at Albert, Beadwork for Adults on Tuesday evenings and
an afternoon Reading Circle for kids. The Dunlop Art Gallery had
three excellent shows I'd seen, "Aerial Farm Photography," Everett
Baker photography, a Myles MacDonald show from the Mendel, as
well as an "Our Town" show celebrating Regina artists as part of the
city's centennial celebrations. RPL had a year-long program to celebrate the centennial, "Urban H.U.M.M.," a storytelling project.

SPECIAL FEATURES, SASKATOON – PLEA

When I was a member of the Saskatoon Public Library (SPL) board
the most innovative program the library was involved in was PLEA
(Public Legal Education Association of Saskatchewan), which was a
partnership between the SPL, the Saskatchewan Branch of the
Canadian Bar Association, the College of Law, Legal Aid Clinics,
Law Society of Saskatchewan, and the Regina Bar Association,
according to the membership on the original 1980 PLEA board. While
the Saskatchewan Bar Association was already at work in 1977 trying
the raise money, the catalyst action was taken by Gordon Ray, adult
coordinator at SPL, when he invited participants to a founding
meeting, January 30, 1980 at the library; a steering committee was
formed at the meeting with Ray the first president, and a grant of
$65,000 from the Law Foundation of Saskatchewan already in place.
In his letter of invitation, Ray said such programs were already active
in British Columbia – the Vancouver People's Law School, the
Interior Legal Awareness Society. Ray had most recently worked in

the Cariboo Thompson Nicola Library System before coming to Saskatoon.

The first full-time director of PLEA was Peg Richeson, who had managed instructional services at the justice institute of BC. The BC Connection. The SPL housed PLEA for its first year, purchased a law library, still extant, and appointed a librarian with skills in legal librarianship. In that first year there were twenty-four PLEA classes at SPL, eight at RPL, others in Melfort. The program would spread quickly through the regions, with libraries the first hosts. *Focus,* January 1982, lists the PLEA classes in libraries for February and March: programs on taxation at Bankend, Regina, Saskatoon, Hudson Bay, Avonlea, and North Battleford; programs on wills and estates at Quill Lake, Rosthern, Silver Stream, Regina, and Saskatoon; programs of interest to women, at Willowbunch ("Women and the Law"), at Lloydminister ("Women's Rights"), at Nipawin (Matrimonial Law"); programs on "Children's Rights and Vandalism" at Glaslyn; "The Law of Day Care" at Saskatoon; "Mental Health and the Law" at Moose Jaw; "Drinking and Driving" at Nipawin; and "Dog Control" at Swift Current. Listing the topics for this one small window shows how fascinating and useful such programs would be, and how rapidly the program spread. In March of 1983 there were programs, sponsored by the Open Door Society, for Polish, Vietnamese and Laotian Canadians. PLEA was a great success. "The public response to PLEA programs has been phenomenal; new records for attendance at public legal education programs in Canada have been set."[3]

In its twenty-year "snapshot history" PLEA has written its own year-by-year history, which shows how many successes it has achieved outside the library world, though PLEA library programming continues today. Here are two snapshots of its history: In 1983, clearly a banner year, PLEA served 41,000 people in 128 communities, had created 200 programs since 1980, had a speaker's bureau of 200 volunteers, and had 79 publications in print with over 700,000 distributed, while a Provincial Legal Resource Centre, staffed by a law librarian, was established at SPL. One of the new incentives from 1986 on was a program on and in schools. A research project was undertaken to study knowledge and attitudes of grade eight students, workshops were held for school administrators to develop policies on alcohol and drug abuse, and in 1988, 35 workshops on human rights were held in schools. The PLEA newsletter became school oriented: in 1991 easy-to-read pamphlets were written (72,000 booklets and 100,000 pamphlets distributed that year in 600 locations); new booklets were produced on Youth and the Law for grades 6-12. In 1995 and 1997 PLEA began publication and workshops for Aboriginal youth. That invitation by Gordon Ray for a meeting at SPL led to an amazing success story across the province.

SPECIAL FEATURE, REGINA – FILM

RPL has had the most elaborate of any film program in the province, which can be presented in three jump cuts. The *SLA Bulletin,* April 1950, has a piece by Regina Librarian Marjorie Dunlop on the increased film programs between the declining use in 1948 and the successes by 1950, when there were weekly films at Central, a Travel Through Films series, information film evenings on nutrition and on mental health, and showings at Eastview and Albert. "People who had never seen a 16mm film, and who probably never would see any as they belonged to no club, saw them at these public showings." Over 1,600 films were loaned (225 in 1948), while the National Film Board (NFB, at the time the greatest national filmmaker in the world) doubled its deposit at RPL, and the Regina Film Council had reorganized. "The recollection of children's laughter at Eastview on seeing *Here Comes the Circus* or *Three Little Bruins Make Mischief* and the response of adults to *Atomic Energy* or *Bird Dogs* dispels any doubts on the value of film." Last summer, 2004, the public response to Michael Moore's *Fahrenheit 911* was as gratifying as the expressions of delight in 1950.

Cut to 1977 when Gary Deane, audio-visual coordinator, and Regina's foremost film fanatic (I went to a number of weekend screenings with Gary, he for the RPL, a number of us for the University Film Society) was complaining to the Museum of Natural

History because it cancelled a Contemporary European Film Festival at the last moment, and for spurious reasons: concern that it might compete with commercial cinemas (an unwarranted concern, according to Deane, as cinemas always had first choice of films), and that it might exclude part of the public (what doesn't?). Deane's own early programs are appended to his letter. They have nothing in common with the 1950 films. Series one, 1974, offering fourteen Canadian films, didn't do well. Next a Contemporary European Film Series, 1975, was a success with two films selling out (140 seats). A second European Film Series was less successful. Then the library tried longer runs of single films. Michel Brault's *Les Orders* (it was on arrests made during The War Measures Act), ran at a loss, recouped by Bergman's *Scenes From a Marriage,* while John Cassavetes' *Woman Under the Influence* broke even. We are now in the world of alternate cinema, featured in Saskatoon's Broadway Theatre and in RPL's popular film program, both helping people escape mainstream American stories.

Cut three, and 140 films screened a year at RPL, as good as any repertory cinema in Canada.

Chapter Fifteen

Saskatchewan Library Association
1914-1994

HERE WERE TWO ITERATIONS OF THE SASKATCHEWAN
Library Association (SLA), the first between 1914 and 1916,
the second beginning in 1942 and remaining active today.

The first SLA meeting took place in Moose Jaw, April 13,
1914, with seventeen delegates, representing Moose Jaw, North
Battleford, Prince Albert, Regina (four delegates), Saskatoon (five
delegates), and Weyburn. The meeting adopted a constitution,
whose objects were:

> To promote the welfare of libraries, by stimulating public
> interest in founding and improving them, by securing any
> needed legislation, by furthering such co-operative work as
> shall improve results or reduce expenses, by exchanging views
> and making recommendations in convention or otherwise,
> and by advancing the common interests of libraries, mem-
> bers of boards, of management and others engaged in library
> and allied educational work.[1]

There were two resolutions on providing rural communities with
libraries, including ways to combine public and school libraries. The

first chair was A.W. Cameron, a teacher at Saskatoon's Collegiate Institute (later Nutana), who had been an officer of the Ontario Association, and who would for many years be a trustee on SPL. Regina Librarian J.C. Honeyman, clearly a moving spirit behind the organization, became secretary-treasurer.

There was a second meeting in Yorkton in 1915, with eleven people in attendance; that meeting passed a motion asking the minister of education to circulate materials on libraries so free public libraries would be available in all towns. Then the organization dwindled to the precious few, only four of five members present at the last meeting of the organization in Prince Albert in 1916.

The remaining materials in the SLA file are letters from Honeyman, mostly to Moose Jaw Librarian A. H. Gibbard, who had become SLA president. Clearly Honeyman was frustrated. In a January 19, 1917, letter to Education Minister W. M. Martin, minister of education, one of his frustrations is clear, that no public report on the travelling libraries had been made and that no provincial librarian, a position provided for in the 1913 Act (little different from the 1906 act), had been appointed. Legislative Librarian John Hawkes replied to the minister on that letter. Honeyman's letter also detailed Ontario's legislation and practice as a model, said that the Saskatchewan SLA needed public assistance because it was "hampered by lack of funds." By January 24, 1917, Honeyman wrote Gibbard, "So far as diplomacy is concerned, I am sick of the whole business." The association met with Martin in the summer of 1918 but no changes had been made. Perhaps the SLA was unaware of the government's stringent financing in the war years, which made library funding highly unlikely. The organization was unfortunate in its year of beginning, just before war broke out in Europe. Had the organization begun after the war it might have survived.

SASKATCHEWAN LIBRARY ASSOCIATION (2)

"I have great hopes that in the near future there'll be satisfactory news for you about the formation of a Saskatchewan Library Association,"[2] wrote J.S. Wood April 13, 1942. Two weeks later the

SLA was reborn. It was Wood, Saskatoon's librarian, who wrote the early history of the SLA. The organization met first April 27, 1942 in Regina, with nineteen members present, sixteen of whom were women. A Regina Library Association had been formed earlier, in 1941, with Regina Librarian Dr. Lingard as president. A Saskatoon branch of the SLA was formed in October of 1942. Much of the early work concerned the national body, the Canadian Library Council (CLC), and its constitution, to which Saskatchewan made a full response. Its first representative on the CLC was John Lothian of the English Department of the University of Saskatchewan.

The key early document was that SLA brief to the Saskatchewan Reconstruction Council, 1944, the best document on the terrible library conditions before the hiring of Marion Gilroy and the beginning of the regions. The recommendations of the SLA brief appeared in the Reconstruction Council Report, the first public document that supported radical change in library service. The brief was widely distributed and appeared in the *Ontario Library Review*. The annual meeting of 1946 celebrated the CCF government's new programs. Wood, as chairman, said, "Prior to the present government, the Association, never powerful, received no co-operation or support." As well, "There has been a pouring of money into the government libraries which hitherto had been in great need." Carlyle King explained the new SLAC he chaired; Miss Brandon the Travelling Libraries, with a box on display; Miss MacKay the Open Shelf Library. Education Minister Woodrow Lloyd was guest speaker. The minutes, taken by librarian Ruth Murray, are quite detailed and useful. Wood made one amusing comment: "So a great many adults looked upon a library as a respectable edifice no community should be without so long as no one went into it."[3]

By 1950, when there were thirty-nine members plus two library boards, the committee structure was elaborate. There was a Library Legislation Committee (King, chair), a Bio-Bibliographical Project (archivist Lewis Thomas, chair), a Membership Committee, a Publicity Committee (with thanks to Violet McNaughton, with Mary Donaldson chair, Marion Gilroy a member), a Personnel Committee (Regina librarian Marjorie Dunlop, chair), a Booklist

Committee, which asked its members to create ten booklists, all literary, a Radio Committee (Ruth Murray and Lyle Evans chairs, programs in concert with the Saskatchewan Arts Board, and including a series of reviews, "All about books"). An amazing committee structure for an organization with so few members. The Personnel Committee presented information on library salaries, all of which had gone up during the year. A librarian with a BA and a BLS started at $1,920 to $2,076 per annum and rose to a maximum of $2,280 to $2,529. The teacher librarians did better. Two libraries were unionized. Benefits included three weeks of holidays and pension plans in five of six reporting libraries. The work week was from 35½ to 39 hours. There had been a modest increase in the number of trained librarians in the province. Four years later, according to the Annual

SLA Tea at Mrs. R.J. Brandon's, early 1950s when she was president. *From left to right:* Lyle Evans, Teacher's College; Betty Carnie, RPL; Eileen Healy, RPL; Mabel Littlejohn, RPL; Marjorie William, RPL; Adrienne Llewellyn, RPL; Mary Young, RPL; Mrs. R.J. Brandon, Travelling Library; Christine MacDonald, Legislative Library. *Seated,* Mary Donaldson, Provincial Library.

Report, professional librarians began between $2,500 and $3,300, rising to $3,468 at the Provincial Library; with higher rates at the Regina Collegiate Board, from $3,150 to $5,300. CLA recommended rates for 1953 ranged from $3,000 to $4,300 for the BA, BLS graduate.

The following year there was a Film Committee (chair Mable Littlejohn of SPL); a Library Course Committee, which couldn't recommend a library program in Saskatchewan; and an Archives Committee (chair Emma Bell), a committee crucial for this book. In 1951, Bell planned to cull and preserve letters between the SLA and CLC (and CLA) of significance. The following year she listed her categories of organization. In 1953 the committee on films reported on a new Northern Saskatchewan Federation of Film Councils, whose object was to operate a film pool for members. There were film festivals in Regina and Yorkton while the Saskatoon Film Council was planning a British Commonwealth film festival. Regina and Saskatoon libraries lent 4,772 films during the year, not counting the NFB or the Saskatchewan Film Board. Year after year films were part of annual reports in the cities and sometimes in the regions.

By 1953, a number of SLA members held important position in the CLA: Gilroy was past-president; Frances Morrison of SPL, chair of the Inter-Library Liaison Committee; Grace Crooks of Prince Albert, chair of Young Canada's Book Week; while the following year John Archer was a member of the CLA Council; Muriel Clancy of SPL president of the Children's Section; Lyle Evans president of the Young People's Section; Mrs. J.B. Harrington, president and Mr. Singleton, secretary of the Trustees Section; King, chair of the Library Legislation Committee.[4] There was another excellent brief from the SLA with Betty Davis as chair, presented to the Royal Commission of Agriculture and Rural Life. It said rural people were discriminated against in library service, the solution being regional libraries. The report included a breakdown of provincial government expenditures on the basis of $100 – education getting $18.16, highways $10.79, agriculture $4.01, libraries $.14 or ½ of a penny. Enough said.

There was a coming of age of the CLA in 1955 when Saskatoon hosted the annual CLA meeting as part of the province's Golden Jubilee.

An SLA brief, presented to minister Ed Tchorzewski in 1975, is a good cross-section of library interests that year, praising the completed regional library system but reporting that rural service was still inadequate, "often in crowded or shabby buildings, operated by a dedicated staff who receive only minimal training, due to budget restrictions" (p. 3). The level of service in the regions was a quarter of the service in Saskatoon and Regina. There wasn't enough professional staff (a perennial problem), while the new community colleges had shown the weaknesses in both regional and Provincial Library collections. The brief asked that both standards and compulsory legislation (the perennial demand) be legislated; that grants be increased to regions and cities (the perennial request); that 16mm film service be centralized under the public library system; that government documents be catalogued and a distribution set up at the Provincial Library; that services in languages other than in English (and including audio-visual materials) be increased. The brief also urged the government to consider contributing to the Library School at the University of Alberta as a way to guarantee spots for Saskatchewan students. As well, the SLA had its own agenda, asking for funding so it could implement its programs: a catalogue of Saskatchewan publications, the annual conference, its magazine *Saskatchewan Library*, and the one-year-old Saskatchewan Library Week.[5]

Saskatchewan Library Week began in 1974 when the SLA replaced in the province a program the CLA could no longer afford, the nation-wide program called Young Canada's Book Week (a year-by-year account of that program in Saskatoon was made by children's librarian Muriel Clancy in the SPL annual reports, beginning in 1949). That year librarians in Saskatchewan formed a committee to find a provincial replacement. Under chair Pat Cuts the first Saskatchewan Library Week (SLW) was celebrated in March 1975, with former Prime Minister John Diefenbaker as patron. Feedback included all the stories about the event in newspapers across the province. In later years radio and TV spots would be added. In one response that week, a boy in Palliser asked, "Why aren't there more acres to a square mile on rolling land rather than flat land?" There was a mixed response to the inaugural year but the Saskatchewan

Library Week was a go, the week proclaimed that first year by Premier Allan Blakeney. In the next two years Karen Labuik was chair, author Max Braithwaite and folklorist Edith Fowke patrons. In the Provincial Library *Focus* for February 1977 Fowke spoke of library service when she was young:

> When I was a girl growing up in the small town of Lumsden, I was starved for books. I read all the books my parents owned and all I could borrow from neighbours. There was no library in Lumsden...but I used to go into Regina with father and come back loaded with books I borrowed from the Regina Public Library.

Look how much luckier children are today, she suggested, with regional libraries.

The other reading week in Saskatchewan was initiated by children's librarians talking to Bill Johnson of the Provincial Library who made a button and some notes, inherited by Wenda McArthur when she became the first children's librarian at the Provincial Library in 1977. The week was launched the next summer, became a success by 1978, a partnership between the Provincial Library and regions, until, in a money crunch, the program was dropped. Fortunately, the credit union came to the rescue. Campaigns included Read for the Stars (image a rocket and night skies), Sea Deep in Books (sea horses, etc.), Go For Books (gopher logo).

In 1977 the SLA was involved in the Max Braithwaite book on the Wapiti region. Publisher J. J. Douglas wanted $12,000 to publish it. Ken Jensen said $6,000 was more realistic for 1,000 paperbacks. They'd approached the Provincial Library to buy copies to distribute to regional branches ($2,500), had secured $1,500 from the SLA, had passed a motion requesting SLTA contribute $1,500, and had received $2,000 from Wapiti itself.[6]

Finally, there was a cross-section of SLA at work in 1993 and 1994, according to SLA *Forum,* for June 1993 and April 1994, Bryan Foran serving as chair both years. In the second year, new chair Maureen Woods became provincial librarian and Foran stepped back in. There were fifteen active committees, with one amalgamation – the Children's Library Services Section and the Young Adult Caucus merged. The organization was especially active because of support by Sask Trust, which provided 71% of the funding by 1993 (5.8% from memberships, 8% from programs, with the major expense programs at 61%). Two major publications from the fiftieth anniversary of the SLA in 1992 appeared in 1993, a collection of the Mary Donaldson lectures, *Survival of the Imagination,* edited by Brett Balon and Peter Resch, and the following year the *Saskatchewan Bibliography, First Supplement, 1979-1993.* Special programs included an Aboriginal Services Conference in the fall of 1992 (with special funding from Sask Trust), and participation in the first annual Saskatchewan Book Awards, which SLA helped to found. The archives committee remained active thanks to Frances Morrison and Alice Turner McFarland of SPL. The organization was pressing for the appointment of the Multitype Library Board (see chapter 18). Of the presentations at a forum on one-person libraries, that by Wendy Rounce of Carlyle Branch felt especially real. "My only real training for this job is a love of reading and an enjoyment of working with the public, accompanied by on-the-spot training," she said. She read books she wouldn't ordinarily, to learn what was on the shelves. "I have to be a publicist, a long-range planner, a repair person, and a book binder." She had to use a coat hanger to get a patron's keys out of a locked car. That's service. Patrons sometimes browsed through books waiting for the bus or taking a rest on the way home. Teens after school and board members offered volunteer help, while she contributed about 25% volunteer time beyond her paid hours. The one-person library, all over the province.[7] The SLA, all over the province, the central forum for library service in Saskatchewan.

Chapter Sixteen

The Saskatchewan Library Trustees Association 1965-2003

HE BIRTH OF THE SASKATCHEWAN LIBRARY TRUSTEES
Association (SLTA), the sponsor of this book, was a four-year
process, begun in 1965, when Rusty Macdonald agreed to
seek reactions from library boards. In 1966 a pro tem board
was followed a year later by the establishment of SLTA, J. S. Porter,
Weyburn, as chairman, George Bothwell, Regina, as vice-chairman.

In 1968 trustees were invited to attend the next SLA meeting (SLTA
began as a part of SLA). A year later, on September 13, at the Regina
Public Library, the first executive met, Porter and Bothwell in their
posts and representatives from the cities in all regions present; three
regions had yet to be formed but there were trustee boards in the
cities of Moose Jaw, North Battleford, and Swift Current.[1] The SLTA
story will be told in a special way, through a selection of their briefs
to the provincial cabinet, and which form a kind of summary to this
book because the briefs draw together so many of the library concerns.

The first SLTA submission was on November 3, 1969. The document praises the Library Inquiry Committee plan, "probably the
most practical in Canada," (p. 2). The Provincial Library is the keystone for the on library system but reduced funding had meant

sharply reduced cataloguing service, so other libraries had to absorb the cost (not for the last time, including as late as 2003). The submission made the kind of money points that would be made year after year, more money needed by the cities (20 cents per capita), which offer services to the regions. Three regions had met their population quotas but weren't funded. There were problems within regions. "The North Central Regional Library, after twenty years of existence as the pioneer region, would be able to struggle on one more year at present levels of support but if no increase in the grant structure was forthcoming it would then fail.... Local support in rural areas has reached its limit" (p. 6). As well, "In the past three years the cost of books and librarian salaries has increased 30% without corresponding increases in government support from the $1.00 per capita" (p. 10). The trustee's submission asked for $1.25. Graphs in an appendix show the rise in the cost of books, as well as costs at the Provincial Library ($45,000 would restore levels to 1968 levels) and a table on increased needs for the whole system ($220,000).

By 1972 it was clear increases had been granted by government (40 cents per capita to the cities, $1.50 establishment grants and $1.30 operating grants for regions, and good funding for the Provincial Library). Now the trustees wanted considerably more, including an incentive plan to encourage RMs to join regional libraries; a proposal to compensate regions for bookmobile service; a survey of grants, boundaries, service, standards – by the SLTA and the Saskatchewan Library Development Board (SLDB). They also requested that the provincial librarian create a cost-of-library service index (something never undertaken).

The SLTA now had one hundred members and its objects were to promote and foster libraries, to provide for the exchange of ideas among trustees, to assist trustees to learn their responsibilities, to seek necessary changes in library legislation, and to co-operate closely with the SLA.

Why should grants increase? In 1956, books cost an average of $5.29 compared to $13.25 in 1972 (according to *Publisher's Weekly*). Levies had risen a great deal in some regions, North Central up by 85% from 1959 to 1971. There was a third problem: "Library service is extended to communities which lacked such services; *but* this service is given at the expense of established libraries [which] find their service deteriorate" (p. 8). There were appendices, from North Central and Lakeland, on such prohibitive costs. There was also a telling image, "what we are trying to do here is to work five sections of land with the same old team we used to break the homestead quarter!" (p. 10). A table showed how many RMs were in regions, 147, and how many were out, 120.

By the 1973 brief SLTA and SLDB had conducted their survey, with a 70% return rate. There was a recommendation for compulsory legislation once a region reached 70% of its total population. A new grant formula was proposed to replace the original per capita grant. The new formula consisted of two parts, fixed costs for all regions (and tied to Canadian price indexes), and equalization grants, based on geography, population, assessment. There were good appendices, the first showing how the 1974 increase in grants was used. Palliser used its $41,000 to retire its deficit. Regina spent 100% on materials, Saskatoon 67% on staff, North Central, Parkland and Lakeland a majority on materials. The second table was on population and

Library Display: hundreds of delegates to the annual conference of SARM visited the Saskatchewan Library display on library services in the province. Shown above are George Bothwell of Regina and Don Burton of Springwater manning the display.

assessment, with a column on assessment per acre, highest in Southeast, Parkland and Wheatland, lowest in Chinook and Lakeland. The third table was a Consumer Price Index, showing increases every year since the 1961 base of $100, with greater increases after 1968 and huge jumps between 1972 and 1973, and 1973 and 1974, up 12% in that year. Pity the three new library regions born into such economic times. The growing pains and resistance of the cities must have been partly a result of such money pressures.

That year the SLTA had a membership of five hundred and Saskatchewan "was the only province in Canada with an autonomous trustee organization" (p. 1).

In 1976 there were two presentations by SLTA, first a brief with four principles for regions: that a standard materials budget be set of at least 17.5% of total operating budget (regions did indeed use that figure as a measure of how well they were doing); that more trained librarians be hired (in the regions 21 professional librarians served 549,000 people, for a ratio of 1 to 25,000 people, while in Regina and Saskatoon the ratio was 1 to about 7,000); that mandatory legislation be introduced; that the capital grant, which "is credited with improved Branch library facilities" (p. 10), be increased; that the new grant structure be fine-tuned. Information on the effects of new grant formula was given in an Exhibit. Every region received a basic $200,000 grant; there were minor differences in a smaller grant based on distribution, except Palliser which was 20% below the others; there were major differences in equalization grants, from $123,000 to Wapiti, with the largest participating population, to $30,000 to Lakeland which had the lowest population; geographical grants benefited Wheatland and Wapiti most, Palliser again least by far. Yet per capita equivalents favoured Lakeland, while Chinook and Palliser also did well. It was a complex matter, and it wasn't clear who the winners were. A later presentation (in 1978) included this passage: "regions with larger participating population support the premise that more weight should be given to population when grants to the libraries are processed. Regions with smaller populations do not support that proposal, because a small reduction or shift in population adversely affects their incomes."

The second brief, the Guidelines document, January 14, 1976, was primarily about money, with this new information: that telex increased ILLO (which had been increasing by 30% a year) and that 16 mm films cost between $200 to $450 each. Exhibit 1 showed the government grants for 1974, and suggested that where the ratio of government grants was highest (Chinook, Southeast), municipal levies should be increased, and where it was lowest (Palliser), government grants should be increased. A second table showed that the government grants between 1971 (four regions) and 1974 (seven regions) increased from $740,000 to $2,153,000, while as a percent of total library expenditure, government grants had risen from 58% of the total to 70%, showing the remarkable generosity by the Blakeney government, though inflation ate at some of the increase.

Frances Morrison told me that Saskatoon and Regina had foregone grant increases so the regions could form, and not for the first or last time in their briefs, SLTA agrees: "Regina and Saskatoon municipal libraries also waited many years for increased provincial support, believing that the establishment of all regions had priority over their own increase" (p. 14).

In the 1978 SLTA brief on public participation, Exhibit II shows how participation had increased, with 125 towns (five outside regions), 263 villages (53 outside regions), 260 RMs (39 outside regions), 29 Indian bands (40 outside regions), for a total participation of 91%, Chinook leading all the rest at 98%, Lakeland lowest at 87%.

A brief two years later, January, 1980, was important for two reasons. It was the first that included recommendations on automation (they were catching up with what was already occurring). It took its background information from *Feliciter,* the CLA magazine. The brief recommended government financial aid to installing automation in the library system. It also presented a new grant structure, created by a Grant Study Committee, and prefaced with recommendations on universal participation, on the uniform presenting of statistics, and on a three-year planning process. The heart of the matter was the 30/70 proposal, 30% for cities, 70% for regions from government grants, with caps ($8.00 per capita for cities, $12.00 per capita for regions, but some regions would have to bring their levies up to the 30% levels). It was a simple and expensive formula, not finally to be accepted by government.

The 1981 brief, including the same grant proposal, had a condensed history of grants (pp. 5-11). The per capita system had been changed in 1974. "The problem with the current formula...is that it provides no incentive to substantially improve the level of local support" (p. 7). By 1987, the government would discover harsh means to make that happen: reduce provincial funding by 10% and never catch up again. The rational world of the Blakeney government would soon disappear. A table for 1980 shows Regina contributing 91% of its own funding, Saskatoon 89%; then Wapiti at 46.8% and Palliser at 45% were the only regions to pay considerable levies but they contained major cities, Prince Albert and Moose Jaw. Wheatland was always most dependent on government, raising only 20% from local levies. Funding per capita ranged from $22.30 in Regina to $1.32 in Wheatland.

In 1982 the SLTA was disappointed that "even after the reconciling work of the Library Automation Committee, very little progress has been made in automating the provincial library system" (p. 5). The trustees also responded in detail to proposals made by the Committee to Review Library Legislation.

The 1990 brief, the twentieth annual brief to cabinet, offered resolutions on automation, with grants sufficient to automate with Dynix, on school and public libraries – not compatible. There was a third resolution on emphasizing literacy work (A report entitled *Literary Learning in Saskatchewan,* concluded that 42% of all learners were enrolled at READ Saskatoon and at RPL; 10% in SIAST programs, 48% in regional college programs). As usual in all its briefs, SLTA explained the function and importance of trustees (all 2,200 of them now).

There was an especially strong brief from Palliser in 1992 explaining the harsh results of poor provincial funding for 10 years, 1983-92, from $509,976 in 1983 to $509,500 in 1992. In 1983 dollars that meant a decline to $315,000, a loss that is "having a disastrous impact on library service" (p. 3). The region purchased fewer books each year until books withdrawn exceeded books purchased. "Since the devastating cut in Provincial Grants in 1987, the staffing and hours of opening have been reduced" (p. 4), including a 10% cut at headquarters. The 5% cut in 1992 would result in the whole system closing for two weeks. Nor could regional libraries match increases to provincial government employees: settlements in 1986, 0%; in 1987, 0%; in 1988, 1.5%; in 1989, 2.5%; in 1990, 3%; in 1991, 0%. The offloading of financing to local boards was being paid for by workers as well as patrons. The Provincial Library had been cut sharply too, to eleven fewer staff members than in 1983, which meant delays in ILLO and cataloguing (Palliser and other regions still received help on automation and programs like the Summer Reading Program and Saskatchewan Library Week). The cities too were in trouble, with a 30% cut in 1987 and a 25% cut in 1992, so they had reduced resource centre purchases. Conclusion: "We can no longer boast that Saskatchewan has the best library system" (p. 6). Nor could the system implement its new vision, "Independent but together," because there wasn't enough money.

A February 1993 SLTA brief expanded on the effects of the 1992 cuts. Bookmobile service was reduced in Chinook, Lakeland, and Parkland, and was closed entirely in Southeast. Chinook cancelled paperbacks by mail; Lakeland reduced the book budget by 5%; Palliser slashed the materials budget and closed for two weeks. Parkland left two headquarters positions vacant and cut the materials budget; Southeast closed three branches and three positions at head-quarters; Wheatland reduced block exchanges and cut delivery serv-ices to senior citizens homes; Wapiti cut hours of service; Pahkisimon had a zero increase, no cuts, no new services; Regina closed all branches Sundays in summer and increased fees to non-residents, as did Saskatoon, which also cut hours of service and increased fines (cuts expanded on in a 1992 document in SLTA, Saskatchewan Archives Board). You'd need a heart of stone not to respond to those needs. The government, faced with deficits, succeeded in developing such a heart of stone.

There's a 1994 brief to SaskTel from the SLTA, the Provincial Library, and the Province-Wide Library Electronic Information

System Committee (you can see the usefulness of acronyms), which spoke of all libraries as a unit – public libraries, special libraries, academic libraries, school libraries, all those which would make up the Multitype Library System, "a network of working relationships, between any combination of libraries and information providers established to share resources for mutual benefit"(p. 5). The basic requirement for a multitype system to work was an electronic network linking all libraries in the province. The situation in 1994 was automated catalogues in Regina and Saskatoon, in the two university libraries, in many special libraries, and in some regions – Palliser and Southeast the leaders. All public libraries (other than Saskatoon, Wheatland, and Chinook) were using or about to use Dynix Automated Library System. (Chinook would later shift to Dynix.) The object was a virtual union catalogue (virtual as a new word for machine readable), to be available in a seamless way for libraries and home computers (for home computers now say "individual access"). The virtue of virtual reality was the public right to free and quality information (quality control was a new function for librarians), and the provision of equitable access to information in remote and rural communities. Computers were the great equalizer – and for many the great mystifiers – so libraries assumed a new duty: offering programs to help people become comfortable with the new world. (My favourite comic image of the world comes from *Rocky and Bullwinkle* when Moose gets caught in a very dangerous information highway.) In 1994 there was good news for rural users of the information highway. "SLTA welcomes the October 14 announcement that SaskTel will offer a ramp to the highway"(p. 4).

The 1996 brief has a ministerial response attached to the minutes, by Carol Teichrob, a responsive minister caught with a no-budget increase. One issue was SaskTel service to rural libraries. The SLTA brief says a subscriber "in Swift Current, at the standard rate, could access the net for 25 hours at a cost of $19.95 per month plus $15.00. A subscriber in Prelate would pay $19.95 plus $130.00. This is $115.00 over and above the Swift Current rate" (p. 7). Response: "Watch for an announcement very soon from SaskTel." But the introduction of long distance competition would make subsidizing local services more difficult. As well, the important Canada-Saskatchewan Infrastructure Works Program had provided funds to the Provincial Library to make matching grants for PLEIS and the ten public library systems – $560,000 over three years. The importance of cities to remain part of the one-library system was recognized with an increased grant pool of $170,000, Saskatoon the major beneficiary because it had more bedroom communities.

The 1997 brief thanks the government for legislating mandatory participation in the 1996 Library Act, praises its involvement in PLEIS and its support of a one-province rate schedule for the net. The Review of Regional Libraries Committee proposed five levels of service, equitable access to information and library service and a new funding formula. Negatively, the Provincial Library service levels had dropped – no central reference service, reduced cataloguing support, disbanding of key collections (non-fiction large print books, talking books) – "the public library system must either refuse to deliver these services to the general public or they must absorb the functions into their home operations"(p. 4) with no additional funding.

By 2002 Community Net had been extended to libraries, 298 of which had received computers and internet service by 2000. A successful program funded by the provincial Information Technology taught computer literacy to Aboriginal and low-income people. Palliser and Southeast combined to deliver training sessions in rural libraries. Saskatoon developed a CD-ROM as a step-by-step interactive training. Pahkisimon translated the Saskatoon models into Cree and Dene. "The pilot projects are unique in the Canadian context and have attracted international attention," said Provincial Librarian Joylene Campbell as part of her response to the SLTA Brief. There had been a decline in population in all regions, Wheatland and Parkland most seriously affected.

Where do things stand in 2003? Automation (an old '70s and '80s word), now called E-Library, is a central issue and a great accomplishment, with the help of Gateway in 2001 (one electronic search from anywhere in Saskatchewan) and Community Net, 2002, with greatly increased line speeds. Costs for these services are rising (life of a computer estimated at three years). As government puts more and more services online can they be downloaded at libraries? Won't that mean more computer terminals? As well, only 162 libraries, about half, are connected to the Community Net so there is still a digital divide.

There remain needs for capital funding for aging buildings, for more professional librarians because so many are about to retire and there is a national shortage. The three-year phase-in of the new funding formula resulted in some losses, but the situation was somewhat ameliorated by the 3% increase to libraries in 2003-04, and municipal grant increases of 50 to 60% over the past decade. There is still the hope, expressed for many years, of a universal library card, but it does cost money – hardware and software upgrades, the cost of returning books to home libraries, plus the need for policies on borrowing status, privacy, exchange of user data – no easy matter.

The final issue is an important one, praise for the Minister's Advisory Committee on Aboriginal People and for the $250,000 grant to assist libraries responding to the goals of the document.

Chapter Seventeen

Indian and Aboriginal Libraries
1967 to 2005

By 1967 THE FEDERAL INDIAN AFFAIRS BRANCH, responding to requests from First Nations communities across the country, established a program to assist bands to gain library service from provincial public libraries. The band had to pay 10 cents per capita and could receive from Indian Affairs $1.00 per capita.[1] A document a year later, June 20, 1968, gave increased information on libraries and said bands could now join regional libraries. The band would run the library, through a committee and with a band member as librarian. The library could be housed on the reserve or a library in a neighbouring community could be used.

In Saskatchewan the Provincial Library and other libraries made initiatives to hire Indian or Metis personnel, permanently or for the summer. This early attempt to train Aboriginal librarians met with mixed success. The Provincial Library hired and trained some excellent people, according to Provincial Librarian Harry Newsom, but "all of them have disappeared suddenly without explanation."[2] A list of Indian Affairs teachers for 1968 shows very few Indian or Metis names. By December 18, 1968, fifteen bands had joined regional library service. Saskatchewan's claim to have the first band join a library region was false, according to Edith Adamson, library consultant with the Department of Indian Affairs and Northern Development, since there were nine bands in the regional system in Ontario by then, while others were active in the Maritimes and Quebec.[3] By 1969, four bands had joined Southeast, three North Central, two Parkland, with five more bands likely to join in 1969-70. That was a small proportion of the reserves, 28 in North West, 15 in North Central, 10 in Southeastern, 13 in Parkland, plus reserves in the North. By 1971, 17 bands were in regions, for a total of 8,436 people, 19 bands, by 1973.

In January, 1969, David Sparvier, the Provincial Library's librarian on Aboriginal matters, wrote a report on "Library Service to Indian Bands in the Broadview and Grenfell Areas."[4] He came to a number of conclusions. "The Branch Libraries at Broadview, Grenfell and Whitewood are too far from Indian communities and most Indians lack transport to use the branch libraries." There was little material of interest to them. Nor were there reading rooms for people who lived far from the branch. There was a particular injustice because everyone in Southeast paid 75 cents per capita "except for the Indians, they pay $1.50 per capita" (up from the original Indian Affairs grant of $1.00). They didn't get increased services, "but access to a library service that [was] almost useless and irrelevant to the majority of Indians in the area." First Nation people wanted periodicals or magazines published by First Nation organizations. As well, "when a book is lost the librarian makes the chief or councillor feel that their children have defrauded the white taxpayer." He concluded that he expected the bands in Southeast would withdraw within the year. They didn't.

People in Southeast were angry. Board chair Jim Porter said they were doing their best, and, in a letter to the provincial librarian he looked forward to "a meeting with you, with federal persons, with band library people and with the Indian people."[5] When Porter asked for "qualified and understanding people" he may have been implying dissatisfaction with Sparvier. There was a second response to Sparvier's report, without date or author, but two people visited Cowessess, Khkewistehaw, and Ochapowace. Sparvier had talked with the last two boards but not the first. Cowessess had a trustee attend local board meetings and the band valued their children's use of the library. All three communities said they'd like bookmobile service at their community centres, would like "books and materials on beadwork and Indian handicrafts, and books that tell the truth about Indian culture and how the whites took their land." They suggested two periodicals, the *Saskatchewan Indian* (Federation of Saskatchewan Indians) and *Tawow*. The final conclusion – bookmobile service was needed.

At the Provincial Library Sparvier expanded the Native Collection to 600 titles (in a collection of 1,500 volumes), and it was especially well-used in La Ronge. By 1972, Sparvier had left his position to join the Federation of Saskatchewan Indians Cultural College (FSICC) in Saskatoon.

A preliminary report on "Regional Library Service in Indian Bands" accepted the regional system and wanted to make it more responsive. "The experience of librarians in providing library service to Indians is as limited as the Indians' experience of using libraries" (p. 1). Again, "The library needs to be fitted into the Indian's background culture and way of life by providing books, periodicals, reports and studies published by Indians, Indian Bands, Indian Affairs, Indian associations, and other such organizations" (pp. 3-4). Only by providing information of interest to Aboriginal people would library services attract them, the report says. It recommended that branch libraries on reserves or bookmobile service should be provided. The chief should not "be approached every time a band member is delinquent [not returning a book]. You don't approach a Mayor when a member of his town loses a book, do you?" (p. 6). Outdated books or tourist brochures should not be sent to bands. Finally, the report concluded, the federal grant "belongs to the Band, not the region. The Band is free to choose the type of information service on which it will spend its library grant" (p. 8). I expect, from regional tariffs at the end of the paper, that this preliminary report dates from 1971 or 1972; it's the earliest general paper I've found on service to Indian bands.

In 1976 a major document by Sparvier, now administrator of the FSICC, and John Rafter of the Provincial Library, "Survey/ Investigation of Library Services to Indian People in the Province of Saskatchewan" (31 pages), began by responding to a request by the Federation of Saskatchewan Indians (FSI) to Provincial Librarian Don Meadows for a survey on library services afforded to Indian people. The document had seven recommendations, of which the central one was number six, to establish a regional library "for Indian people under the direction and control of the Federation of Saskatchewan Indians" (p. 7). Other recommendations emphasize the central role of the FSICC; library training for people at the reserve level, through FSICC, regional headquarters and the Provincial Library. The report recommended that the FSI appoint area coordinators and be given responsibility for all the residents of northern Saskatchewan (a controversial proposal). Bands should select delegates to regional board meetings "to protect" (p.5) the rights of Indian people.

That document led to a second one, a Budget Submission for the Indian Federation's Regional Library and Resource Centre, submitted June, 1970 by the FSICC.[6] Sparvier created the budget, after a meeting with Rafter and Turnbull of the Provincial Library, based on the assumption of thirty new branches. The budget was presented in detail, putting the cost of the system at $1,667,493, of which the province was to provide $582,836 (at $8.00 per capita plus other grants), and the Department of Indian Affairs and Northern Development a similar amount. "This is what Saskatchewan Indians contributed to Saskatchewan and Canadian economics in 1974."[7]

One group, the SLDB, passed a motion of support. "The Development Board unanimously endorsed, in principle, the Federation of Saskatchewan Indians' proposal and we look forward to working closely with you in the eventual approach." (p. 2) Other responses were not so positive. Indian Affairs official J.D. Leask said there was no money available, and detailed discussions were needed to add a budget item. A telephone call by Rafter to Jim Freeman, also of Indian Affairs, was received with a "My God." Rafter suggested that implementation of some recommendations would take five years, "after priorities have been decided upon, while the province might make a maximum grant of $2.30 per capita (or $100,000, not the $500,000-plus suggested in the Survey/Investigation)."[8] Indian Affairs recommended the exploration of alternate means of attaining the objectives, all within the current system (training Indian librarians, better book lists).

When the FSI held a meeting November 1, 1976, with Cabinet, they had eleven issues to discuss, including land settlement, special RCMP constables on reserves, and a regional library. The summary for premier and Cabinet, November 3, 1976, included Tchorzewski's statement: "With respect to the [Indian] Regional Libraries...there is a Provincial Library network now in existence... [the] government [has] to be careful about duplication of services." It also had to determine the federal commitment to libraries before it could act.[9] Meadows wrote a status report November 10, 1976, saying the original report had been accepted in principal by SLDB and by regional directors. At an April 12, 1976 meeting it was agreed that the cultural college would create a five-year implementation proposal, with a clear narrative outlining how a delivery system to Indian people would work. It was to be a complementary service which had no duplication of services (in effect a rejection of the original financial proposal). There must be strong financial support from Indian Affairs. Then nothing happened. The Provincial Library tried to contact college staff to assist with shaping a system. No response. There was a budget submitted by FSICC to the federal department which the Provincial Library received after much difficulty. That document "lacked well-defined program planning in many areas," six of them listed. In late October Cultural College staff were told the budget did not reflect the joint "Survey/ Investigation".[10] A new budget was requested. That's the last word I've found in archives.

What happened next, though, was the creation of the northern library, already recounted in Chapter Thirteen.

ALBERT BRANCH, REGINA

The Albert Branch Library in Regina is the first urban branch in the province to concentrate on providing service to Aboriginal people, who make up about 40% of the people in the North Central area of Regina and 90% of Albert's library patrons." This account is based on an interview with Wendy Sinclair September 17, 2003, and her thirteen-page single-spaced article "Improving & Delivering Effective Library Service for Aboriginal Peoples in Saskatchewan, 2002."

In 1979, RPL was planning to cut hours at Albert. Maureen Woods, then working in the Regina system, moved from Connaught branch to Albert branch. Meetings were held between RPL and the North Central Community Society, which had protested the cutback. The meetings led to a formal agreement between the community society and the RPL, establishing for the community an advisory role in staffing, in programming, in collection – and in fundraising. The library committee meets ten times a year.

Wendy Sinclair, currently the librarian at Albert, began library work in a four-week summer placement at Connaught. She applied for and got a job on a book trailer and worked her way up, was a library assistant at Albert under Woods, whom she replaced as branch head twelve years ago.

There's been a distance to come for the branch. When Sinclair did a puppet show at Albert School for 80 or 90 students, with some Aboriginal content, "There was a sea of brown faces. I asked how many were Aboriginal and only two or three put up their hands." They were ashamed.

The branch increased Aboriginal programming, including Aboriginal art on the wall from students of the Saskatchewan Indian Federated College's Indian Fine Arts Department. The art changed annually and was offered for sale. Library staff visited schools and daycare centres with this goal: "Target the kids." Literacy work was important too. Albert branch formed a partnership with firemen to offer Community Stories: Firemen, trained in storytelling, read to children in schools, demonstrating that not all men in uniform are

to be feared. The branch is also partner in a program of family literacy, Sowing the Seed: A Family Literacy Project, which teaches parents how to read to their children; and in another for fathers who are
incarcerated, teaching them to read to children, a program Sinclair
says the men enjoy. A computer lab in the basement of the branch,
provided by a federal Community Access Program in 1998, gives
access and training to people with little personal access to computers.
When the library has the funds, a lab facilitator gives fifteen minutes
of training an hour, so users don't just disappear into chat lines but
improve their skills.

The Albert Community Library Committee has been an important fundraiser. In 1998, it funded and hosted the first Canadian
meeting of inner city library patrons and staff. It received a grant in
1995 of $10,000 for programming, and that led to Cree classes,
powwow dancing, beadwork, storytelling programs, and a field trip
to Wanuskewin, the First Nations heritage park near Saskatoon. In
1996, a grant enabled the library to hire a teacher and storyteller, Wes
Fineday, for a year. The committee did fundraising to send representatives to attend the international Aboriginal forums in Norway,
New Zealand, and Sweden.

When my wife and I drove on a Thursday afternoon to central
libraries in Regina we saw at both Albert and Connaught about a
dozen Aboriginal high school students as the main clientele, mostly
at computer stations. It was exciting to see part of the new demo-
graphic world that is working.

LSSAP

In 1991 a new committee, Library Services for Saskatchewan's
Aboriginal People's Committee (LSSAP) was formed to share information and issues on library service for Aboriginals. Its membership has
varied over the years, but as of August 2004 it consisted of
Saskatchewan Indian Cultural Library in Saskatoon (SICLS); First
Nations University of Canada, Regina and Prince Albert campuses;
the Prince Albert Grand Council; Gabriel Dumont Institute, Regina

and Prince Albert campuses; the northern library PNLS; the two city libraries, RPL and SPL; University of Saskatchewan; First Nations band school/public libraries; Parkland and Lakeland regions; Touchwood Files Hills band; with support from the Provincial Library and SLA. It meets six times a year, in Prince Albert, Saskatoon, and Regina.

It held a 1992 conference in Saskatoon at which it worked on basic goals: library training for Aboriginal people, creating linkages between services, learning options for service at the local level, promoting literacy, and identifying information sources on Aboriginal people. By 1996, Industry Canada had provided computers to many band schools, leading to training workshops by LSSAP. It also contributed to a program of SICLS to index periodicals of interest to First Nations people. LSSAP gave presentations at an SLA conference, and attended international Aboriginal forums in New Zealand and Sweden, at which Phyllis Lerat and Wendy Sinclair conducted a workshop. After the 2001 "Information is for Everyone" report (see below), members spoke at SLA, CLA and at an Alberta Library Conference about that important initiative. The major new initiative is to hold, this year, the Fourth International Indigenous Library Forum in Saskatchewan.

INFORMATION IS FOR EVERYONE, 2001

The major document and proposal on library service for Aboriginals appeared in October 2001, *Information is for Everyone,* the final report of the Minister's Advisory Committee on Library Service for Aboriginal People. The committee was created in the spring of 2001 by Minister Ron Osika, was co-chaired by Ava Bear and Sinclair. The committee held six meetings between May and August, spoke with key groups and completed its report in October, another example of an efficient committee.

It's hard to summarize so complex a report, with forty-six recommendations. The committee was created to address two areas of concern: "First, only a small proportion of First Nations communities in southern Saskatchewan (20 of 57) chose to join the public library system." Second, "public libraries are not attracting off-reserve First Nation and Metis people in numbers reflecting their proportion of the population" (p. 1). One feature of the document are a number of boxes quoting briefs or presenting information. Aboriginals were 11.4% of the province's population in 2001, while by 2006 one of three school entrants would be Aboriginal, according to some estimates. "The employment rate for Aboriginals is 38 per cent compared to 65 per cent for Non-Aboriginal peoples (1996 census)" (p. 8). One of the most shocking pieces of information was included in the Southeast Regional Library brief: "Only 21 per cent of residents of participating First Nations have current library cards. Of these only 4 per cent are truly active users of the public library system" (p. 10). That passage shows how crucial such a report as this is.

Solutions were based on two central library principles, universal access and equitable access. One successful outcome of the report, said Sinclair, was that First Nation people on reserves could now get a library card from a branch near them whether or not the band had joined the region. That was a step toward universal access.

Suggested ways to achieve equitable access included adding Aboriginal people to library staffs and boards, including Aboriginal consultants at the Provincial Library, and in the regions – especially Lakeland, Parkland, Southeast, Wapiti, and the north – and at Regina and Saskatoon. Create a welcoming atmosphere for Aboriginal people, partly by having cultural awareness and sensitivity training. There were seven recommendations on training Aboriginal librarians, from training programs to bursaries, to mentoring, to public forums. Libraries should have Aboriginal collections, and outreach programs – including an annual story-telling week as one way to celebrate oral culture.

Looking at one section more closely can give a sense of the detail of the whole report – Chapter VI, "On-Reserve Public Library Service Points and Agreements." There were five recommendations, of which the first was most important, "That First Nations have ownership of, and primary responsibility for, on-reserve public libraries and public library services..." (p. 18). There were five examples of what that might mean, from stand-alone libraries to computer access and van delivery of books. Barriers were identified, too.

> First, libraries are often not seen as a priority, when First Nations Chiefs and Councils budget for such urgent needs as housing, infrastructure, etc. Secondly, there is often no suitable infrastructure to support the creation of public libraries on reserves. Many of the First Nations have school libraries but are not equipped to establish a public library. Third, First Nations lack experience in how to establish and operate a public library or a combined school-public library (p. 18).

One need was for trained library staff, while one on-reserve preference, the bookmobile, was no longer available – a victim of low provincial grants. (Can a bookmobile for First Nations ever become a reality? John Edgar of the RPL attended a recent bookmobile conference and he says they are now self-contained and much more sophisticated – the cheapest bookmobile is now worth $100,000.) There was one good example of service – Southeast assisted Pasqua First Nation with a library for elders.

The report made two financial recommendations – item 2, that the regional formula be changed to include on-reserve residents in a region, so no region was disadvantaged by such service; and item 14, that the government add project funds for initiatives to address concerns of Indian and Metis communities. The provincial government has indeed added $250,000 a year for such projects.

ABORIGINAL PROJECTS, 2003-4

Regina promoted cultural awareness, through workshops for staff and the public, delivered by consultant Clayton Dejarlais, who also made presentations at Chinook, Parkland, and Palliser. The latter region also emphasized awareness through three talks on Aboriginal issues and one reading in Assiniboia. Of the Dejarlais presentation there were two comments reported: "He succeeded in turning the outlook of several very biased individuals around," and "put to rest many a fear of the mostly white audience."[12]

Southeast region (which lost $27,000 in band grants for the year) spent $18,000 on a consultant who mapped out a time line for Southeast to complete all recommendations for regions from *Information is for Everyone* – and to complete them between 2004-2006. One interesting item in the report: "attitudinal themes" (a long way to say attitudes), that the consultant says must be overcome – Aboriginal people are but one of many cultures in the province; they are responsible for using libraries themselves; librarians in communities with few or no Aboriginal people saw the report as irrelevant.

Cancelling fees for service to on-reserve readers was central to Lakeland, Wapiti, and Wheatland. Chinook worked primarily to increase Aboriginal resources, at Maple Creek and Swift Current. Wheatland added bookmobile serve to the Whitecap Dakota First Nation Community, the only reserve in the region.

In the north, PNLS had two speakers at its annual conference, added to the resource budget for Cree, Dene, and Michif materials, spent the lion's share of the money on training band library staff, at a La Ronge meeting, on databases, ILLO, and web training. As a separate item PNLS added 2% to the government's 3% increase to branches (up to $15,750).

Lakeland added $17,000 to its Aboriginal collections, including $1,500 each for the three branch libraries on reserves. It also hired a library technician of Aboriginal ancestry, and she made a report on her extensive activities. There was some increase in borrowing from reserves but "lack of transportation [could] be a serious barrier to library access," still. Lakeland had a $40,000 grant. The region also participated in the 2004 Aboriginal Storytelling Festival, at North Battleford and Little Pine First Nations, with the help of eleven partners, including LSSAP.

Wapiti did cultural awareness projects for staff. The removal of barriers for on-reserve people led to a 40% increase that was still only 5% compared to an off-reserve figure of 60%. Wapiti put most of its grant into a reserve fund and plans to hire an Aboriginal library consultant, and included in their report a timetable for implementing seventeen recommendations from *Information is for Everyone.*

Saskatoon reached out to Aboriginal organizations and people through three programs: Stories in the Park for July and August; Family Day parties during Saskatchewan Library Week to introduce Aboriginal residents to the library and to two Aboriginal performers; and readings at two Aboriginal centres. The project leader was children's librarian Michelle Gowan, of Aboriginal ancestry. She analyzed the three projects – the first two successful – and included in an appendix a list of 43 organizations – 38 contacted, 20 responses.

Parkland had the most ambitious program of all, partly because it raised other money, $10,000 for a Family Literacy Initiative and $15,000 for the Storytelling Week Festival, for itself and for other regions. It had a series of literacy projects in Yorkton in concert with the Aboriginal Head Start program, including presenting Babies Plus Kits to all Head Start participants in the city and on reserves. Indian and Metis elders were encouraged to participate in Family Literacy Day. The Aboriginal Story Telling Festival was a great success, with 2,813 people attending programs in twenty-one communities, with good attendance at Pelican Narrows (400 over a week-long festival), Fort Qu'Appelle (380), Beardy (300), Regina (300), Canora (200), Watson (140), Kelvington (100), Broadview (p.90) and so on. The planning process included LSSAP, while thirty Aboriginal storytellers took part. The program will continue in 2004/05.

Chapter Eighteen

Multitype and Regina
2003-04

ECHO VALLEY AND MULTITYPE LIBRARY SYSTEM

THE ECHO VALLEY LIBRARY FORUM, NOVEMBER 3-6, 1988, was the first attempt to redefine the Saskatchewan library system since the Library Inquiry Committee of 1967. It was the creation of motions passed by SLTA on May 1985, and SLA on May 1986. A steering committee was appointed, which imagined a grassroots conference that would involve a variety of participants. Linda Fritz and Audrey Sullivan of SLTA contacted people, Ernie Ingles of the University of Regina raised the money, Tim Plumptre of Ottawa was chosen as facilitator. At the event there were 115 delegates representing the public library system, post-secondary libraries, and a variety of organizations, including SARM, SUMA, SIAST, PLEA, NFU, and so on. The report on the forum (121 pages) includes accounts of sessions and a series of presentations, including one, by Sheila Farden, on demographics, in which we're told: population was shifting to cities – Saskatoon one of the three fastest growing cities in Canada; the senior population is growing, 21% seniors in towns; more people were more educated – a doubling in a decade; the Aboriginal population would grow to 24% of the total by 2000, while 14% of Regina's population was Aboriginal.

Two sessions, one on Native Peoples, one on User Fees, give a flavour of the whole. The sessions on Native Peoples (the document's term) reads like an early version of *Information is for Everyone.*

In the summary page on that session, recommendations included adding more Native people on library boards and as staff; educating trustees and staff to understand needs of Native people; developing appropriate collections and programs; and assisting with collecting oral histories, and so on. The limitation of the forum was that people talked together (useful) but specific recommendations had no place to go.

The session on user fees is interesting because there were diametrically opposed views; ILLO in Saskatchewan was free, partly because the Provincial Library absorbed the fees for some out-of-province requests. The dilemma was whether they could afford to abandon this service (p. 95). Database services were also provided free. Library legislation didn't deal with non-print media, and people wanted it legislated, clear one way or the other. (In an earlier world of 16mm, film projectors were rented.) One possibility was to charge commercial users of information. Yet "If libraries obtain revenue from user fees will they be forced to give more priority to the development of 'user-pay' services over 'free' services?" (p. 94) The advantage of user fees was more money for other services, yet there was this objection, that libraries ought not to treat information and knowledge "only as an economic commodity" (p. 95). The conclusion of the session came down on the principle of equal access and the need to explain how each person "contributes a little so that everyone enjoys the final result" (p. 96).

The *Summary of the Forum* had different components. There was a Five Key Issue Summary for post-secondary institutions and for all participants in the one-library system. Because planning for the forum began in good economic times for libraries but it was held after the 10% government cut, four regions and the two cities placed funding as first priority, while it was included in all groups. The most interesting response was by Lakeland, which put Native services first, the one-province system second, technological change third (it appeared in seven accounts), funding fourth. A second part of the summary was a Proposed Action Plan, which included publishing the proceedings, and keeping the momentum going; but more specifically, a new vision was thought so necessary that a Vision Committee was formed with terms of reference, which included as item three – "focus on what libraries can achieve collectively on a province-wide basis" (p. 119). The steering committee had proposed those terms. Tim Plumptre in his closing reflections included this point: "I also had some sense of an emerging awareness of the need for co-operation among different institutions if libraries in Saskatchewan were effectively to meet their responsibilities for service to the public" (p. 121).

Eight years and two reports later, in 1996, *Think Globally...Search Locally, a Strategic Plan for the Multitype Library System in Saskatchewan* was published. It gave a brief history of the concept, from the *Echo Valley Forum* to the vision committee's *Vision: Independent...But Together,* 1990; followed by a subsequent vision committee 1992 report, *Independent But Together: A Vision for a Province-wide Multitype Library System;* and now the 1996 plan and a *Workbook* as part two. The 1996 report was created by consensus, which consumed time early on, by consultation with partners and target groups throughout the process, so it had a sense of how partners were different – in roles, clients, size, structures – but shared common needs. The Provincial Library was the centre of the implementation plan. Any information providers could join: one model for Multitype is the one-library system of the public libraries, another the distance-education projects of post-secondary institutions, a third the automation of public libraries though the Provincial Library (UTLAS, 1980; Dynix, 1990; PLEIS under development). There were multitype projects underway in Weyburn and Estevan (the Souris project to provide access to CD-ROM databases); in Prince Albert including Woodland Campus and Gabriel Dumont Institute, and called PANet; a multitype library discussion group in Saskatoon; while Chinook and Wheatland had working relations with some schools.

The vision of Multitype was access to all, while the title *Think Globally...Search Locally* meant beginning at home and then sharing resources regionally, nationally, and internationally. Four goals were identified: To Develop, To Implement, To Connect, and To Promote. To achieve them, eleven strategies were identified, key among them: Establish, Involve all libraries, Research, Set Standards, Secure Funding, Provide Training, Develop a province-wide electronic system (PLEIS as cornerstone), Communicate, and Educate. A section on funding made an essential point – that systems would be responsible to contribute "as appropriate to the benefit they expect to receive" (p. 21), or again "contributions should be in proportion to their expected usage." The aim of the program was simple, "to save money through greater resource sharing" (p. 22), while volunteer staff could be part of the budget of a partner library. The Provincial Library had money for its coordinating role. The system would progress depending on the funding it and partners provided. If new provincial money was granted to the Provincial Library, multitype activity would remain a priority, but there was no specific request for provincial funding.

The *Workbook* is of little interest historically except that it defines the Mulitype Library Board of fifteen members, at least two from each of four sectors, public, special, school, post-secondary, and including representatives from SLA, SLTA, as well as five members at large, including representatives from SUMA and SARM. It still sounded like Echo Valley.

The 2002-2003 Annual Report of the Multitype Board gives a good cross-section of its nature and actions. A board of sixteen from the various user groups governed its actions. The report was based on the five goals and then on databases licensed that year. The Literature Resource Centre was a new database and offered access to 600 journals and information on over 120,000 writers across the world. Its acquisition was financed primarily by the two city public libraries and the two universities. A new provider of national daily and Saskatchewan newspapers was negotiated. Saskatchewan Learning (the new name for the Department of Education) set up a licensing fund so the Provincial Library would have the capacity to sign agreements on behalf of the members. Fourteen new libraries joined that year, from government departments like Social Services, to corporations like Potash Corporation, to other companies like McKercher, McKercher & Whitmore. For the future Multitype planned to create access for home computers with a single authentication. The March 2004 AGM report said that use of databases was up 46% while each partner's contribution declined 12%, and 284 people were trained in the system in six centres.

Multitype service is the most recent example of the Saskatchewan library system working at its best – cooperative, innovative, sophisticated.

REGINA, 2003-04

November 26, 2003, was a landmark day for Saskatchewan libraries. There had already been the bad year of 10% cuts in 1986, the cancelling of the bookmobiles, but the announced closure by the Regina Public Library (RPL) Board of three inner-city branch libraries (Connaught, Glen Elm, and Prince of Wales) plus the Dunlop Art Gallery, and significant restructuring to the Prairie History Room (and the loss of twenty-seven jobs) was as major an event as any in the province's library history. There had been many closures in regions, but their governing structure is different than cities, and probably superior. Every municipality has a representative on the board which elects an executive. In the cities there's a board of ten or twelve appointed by city council, but the members have no constituency to report back to. The arm's-length principle of such boards is useful both to the council, since one important service is removed from politics, and for libraries, because an independent board can best serve libraries.

There were two difficulties with the RPL Board decision: it was extensive and it came as a surprise, indeed a shock. There had been no public consultation – though there had been in earlier years on similar topics. The board said the immediate financial causes were underfunded pensions, of $300,000 a year for five years, and a loss of property tax revenue (between $150,000 to $400,000 a year) because of tax appeals. Later it talked of the costs of repair and upkeep of the physical plant.

The response was immediate and ferocious. When Library Director Sandy Cameron gave a press conference the next day to explain the action, he was "repeatedly challenged by employees and community members frustrated"[1] by the decisions and the lack of consultation. Groups formed to fight all or each of the cuts. There was an immediate defence of the Dunlop Art Gallery, with e-mail bringing support from across the county. People enjoyed contrasting a Regina that had just been proclaimed a Cultural Capital with a Regina that was going to close one of its cultural treasures. On the Prairie History Room, board chair Faye Cameron was reported as saying "the bulk of the room's collection will remain where it is, but materials that go beyond the three prairie provinces will be relocated," while the room would be staffed from the reference desk. How long, asked a nineteen-year employee of the room, would the collection last without local history expertise? A group supported the history room, again in part from outside the city including a petition of twenty-two from Saskatoon. Groups formed, friends of the Connaught Library, of Glen Elm, of Prince of Wales, with one overarching group, Friends of the Regina Public Library.

The pressure on Mayor Pat Fiacco, who was a board member and who supported the closures and no tax increase, was intense. On the same day that a 300-person noon rally took place, organized by the Friends of the RPL, the mayor said, "I want the community to decide on the future of our library."[2] The next day the library board gave a two month stay of execution until May Day, 2004, and appointed a new task force to solicit public opinion, after the fact, and make a report. The Friends called it a "Mask Force," assuming it had a limited mandate, and said they'd create their own task force, though it would be limited because it wasn't given access to all library information except though access by Freedom of Information, a slow process. The Friends also began a campaign to collect enough signatures to force a referendum demanding increased city support for the library, (19,000 or 10% of the population were needed). The city solicitor questioned the wording of the petition since the library board was autonomous. The Friends ultimately collected 26,048 signatures, a significant show of support in Regina for its libraries and their services. The city clerk validated 24,347 signatures, but the solicitor said the petition could not go forward because "it leaves too many questions unanswered," didn't say how much money should be provided or for how long.[3] The Friends went to court and lost again when a Queen's Bench judge upheld the city's position, saying the city doesn't have the authority to open or close libraries.[4] Council chose not to go ahead with a referendum.

I was once centrally involved in an attempt to force the city of Saskatoon to hold a referendum on preserving the Capitol Theatre. We collected 10,000 signature in two weeks, were legally a week late and were turned down by a vote of ten to one. I can add from my own experience the hatred I still feel for that decision, the demolition taking place on December 1, 1979, a long time ago. When you love something that is destroyed by human agency that might have chosen differently, anger can live on (in me, at any rate). People in legal bodies normally act reasonably, in good faith, judiciously, with good advice, intelligently, yet when they come up against love they may win, but they can never *truly* win. People have long memories. It's hard to close libraries.

The RPL board made two public statements, the first a letter by chair Cameron, explaining the financial dilemma with these additions: the RPL lost about $800,000 when city council removed the business tax (there were responses that it was now revenue neutral but the loss was originally a loss); the RPL had attempted to maintain its mill rate at zero or at the rate of inflation over the last five years. To do so, RPL had cut back on maintenance and capital improvements. A serious admission. She added two damning statistics. First, the RPL hours of opening were 26th of 32 libraries serving roughly the same population. Second, "The RPL rank[ed] 4th among those 32 libraries in the number of holdings it ha[d] in its collection, but only 14th in the number of titles, because materials [had] to be duplicated in several branches." Finally, "While the RPL may have been among the best in Canada a decade ago, that is no longer true."[5] A separate chart did show that Regina had more branches per capita than seven other libraries including Saskatoon. That is an attractive statistic for Regina from one viewpoint, an expensive one from another viewpoint. She urged people to talk to the Task Force.

The RPL Board itself published an ad in the January 31, 2004, *Leader-Post,* repeating the causes of the shortfall, including wanting to hold the line on tax increases by postponing "building and equipment challenges." The ad then listed the costs of upgrading the proposed closures:

CONNAUGHT
- The building has a major foundation problem. Engineering estimates made in late 2002 indicate a repair cost of over $500,000.
- Connaught is quite close to the central library.

GLEN ELM
- The building has a range of maintenance and accessibility problems.
- Glen Elm has the smallest circulation of any full service branch.

PRINCE OF WALES
- The building has foundation problems and is very small.
- Prince of Wales has a very small circulation.

DUNLOP ART GALLERY
- The cost of operating the Dunlop is about the same as operating a full service branch.
- Public libraries across Canada do not operate full service art galleries.

PRAIRIE HISTORY ROOM
- Considerable resources are devoted to maintaining the unique components of the collection and offering specialized research services.
- There is not enough room available to expand the system.

The public spoke in many letters to the editor. Kjristen Hordern, clearly a reader, said she now had eighteen items borrowed (maximum allowed, forty) and she costed those items, books, CDs, DVDs, on Amazon.ca and learned "it would have cost me $809.59 to buy what I currently have on loan from the library." All for twenty-four dollars a year in taxes.[6] Again, "My family did not have a lot of money, but our library picked up where our bank account left off." Sabrina Calaldo checked out thirty books at a time, read a book a day so she could borrow more.[7] Andy Tate said, "I discovered the local library branch one summer when I was just eight years old. It was so close to my house I could walk or ride my bike. I went there practically every day."[8] Gail Chin said how libraries were her salvation when young in Vancouver, born of parents who worked all the time. She found the South Fraser branch, "which provided a lonely child a place of refuge." She also went to the free and famous Bau Xi Gallery (the Vancouver Art Gallery closed to her because of fees, still a barrier today). "Now the city of Regina is planning to close three library branches, two of them in the inner city and the Dunlop Art Gallery; the city fathers will deny children, such as I was, the right to develop and become useful citizens."[9]

One advantage of the proposed closures were the detailed and loving defences of libraries.

The library task force was created December 16, 2003, by the RPL Board, at the request of the mayor, as a reaction to the "public outcry." It called its report "Reading within our Means: Building for the Future, Towards a Sustainable Public Library System" (123 pages) and presented it to the board in March. As part of its consultation it received almost 1,400 responses, by e-mail, telephone, mail, and at five public meetings (63 presentations). It gave no breakdown of responses. It was guided by these principles: focus on the core mandate (which excluded the Dunlop Gallery, the Prairie History Room and the Film Theatre —which was not under threat); lower costs (reduce costs in non-core activities, reduce materials budget); realign the system (create "community resource centres" for branches that were to be closed, distribute collection and services across the six full-service libraries, including two new ones, and replace the aging Central Library with a modest branch).

The document didn't define what a "community resource centre" meant and didn't come to grips with how the central library functions (cataloguing, children's services, management and so on) could usefully be decentralized. It valued the Dunlop and the Prairie History Room and suggested transition teams to transfer them out of the library over a three-year period. The Film Theatre should be closed immediately, though during this time RPL was engaged in a campaign to sell seats in the theatre. Of the branches under threat, the task force recommended Glen Elm should receive new capital development of $850,000; Prince of Wales should be moved to a new location, construction at $800,000; Connaught, especially valued, should receive a re-investment of $1,200,000, with capital fundraising undertaken. Other branches should be retained, though Albert should become a community centre. As well, a new branch in west Regina ($3,500,000) was recommended, while downtown the ailing Central Library should be phased out and replaced with a small leased space ($375,000). In effect, the report argued, the branches could all be saved at the expense of the Central Library and its costly major renovation. The task force concluded that new technology meant a centralized system was no longer mandatory.

The task force talked of money. Over the past ten years the average annual library tax increase was 3.2%, or about 1% over the C.P.I., while the library plan for the next ten years would include mill rate increases of 0.5% above the projected C.P.I. It also said that the RPL Board had acted prudently and could not have foreseen the downturn in equities (though it was clear by late 2001) and only learned of the pension shortfall well into its budget year.

The task force presented three models for the future: Stay the Course – the public view, to save everything, which would create a substantial debt within a decade; Consolidate and Continue – the RPL Board model, keep the model intact but cut off extremities; and the Reconfigure and Focus – the task force model, already presented, though it also suggested debt financing in these days of low mortgages.

There were useful discussions in the document, of pensions (pp. 59-60), of earlier RPL reports (pp. 45-46), a detailed defence of the

Connaught Branch (pp. 87-89). The report was filed in March and received almost no notice by the public or response from the board.

Over the summer of 2004 there were two developments. The city council appointed new board members. By June only two sitting members of the board, the mayor and a councillor, had been on the board when the controversy began. Some quit blaming the Mayor and council for political interference. The new board said no actions would be taken until a process of public consultation was complete, sometime in October. A public opinion poll will be part of the consultation as well as a series of meetings. Stay tuned.

Afterward

THE WRITING OF THIS BOOK HAS LED ME TO THREE CENTRAL
conclusions. I'm a city boy and have always dreamed of larger cities,
but now I identify more with the small over the large, the rural over
the urban. My imagination travelled with the travelling libraries to
all those small communities it served, and then lived especially in
Trossachs and Stranraer, two small places where the concept of
regional libraries was born. When I looked at the local history of the
RM of Brokenshell, in which Trossachs is located, I saw what vitality
of the early years has been lost, Weyburn too close, automobiles
better, highways better. Will the Information Highway make all
places more equal?

I've been inspired by all those early heroes of the regional
libraries, all those trustees who made libraries their life work. Today
the dedication remains. I found it in many of the libraries we visited
on our peregrinations. Wherever we were, we dropped in to libraries.
A Sunday afternoon visit to the Blaine Lake library, located in a train
station, found a library fully occupied. A children's reading hour had
just finished upstairs. A woman and two daughters were choosing
their fifteen books. A young man offered us a tour of the museum.
Downstairs, one older girl was teaching one younger boy how to use
the internet. Library life on and on and on. Splendidly.

My third response is on the underfunding of regional libraries by
provincial governments. The province was once the great creator of
the one-library system. A 3% increase in 2003 was gratefully received.

I hope this book will have one practical use now – by seeing how marvellous the Saskatchewan one-system library is, perhaps public officials will rededicate themselves to the health of this great service. It helps stitch the province together. It keeps a service alive in towns and villages. It says what democracy is, the free access to information, ideas, and pleasure.

When I was a trustee at the Saskatoon Public Library in the 1970s I was also a socialist and remember thinking that if Saskatchewan and Canada were transformed by a socialist vision, libraries would have to stay just the same. They were already democratic and accessible. How could anyone invent anything better than a library?

Acknowledgements

THIS BOOK COULD HAVE NEVER BEEN WRITTEN WITHOUT THE gracious help of many people. It was a delight to return to archives again, in the regions, in the cities, and at the Provincial Library. I'd forgotten the pleasure of turning pages that hadn't been turned for some years. I visited all of the regional libraries in the south, and I'm pleased to thank: in Chinook, Michael Keaschuk and Shirley Syrenne, and Jean Murch who sent me early material on organizing the region; at Lakeland, Lane Jackson (and the pleasure of coffee time there explaining to the staff what I was doing); at Palliser, Carolyn Graham, who like others had boxes of files lined up for me, so one day while she was out training a new branch librarian everything was at my disposal; at Parkland, Deirdre Crichton; at Southeast, Allan Johnson who was always available to give me good advice; at Wapiti, Kevin Phillip, and Christina Petrisovar, who when I asked for photos from their archives, sent a note saying how delighted she was to offer help for such a book; at Wheatland, Don Lepp; whose files were the most fully organized by month and year. At the point where I thought the book was finished, I discovered the amazing archives at Provincial Library. The library acts, from 1953 on, have mandated all regions to file materials with the Provincial Library, which has also preserved early correspondence with the regions. I must thank Provincial Librarian Joy Campbell for her courtesy, and especially I thank Marian Buddens, who was archiving the enormous resources at Provincial Library preparatory to a move from their spacious Winnipeg Street location to a smaller space, and who found materials for me. I arrived at the right time. Two years earlier material was not yet organized and there would have been no finding aids. Two years later most of the material would be in storage at the Provincial Archives. Had I examined all the files available at the Provincial Library, the book would be twice as long and perhaps never completed, so rich was the material there. I didn't travel to the Pahkisimon Nuy?áh region in the North, but was able to write a chapter on it through Provincial Library files and particularly through the extensive material (about a foot of it) sent to me courtesy of Graham Guest, Archival Historian of the northern regions – thanks as well to Brian Suetta for making that contact.

In Regina I was welcomed by Librarian Sandy Cameron while Wendy Mohl found materials for me. In Saskatoon I was welcomed by Librarian Zenon Zuzak, who had copies in his office of all the CALUPL files to help me discover just how successful the two urban libraries have been on the national scene. Thanks as well to Cheryl Brown and her staff at the Local History Room.

I was delighted with all the people who granted me interviews: Allan Blakeney, Marilyn Boechler, Isabelle Butters, Grace Campbell, Joy Campbell, Maria Campbell (the Campbells are coming), Patricia Cavill, John Edgar, Cora Greer, Michael Keaschuk, Laureen Marchand, Don Meadows, Frances Morrison, Ned Shillington, Wendy Sinclair, Keith Turnbull, and Maureen Woods. I enjoyed the interviews and the insider view they offered.

My greatest debt is to the steering committee on this project, which encouraged me, raised the money for the publication and promotion of *A Book in Every Hand* – and for expenses and grant to its author. The chair of the committee, Judy Chuey, was the true originator of the book when she was a trustee at the Saskatoon Public Library. Simply said, no Judy Chuey, no book. Her inspiration helped the Saskatchewan Library Trustees Association assume sponsorship of this history. Early on, Judy wrote to trustees in all southern regions who sent a wealth of material. In particular it made chapter two possible. It was a pleasure to spend time again with Frances Morrison, the splendid Saskatoon Librarian I worked with when I was a trustee in the 1970s. Louise Cochran brought her energy and humour to the table as the SLTA representative, from Radisson and Lakeland. André Gagnon of RPL and Zenon Zuzak of SPL, as well as Judy Chuey, were successful fundraisers (over $25,000, which I found amazing). Andre worked on the promotion plan, with the help of Carol Joyner of SPL and the members of the committee. André also made available to me the RLP newspaper files on the Regina controversy of 2003-2004. Zenon was our host and made many contacts for the committee. My role at such meetings was to give updates on where I was, as I missed deadline after deadline. We had pleasure meeting with each other.

I thank my editor Dave Margoshes, who beat upon the manuscript. Most of all I thank Mildred, lively wife and car driver, who drove me sane to all those regional offices. It was a pleasure. Hope you enjoyed it all, eh.

Endnotes

CHAPTER ONE

1. *Regina Leader Post (RPL),* November 19, 1889.
2. *RLP,* July 29, 1890.
3. Carol Budnick, "Books to the People of Winnipeg," *Canadian Library Journal, (CLJ),* December 1981, pgs. 417-421.
4. *RLP,* August 16, 1894.
5. "Recollections and Reminisces," *Saskatchewan History,* Autumn, 1950, p. 101.
6. Jim Blanchard, "Anatomy of Failure, Ontario Mechanics' Institutes, 1835-1895," *CLJ,* December 1981.
7. L.H. Neatby, *Chronicles of a Prairie Family,* Western Producer Books, 1979, p. 34. The story of the father reading in the Watrous library I got from Dick Rempel who heard the story from Hilda Neatby.
8. Neatby, p. 32
9. Fredelle Bruser Maynard, *Raisins and Almonds,* Paperjacks, 1973, p. 24.
10. E.C. Morgan, "Pioneer Recreation and Social Life," *Saskatchewan History,* 1965, p. 50. The article was based on a series of questionnaires sent to pioneers, starting in 1951 and with 287 returned.
11. Meeting of Saskatoon Historical Association, May 17, 1922, Short Collection, University of Saskatchewan, C555/2/400.
12. Evelyn Eager, "Our Pioneers Say," *Saskatchewan History,* 1953, p. 8.
13. Morgan, p. 50.
14. Ibid.
15. Morgan, p. 24.
16. Maynard, p. 24
17. *Library Findings,* 20th Anniversary Issue, Southeast, 1986.
18. *RLP,* November 21, 1891
19. *Qu'Appelle Progress,* November 5, 1891 in *Saskatchewan History,* Winter, 1954, p. 28-29.
20. "The Grenfell Mechanics' and Literary Institute Minute Book, 1892-95," *Saskatchewan History,* Autumn, 1964, pgs. 105-10.

21. In Saskatoon Public Library Local History Room.
22. Miss Janet Etter, Harris, to Wilbur Lepp, Librarian, Local History Room, October 22, 1979, SPL Local History.
23. Stewart G. Mein, "The Aberdeen Association: An Early Attempt to Provide Library Service to Settlers in Saskatchewan," *Saskatchewan History,* Winter 1985.
24. All quotes in this paragraph from John Hawkes, *The Story of Saskatchewan and its People,* 1924, pgs. 1132-36.
25. See Marion J. Powell, "The Early History of the Saskatchewan Legislative Library: A Pioneering Vision for Parliamentary Library Service, 1886-1927," in Legislative Library.
26. John Hawkes, "The Library, *Public Service Monthly,* vol. 12, July, 1916.
27. Marion Powell, p. 6.

CHAPTER TWO

1. "Public Library Grants," February 1, 1949, Saskatchewan Library Advisory Committee (SLAC), King papers, University of Saskatchewan Archives.
2. "Grants," March 15, 1953, Woodrow Lloyd papers, G-15, Saskatchewan Archives Board (SAB).
3. "Statistics," March 3, 1959, Lloyd, G-1 5b, SAB.
4. Mrs. D.H. Truscott, Secretary-Treasurer. Alameda Community Library, to Minister of Education, May 15, 1961 and reply May 31, 1961. Blakeney papers, SAB.
5. Blakeney reply, May 31, 1961, Blakeney papers, SAB.
6. *Saskatchewan Library,* May, 1966.
7. Deputy Minister to Emma Bell, December 10, 1937, SLA SAB.
8. *Palliser Pages,* 10th Anniversary Edition, August, 1983.
9. *Saskatchewan Library,* May, 1966.
10. Information in this paragraph from Judy Thompson, "Going It Alone: a Library stays Independent," *CLA Journal,* December 1981.
11. Newsom to J.C. McIsaac, May 5, 1969, and file, including Virna Thompson to D.T. MacFarlane, Minister of Agriculture, April 23, 1969, J.C. McIsaac papers, 52c, SAB.
12. *Saskatchewan Valley News,* October 6, 1993.
13. "Library Bindings," Southeast, December 1978.
14. "Library Bindings," 16.2.
15. All from *Saskatchewan Library,* May, 1966, an especially informative issue.
16. All material on this year from *Focus,* October, 1984.
17. Material in these two paragraphs from *The Breeze,* the Chinook Newsletter, vol. 4, no. 2, 1979.
18. Material from submissions to Judy Chuey.

CHAPTER THREE

1. John Hawkes, "A List of Appended Reports etc. Re Legislative Library of Saskatchewan, Submitted to Hon. Walter Scott, Minister of Education, July 15, 1913, SAB, p. 5. There was an earlier mention of travelling libraries in a letter in which J.R.C. Honeyman, Regina Librarian, wrote to J.A. Calder, so it's clear the topic was already under discussion.
2. Ibid., p. 18.
3. Ibid., p. 22.
4. *RLP*, December 11, 1913.
5. "Information," December 1914; Scott papers, SAB.
6. Margaret McDonald to Hon. W.M. Martin, January 29, 1919, Martin Papers, SAB.
7. Hawkes to The Speaker, February 8, 1917, Martin papers, SAB.
8. Hawkes to Hon. W.M. Martin, September 13, 1917, Martin papers, SAB.
9. Hawkes to Hon. W.M. Martin, September 23, 1918, "Library Estimates for 1919-20," W.M. Martin papers, SAB.
10. Ibid.
11. Margaret McDonald to Clerk, Legislative Assembly, November 7, 1919, Martin papers, SAB.
12. Hawkes to Hon. W.M. Martin, September 8, 1921, Martin papers, SAB.
13. "Public Information Library," n.d. but 1945, Lloyd papers, SAB.
14. L. Craig to Hon. W.M. Martin, June 30, 1921, Martin papers, SAB.
15. "Statistics for 1922 and 1923," Dunning papers, Y-8-2, SAB.
16. W.A. MacLeod to Hon. S.J. Latta, May 26, 1922, Latta papers, SAB.
17. Report of the Legislative Librarian to the Speaker of the Legislative Assembly, n.d., but inked in 1921, Martin papers, SAB.
18. Jesse Bothwell to J.H. Brocklebank, February 15, 1965, Bothwell papers, IX.6(2), SAB.
19. Information from "Open Shelf Libraries Reports," various years, Provincial Library, Box 30.
20. *SP,* December 31, 1938.
21. *SP,* May 29, 1938.
22. Jesse Bothwell, Provincial Librarian to Hon W.S. Lloyd, February 9, 1951, Lloyd papers, SAB.
23. Mrs. R.J. Brandon to Lloyd, April 4, 1951, Lloyd papers, SAB, and quotations from following two paragraphs.
24. Public Information Library, n.d., but clearly a 1945 report, Lloyd papers, SAB.
25. Saskatchewan Government Travelling Libraries, Miss R.J. Brandon, n.d., but 1946; Mrs. Bothwell to Lloyd, March 1, 1948, Lloyd papers, SAB.
26. Mrs. Bothwell to Carlyle King, June 16, 1947, SLAC, 1948, PL, Box 30.
27. Report from Travelling Libraries, February 10, 1951, Lloyd papers, SAB.
28. Mrs. Brandon to Lloyd, April 4, 1951, Lloyd papers, SAB.
29. Interview with Ned Shillington, Calgary, May 31, 2004.

30. Mrs. Dale Purves to Minister of Education, April 12, 1969, J.C. McIsaac papers, 53f, SAB.
31. Mrs. P.L. Mark to Hon. J.C. McIsaac, McIsaac papers, 53f, SAB.
32. Mrs. Don Carlson, Wauchope, to Minister of Education, April 25, 1969, SAB.
33. Jerrold Malinowski to Clifford McIsaac, October 25, 1969, SAB.

CHAPTER FOUR

1. Commission of Enquiry, *Libraries in Canada, a Study of Library Conditions and Needs.* Toronto and Chicago: Ryerson Press and the American Library Association, 1933.
2. "Partial Summary of Library Services in Rural Saskatchewan, March 1935," SLA, SAB, and reprinted in 1935 *Dominion Bureau of Statistics.*

CHAPTER FIVE

1. Elizabeth Morton, Secretary CLC, to John Lothian, July 21, 1944, Saskatchewan Library Association (SLA), Saskatchewan Archives Board (SAB).
2. Lothian to Morton, CCL, August 14, 1944, Public Archives of Canada.
3. Weweler to Thomas Barcus, new CLC representative for Saskatchewan, October 10, 1944, SLA, SAB.
4. Barcus to Weweler, October 13, 1944, SLA.
5. Weweler to Douglas, September 26, 1944, Box 40, Provincial Library (PL), Weweler File.
6. Weweler to Mrs. Bothwell, Provincial Librarian, November 10, 1944, ibid.
7. "A Memorandum for Premier Douglas in Regard to the Development of a Regional Library Service for South Saskatchewan," SLA, SAB.
8. Weweler to Emma Bell, November 20, 1944, SLA, SAB.
9. Weweler to Violet McNaughton, November 28, 1944, McNaughton papers, SAB
10. Winnifred Barnstead, Director, Ontario College of Education to Watson Thorson, Director of Adult Education, Regina, March 29, 1945.
11. Weweler to McNaughton, November 28, 1944.
12. Weweler to Bothwell, April 13, 1945, PL, Box 40.
13. Weweler to Miss Dawson, April 23, 1945, ibid.
14. Susie Gaught to Mrs. McNaughton, February 17, 1945, McNaughton papers, SAB.
15. Weweler to McNaughton, March 3, 1945, ibid.
16. Morton to Lothian, July 21, 1944, SLA SAB.
17. Barcus to Bell, October 17, 1944, ibid.
18. See Marion Gilroy, "Pioneers! O Pioneers! The Genesis of Regional Libraries," *Survival of the Imagination: The Mary Donaldson Memorial Lectures,* Coteau Books, 1993.

19. "News Story," n.d., "Library on Wheels," CLA, NAC, vol. 92.
20. Commentary "Library on Wheels" NAC, file 92-45. Volume 1. No. 5 of the NFB newsletter "Canada in Action" has a detailed account of the Fraser Valley Region and the film – in the same file.
21. Minutes SLAC, December 15, 1945, C.A. King papers, U of S.
22. Lloyd to King, September 9, 1946, Lloyd papers, SAB.
23. King to Mrs. Bothwell, November 14, 1968, King papers, U of S.
24. Alex M. Derby to Mrs. Bothwell, April 25, 1946, Box 40, PL, SLAC 1946.
25. Saskatchewan Library Association to Mrs. Bothwell, April 12, 1946, ibid.
26. Mrs. E.N. Davis to Mrs. Bothwell, April 6, 1946, ibid.
27. *Focus on Saskatchewan Libraries,* June 1982.
28. Max Braithwaite, *Like Being a Millionaire,* Wapiti, 1965, p. 29.
29. Report of the Regional Libraries Division to April 1, 1947, King papers, U of S.
30. Mrs. Bothwell to King, February 21, 1946, ibid.
31. Braithwaite, p. 62.
32. Ibid., p. 46.
33. Ibid., p. 57.
34. Ibid., p. 34.
35. Prince Albert meeting, January 31, 1948, Lloyd papers, SAB.
36. Mrs. Bothwell to Lloyd, February 3, 1948, Lloyd papers, ibid.
37. Gilroy to Bothwell, February 1, 1948, ibid.
38. Gilroy to Lloyd, June 1, 1948, ibid.
39. Lloyd to King, September 22, 1948, ibid.
40. Gilroy to Bothwell, January 14, 1948, ibid.
41. Gilroy to Bothwell, February 7, 1948, ibid.
42. Ibid.
43. Mary MacIsaac to Lloyd, September 2, 1948, ibid.
44. Gilroy to Lloyd, May 16, 1949, ibid.
45. Gilroy to Lloyd, March 21, 1950, ibid.
46. Braithwaite, p. 52.
47. Gladys Estok to Gilroy, February 21, 1950, ibid.
48. Braithwaite, p. 62.
49. Material in this paragraph is from an interview with Grace Campbell, Victoria, May 26, 2004. Some of her stories are from her first two years at North Central, some from her later long tenure as regional librarian.
50. *Prince Albert Daily Herald,* n.d.
51. "Letter from Executive Secretary," n.d., Box 30, PL, SLAC, 1950.
52. Bothwell to King, November 29, 1950, ibid.
53. "The North Central Library Board, report of Marian Gilroy, 1952, ibid.
54. Mary Donaldson, Provincial Librarian, to Lloyd, December 3, 1956 and Gilroy report November 17, 1956, ibid.
55. Mrs. Sherman to Treasury Board, August 12, 1958, "North Central Saskatchewan Library," ibid.

56. Braithwaite, p. 40.
57. Lloyd to Douglas, February 2, 1959, Lloyd papers, SAB.
58. Treasury Board file, December 13, 1961 as part of Donaldson to Turnbull, April 16, 1962.
59. There is much later material in Wapiti including their submission to the Library Inquiry Committee, 1967, SLTA, SAB.

CHAPTER SIX

1. Mrs. Stephenson's account of early days: in Wheatland file, 1959. Unless otherwise stated all references are from Wheatland files. In his opening chapter Rusty MacDonald provides biographies of the three women, Stephenson, McCuaig, Wiens.
2. Organization of the West Central Regional Library Committee, November 1959.
3. Rose Ducie, "Organizing a Library," *Western Producer*, January 28, 1960.
4. Mrs. Warner Lahti to Helen Stewart, Secretary-Treasurer, WCRLC, Plenty, January 19, 1960.
5. A.E. Nell to Rosetown meeting, March 16, 1960.
6. Ibid.
7. August 1960, Wheatland.
8. Muriel MacLean to Helen Stewart, August 13, 1962.
9. "Proposed Demonstration of Partial Regional Library Service in West Central Saskatchewan," Turnbull papers, 51-4, SAB.
10. Muriel MacLean to Helen Stewart, September 24, 1963.
11. MacLean to Stewart, September 30, 1963.
12. *Western Producer*, October 8, 1964.
13. MacLean to Stewart, July 18, 1963. The 1963 letters from Muriel MacLean are also full of lovely information on people working well or ill from town to town.
14. Elspeth Miller, "Demonstration Bookmobile Service Reports," September 28, 1964
15. "Changes in the System-1971," July 7, 1971
16. Ibid.
17. Interview with Marilyn Boechler, March 24, 2004. Marilyn and I were members together of the Saskatoon Municipal Heritage Advisory Committee.
18. February 20, 1971 minutes of the Board.
19. Wheatland news file, *Saskatchewan Valley News*, May 7, 1997; December 2, 1998; June 9, 1999; November 10, 1999; February 16, 2000; March 1, 2000, June 28, 2000.

CHAPTER SEVEN

1. J. S. Porter, "It can be done, because we did it," in C.A. King papers, SLAC, SAB.
2. Ibid.
3. Bettschen to Turnbull, February 11, 1964, McIsaac papers, SAB.
4. *Broadview Review,* March 6, 1965, Southeastern files
5. Allan Turner to James S. Porter, July 23, 1968, Southeastern files.
6. Donaldson to A., Wakabyashi, Deputy Provincial Treasurer, November 15, 1965, J.C. McIsaac papers, 53a, SAB.
7. Southeastern Annual Report, 1966.
8. Librarian's Report, December 2, 1966, Southeastern files.
9. Semi-Annual Board meeting, October 26, 1968, ibid.
10. Librarian's Report, Executive Meeting, January 13, 1968, ibid.

CHAPTER EIGHT

1. Regina Public Library to George Trapp, November 25, 1965, McIsaac papers, 52C, SAB.

CHAPTER NINE

1. *RLP,* November 10, 1965.
2. Mrs. S. Long to PL, March 10, 1964, Parkland, PL, Box 1, 1964-68.
3. Mary Donaldson to Geoffry Smith, chairman, East Central, October 27, 1965, Parkland, Box 1, 1964-69, PL
4. Thatcher to Trapp, April 25, 1967, including Newsom to Trapp, April 18, 1967, J.C. McIsaac papers, 54c, SAB.
5. Minutes of Executive Meeting, December 8, 1967, Parkland, PL, Box 1, 1966-70.
6. Minutes of Executive, March 1, 1968, Parkland, PL, Box 1, ibid.
7. Newsom to Mr. C. Eggenschwiler, Kamsack, March 11, 1968, Parkland, PL, Box 1, 1964-69.
8. Newsom to Macdonald, April 29, 1968 Parkland, PL, Box 1, ibid.
9. Minutes, Parkland Annual Meeting, May 4, 1968, Parkland, PL, Box 1, 1966-70.
10. Ibid.
11. Interview with Don Meadows, Parksville, May 24, 2003.
12. To the Minister, n.d. but 1972, Parkland, PL Box 1, 1972-78.
13. *Yorkton Enterprise,* January 19, 1977.
14. *Wadena News,* June 22, 1976.
15. *Foam Lake Review,* July 4, 1979.
16. "Report on Bookmobile No. 1," prepared by Frank Clarke, June 1981, Parkland, PL Box 1, 1980-83.
17. Skrzeszewski to Siebold, Provincial Librarian, December 18, 1982, Parkland, ibid.
18. Annual Report, 1975, Evelyne Vandales, p. 5.

19. Ibid., pg. 7.
20. Meadows to Neil Byers, January 19, 1973, Parkland, PL Box 1, 1973.
21. Tony Cote, Chief, to Jeffrey Smith, Board Chairman, May 7, 1973, Parkland, ibid.
22. Libby Griffin to Meadows, March 26, 1973, Parkland, ibid.
23. Patricia Cavill (Cuts) to Skrzeszeweski, January 30, 1981, Pahkisimon, PL Box 1, Library Service to Indian Bands, 1966-81.
24. *Yorkton This Week,* February 27, 1980.
25. Skrzeszewski to Shillington, May 12, 1980, Parkland, PL Box 1, 1980-83.
26. Skrzeszewski to Bilokreli, December 2, 1981, ibid.
27. *Yorkton This Week,* October 7, 1981.

CHAPTER TEN

1. All material in this paragraph courtesy of Jean Murch.
2. Elspeth Miller to Mrs. N. Sillerud, January 5, 1967, Chinook, PL Box 1, 1964-68.
3. Mrs. Jean Murch to RM of Miry Creek, April 2, 1968.
4. Mrs. Ross to Provincial Librarian, September 6, 1967, Chinook, PL Box 1, 1964-69.
5. *Chinook Newsletter,* November 9, 1967, ibid.
6. Newsom to McIsaac, March 19, 1968, ibid.
7. Thatcher to McIsaac, June 18, 1968, McIsaac papers, 54d, SAB.
8. Interview with Pat Cavill(Cuts), November 18, 2003, Calgary.
9. Keith Turnbull Report, September 20, 1972, Chinook, PL Box 1, 1971-79.
10. *Swift Current Sun,* February 12, 1974.
11. Ibid.
12. Keaschuk to Faris, December 19, 1977, Chinook, PL Box 1, 1971-79.
13. "Brief to the Minister in Charge of Libraries re: Headquarters Building," Keaschuk to Executive, December 13, 1978, and submitted January 5, 1979, ibid.
14. Meadows to Shillington, February 12, 1979, ibid.
15. Pat Cavill, "Summary of Correspondence," October 29, 1979, ibid.
16. *Swift Current Sun,* November 4, 1980.
17. *RLP,* December 2, 1980.
18. *RLP,* December 3, 1980.
19. *Swift Current Sun,* February 5, February 10, 1981.
20. Leah Siebold to Pat Smith, December 2, 1989, Chinook, PL, not filed.
21. *Swift Current Sun,* November 23, 1988.
22. *Swift Current Sun,* September 23, 1992.
23. *Leader News,* April 1, 1992.
24. Chinook Annual Report, 1994.
25. Chinook Annual Report, 1997.
26. Chinook Annual Report, 2001.

CHAPTER ELEVEN

1. "Regional Library Service for Battleford and the Surrounding Municipalities," March 31, 1964, Lakeland, PL Box 1, 1964-67.
2. "Progress Report on Regional Library Development up to November 15, 1965," Mary Donaldson to George Trapp, November 17, 1965, McIsaac papers, 54b, SAB.
3. "North West Steering Committee Report to Library Advisory Council meeting," March 5, 1966, Lakeland, PL Box 1, 1966-68.
4. Steering Committee, June 17, 1966, Lakeland, Box 1, 1964-67.
5. Donalda Putnam to Miss E.N. Sutherland, July 29, 1966, ibid.
6. Newsom to Judge Maher, December 21, 1968, Lakeland files
7. Irene Hoskins, Assistant Provincial Librarian, to J.C. McIsaac, August 12, 1970, McIsaac papers, 53g SAB.
8. Lakeland Executive to MacMurchy, June 10, 1973, Lakeland, PL Box 1, 1971-75.
9. Ariel Sallows, Jake Amos to City Commissioner, December 15, 1975, Lakeland, PL Box 1, 1975-76.
10. Cuts to Meadows, December 7, 1975, Lakeland, Box 1, 1975-79.
11. Meadows to Mayor Clements, January 9, 1976, ibid.
12. Cuts to Joe Sequira, Assistant Provincial Librarian, May 12, 1976, ibid.
13. Tchorzewski to Sallows, August 18, 1976, ibid.
14. Lorna Gaudet, October 21, 1976, ibid.
15. "Regional Librarian's Report Given to the Lakeland Executive, Commencing at item 5," July 26, 1977, as part of a long collection of documents presented by North Battleford for a joint meeting with Lakeland, Shillington, 12c 6.2.3, SAB.
16. McDonald to Faris, November 28, 1977, Shillington, SAB.
17. *North Battleford News Optimist,* September 16, 1977.
18. *SSP,* September 22, 1977. The court case was lost but the payout was increased.
19. Lakeland Executive to North Battleford Council, n.d., but 1977.
20. Interview with Laureen Marchand, Saskatoon, January 27, 2004.
21. "Librarians' Report re: Implementation of the Survey of the North Battleford Branch," presented to a Joint Meeting, April 24, 1979, Lakeland, PL Box 3, 1979.
22. Interview with Joylene Campbell, Regina, March 12, 2004.
23. Campbell to Leah Siebold, Provincial Librarian, February 3, 1983, Lakeland, PL Box 3, 1983.
24. John Murray to Campbell, February 22, 1982, PL Lakeland, Box 3, 1982.
25. Patricia Smith to Alan Tanchuk, Secretary Treasurer, Hafford, March 8, 1984, Lakeland, PL Box 3, 1984.
26. Lakeland, PL Box 3, 1984.

27. "Lakeland Discussion Points on the Alternatives to the Equalization Formula," n.d. Lakeland, PL Box 3, 1985.
28. Karen Adams, Provincial Librarian to Pat Smith, December, 1985, ibid.
29. In a document from Meadows to Tchorzewski, January 6, 1976, with attachments, Shillington, 22c, SAB.
30. MacMurchy to Blakeney and Cabinet, n.d. Lakeland, PL Box 1, 1974-75.
31. Cleal, Chair, Lloydminister Public Library Board to Tchorzewski, February 11, 1976, Shillington papers, 22c, SAB.
32. Robertson to Tchorzewski, April 4, 1977, ibid.
33. Gabruch to Pat Smith, March 28, 1985, Lakeland, PL Box 3, 1985.
34. Lakeland Annual Report, 1987, p. 14.

CHAPTER TWELVE

1. Minutes, March 14, 1964, Palliser, PL Box 1, 1964-67.
2. Mrs. Mildred Taylor, "Progress Report No. 7," March, 1966, ibid.
3. Steering Committee meeting, April 30, 1966, ibid.
4. Mary Donaldson to Mildred Taylor, May 30, 1966, ibid.
5. Trapp to Mildred Taylor, February 17, 1967, in J.C. McIsaac papers, 54z, SAB.
6. Bob Ivanochko "Palliser Regional Library," July 23, 1973, Palliser, PL Box 1, 1964-79.
7. Turnbull to Ida Cooke, April 12, 1973, ibid.
8. Palliser Annual Board meeting, February 28, 1974.
9. *Moose Jaw Times-Herald (MJT-H)*, November 23, 1973.
10. *MJT-H,* February 27, 1973.
11. Interview with Cora Greer, January 16, 2004, Saskatoon. She was 24 when she began as Regional Librarian, and retired in 1998
12. *RLP,* July 22, 1974.
13. *MJT-H,* July 6, 1976.
14. *RLP,* July 9, 1976.
15. Greer to City Clerk, Moose Jaw, July 7, 1976, Palliser, PL Box 1, 1964-79.
16. Meadows to Muirhead, Chair, Moose Jaw Board, July 15, 1976, Palliser, ibid.
17. Greer interview, January 16, 2004.
18. Muirhead to Meadows, July 23, 1976, Palliser, PL Box 1, 1964-69.
19. Report, July 28, 1976, Ibid.
20. City Clerk to Greer, January 20, 1977, ibid.
21. *MJT-H,* February 8, 1978.
22. Cora Greer interview.
23. *MJT-H,* June 19, 1979.
24. *RLP,* September 19, 1979.
25. *MJT-H,* February, 3, 1981
26. LDB meeting November 21-22, 1980, PL Box 60.

27. "For the Record," Palliser Trustees Newsletter, December, 1990.
28. Daniel Pugerude, Chair of Palliser, to Lorne Hepworth, May 19, 1987, in "For the Record," July, 1987. Other sources on the resultant cuts to service include "For the Record," May, 1987 and February, 1988.
29. *MJT-H,* March 19, 1987.
30. Cora Greer Interview.

CHAPTER 13

1. "Proposal for a Northern Regional Library," May 30, 1979, no author but from PL, Northern Saskatchewan Archives, with thanks to Graham Guest.
2. Budget submission, on library service to the North, July 6, 1981, Pahkisimon, PL Box 1, Budget Submissions Northern Services, 1980-83.
3. Harbottle, Provincial Librarian, to Bowerman, April 28, 1981, Pahkisimon, PL Box 5, 1980-81.
4. All material in this paragraph from Pahkisimon, PL Box 5, 1983-88.
5. "Issue Paper: Northern Library Grants," February 15, 1985 PL Pahkisimon, Box 1.
6. Interview with Maureen Wood, Victoria, May 26, 2004.
7. "Northern Library Report to the SLTA," October 27-28, 1990, Northern Archives (NSA).
8. "Word's Worth," 1991.
9. "Presentation to the Minister's Advisory Committee on Library Service to Aboriginal People," June 30, 2001, p. 3, NSA.
10. "Word's Worth," March-April, 2000.
11. Maureen Woods interview.
12. Ibid.

CHAPTER FOURTEEN

1. All Regina and Saskatoon vignettes are in annual reports.
2. *Cosmo Civic Centre,* pamphlet, SPL, Local History, B. 60b.
3. SPL, Annual Report, 1981, p. 4.

CHAPTER FIFTEEN

1. SLA, A1, SAB. All material on the early SLA is in this file
2. J.S. Wood to C.R. Sanderson, Chief Librarian, Toronto, April 13, 1942, Canadian Library Council (CLC), Vol. 28, National Archives of Canada (NAC).
3. *Western Producer,* June 10, 1944.
4. For a fuller list see Elizabeth Morton to Lloyd, December 31, 1953, Carlyle King papers, SAB.

5. SLA Brief, December 11, 1975, Shillington papers, 4a, 6.14, SAB.
6. SLA Executive Meeting, October 6, 1977, SLA SAB.
7. *SLA Forum,* April, 1994.

CHAPTER SIXTEEN

1. History in *Focus,* November 1978 and by George Bothwell in SLTA Brief, January 22, 1992, pgs 8-9, Appendix 1 in SLTA *Trustees Handbook.*

CHAPTER SEVENTEEN

1. PL, Box 60, Grants to Indian Peoples, 1967-75.
2. Newsom to Furlong, SaskPower Manager, September 26, 1968, PL Box 60, Indian & Metis Schools and Education, 1960-69.
3. Adamson to Newsom, December 18, 1968, PL Box 60, Grants to Indian Peoples.
4. Sparvier, January, 1967, PL, Box 60, Library Service to Indian & Metis, 1970-79.
5. Porter to Meadows, March 26, 1971, ibid.
6. PL Box 60, Library Service to the Indian & Metis People, 1970-79.
7. "Indian Control of the Federation of Saskatchewan Indian Regional Library and Band Information Services," SCTCC, October, 1976, ibid.
8. Rafter to Meadows, August 24, 1976, ibid.
9. Carol Bryant to Blakeney and Cabinet, November 3, 1976, Shillington papers, FSI, SAB.
10. Meadows to Tchorzewski, November 10, 1976, Shillington Papers, ESL, SAB.
11. Wendy Sinclair-Sparvier, "Improving & Delivering Effective Library Service for Aboriginal Peoples in Saskatchewan, *World Library Journal,* Spring 2002, p. 4.
12. All material in this section thanks to Marian Buddeu, PL, current file.

CHAPTER EIGHTEEN

1. *RLP,* November 27, 2003.
2. *RLP,* December 4, 2003.
3. *RLP,* April 6, 2004.
4. *RLP,* April 20, 2004.
5. *RLP,* December 13, 2003.
6. *RLP,* December 12, 2003
7. *RLP,* January 8, 2004.
8. *RLP,* February 12, 2004.
9. *RLP,* December 6, 2003.

Index

INDEX

C

Cabri 12, 25, 26, 130, 132, 136
Cadillac 142
Calaldo, Sabrina 246
Calder 116, 121
CALUPL. *See Council of Administers of Large Urban Public Libraries*
Cameron, A. W. 209
Cameron, Bruce 90
Cameron, Faye 243, 244
Cameron, Sandy 243, 252
Campbell, Grace 65, 74, 75, 78, 252
Campbell, Jim 96
Campbell, Joylene 155, 170, 224
Campbell, Maria 31, 126, 252
Canada-Saskatchewan Infrastructure Works Program 224
Canadian authors 47, 134
Canadian Library Association (CLA) 61
Canadian Library Council (CLC) 57, 61, 63, 64, 210
Canadian Library Council Conference 64
Canadian Pacific Railway (CPR) 1, 41, 65
Canadian Pacific Railway employee libraries; 1, 2, 16
Candiac 44
Canora 12, 13, 115, 116, 118, 119, 128, 237
Canwood 29, 74
Cape Breton 65
card catalogue 105, 141, 200
Carievale 59
Carlyle and the Soo Line Homemakers 96
Carlyle King Branch xiii, 25, 197, 198
Carnduff 12, 34, 44, 66, 97, 98, 100

Carnegie Foundation 56, 191
Carnegie Library 16, 67, 154, 191, 192
Caron 33
Caronport 28, 175
Carrot River 110
Cavill, Pat 133, 252
CCF. *See Co-operative Commonwealth federation*
Cennon, Zack 80
Central Butte 33, 131, 166
Central Library 191, 192, 193, 195, 245, 246, 247
Chamber of Commerce 15, 24, 96
Chamberlain 54
Chaplin 33, 131
Children's books 27, 44, 45, 46, 71, 75, 78, 151, 152, 181
Chin, Gail 246
Chinook 13, 47, 49, 103, 127, 129-142, 146, 147, 157, 159, 166, 167, 175, 219, 220, 222, 223, 235, 236, 240, 251
Chuey, Judy i, 10, 252, 253, 257
Churchbridge 117, 121
circulation 13, 18, 19, 23, 30, 32, 33, 34, 35, 36, 39, 40, 43, 45, 46, 49, 51, 55, 78, 79, 91, 92, 103, 106, 121, 123, 124, 126, 134, 141, 142, 143, 151, 152, 156, 157, 162, 163, 165, 170, 176, 178, 183, 192, 201, 202, 245
CLA. *See Canadian Library Association*
Clair 44
Clancy, Muriel 199, 212, 213
CLC. *See Canadian Library Council*
Cliff Wright Branch xiii, 198
Cochin 44, 144
Coldwell, Betty 101
Collins, Hilda 102, 103

Collins, Lea 100
Commissioner of Publications *MacLeod, W.A.* 35
Community Access Program 232
Community Libraries 12, 13, 35, 108, 112, 113, 145
Community Net 224, 225
Community Stories 231
computer searches 49
Connaught Branch. 192, 231, 248
Conservatives 51, 104, 158
consumer price index 158, 219
Cooke, Ida 171
Co-operative Commonwealth Federation (CCF) iv, 9, 36, 37, 42, 43, 52-56, 62, 63, 67, 72, 73, 77, 108, 220
Copeland, Carol 94, 114
Coronach 165, 166
Cote band 121, 124
Council of Administers of Large Urban Public Libraries 202
Cowessess 227, 228
CPR. *See Canadian Pacific Railway*
Craig, L. 35
Craik 165, 168
Cree 183, 186, 189, 224, 232, 236
Creighton 184
Crooks, Grace 74, 76, 77, 212
Cross, Susan 93
Cuelenaere, John 66, 72, 74, 78
Cupar 44
CUPE Local 1904 122
Curry, Sonia 143, 145, 149-154
Cut Knife 29, 144, 145, 146, 147
Cuts, Patricia *See Pat Cavill*

268

About the Author

DON KERR is the author of five books of poetry, seven plays, a short fiction collection, a teen fiction novel, and non-fiction books on politics and the history of the city of Saskatoon. He served on the Saskatoon Public Library Board for eleven years, and as chair for five of those years. He was the first chair of the Saskatoon Heritage Society and the first chair of the Saskatoon Municipal Heritage Committee. He is currently the elected Saskatchewan governor for the Heritage Canada Foundation.